# Field Marshal Claude Auchinleck

# Field Marshal Claude Auchinleck

Evan McGilvray

Pen & Sword
MILITARY

First published in Great Britain in 2020 by
Pen & Sword Military
An imprint of
Pen & Sword Books Ltd
Yorkshire – Philadelphia



ISBN 978 1 52671 610 1



A CIP catalogue record for this book is available from the British Library.



Typeset by Mac Style
Printed and bound in the UK by TJ International Ltd,
Padstow, Cornwall.

FSC www.fsc.org MIX Paper from responsible sources FSC® C013056

Pen & Sword Books Limited incorporates the imprints of Atlas, Archaeology, Aviation, Discovery, Family History, Fiction, History, Maritime, Military, Military Classics, Politics, Select, Transport, True Crime, Air World, Frontline Publishing, Leo Cooper, Remember When, Seaforth Publishing, The Praetorian Press, Wharncliffe Local History, Wharncliffe Transport, Wharncliffe True Crime and White Owl.

For a complete list of Pen & Sword titles please contact

PEN & SWORD BOOKS LIMITED
47 Church Street, Barnsley, South Yorkshire, S70 2AS, England
E-mail: enquiries@pen-and-sword.co.uk
Website: www.pen-and-sword.co.uk

Or

PEN AND SWORD BOOKS
1950 Lawrence Rd, Havertown, PA 19083, USA
E-mail: Uspen-and-sword@casematepublishers.com
Website: www.penandswordbooks.com

# Contents

# Introduction

Field Marshal Sir Claude Auchinleck lived a long time and saw service in the British army in some of the most difficult times of the British Empire as it began an inevitable wane from 1914 onwards. Auchinleck was to oversee the ending of British rule in India, a country to which he had given much of his life. India was to have the greatest influence on Auchinleck's life as he was to spend much of his service career there and was very possibly influenced by his own father's career in India. To ensure that when independence came to India (and Pakistan) in 1947, Auchinleck tried to ensure that the transition from British rule to independence on the Indian subcontinent went as smoothly as possible. Therefore to understand Auchinleck's service career we need to return to the situation in India in the 1850s when his father saw action there during the Indian Mutiny as it is considered that the mutiny remained relevant ninety years later in 1947.[1]

Evan McGilvray
Pudsey
May 2019

## *Chapter One*

# The Early Years

The future Field Marshal Auchinleck was born Claude John Eyre Auchinleck at his parents' home in the garrison town of Aldershot in Hampshire on 21 June 1884. His father, John Claud Alexander Auchinleck, was a lieutenant colonel of the Royal Horse Artillery and had as a young subaltern served in the Indian Mutiny in 1857. The father later served as a major commanding a battery of Royal Field Artillery in Afghanistan as part of Lord Roberts' advance on Kabul during the Second Afghan War (1878–80). Later in 1885 Auchinleck senior was posted back to India as a lieutenant colonel to command the Royal Horse Artillery at Bangalore. This appointment allowed him to bring his wife Mary (christened May Eleanor) and the baby Claude to this posting with him. This was an idyllic posting and another child was born there to the Auchinlecks, but Lieutenant Colonel Auchinleck was once more sent on active service in the spring of 1888, this time to Burma. The British in 1886 had annexed Burma from King Thibaw and had made it a province of India. Unsurprisingly, the Burmese resented this and so a series of guerrilla actions began against the British. Auchinleck senior was to take part in the Third Burmese War which was marked by its brutality, both by the British and the Burmese guerrillas fighting them.

Sadly, the Third Burmese War was to be the end of Claude Auchinleck's father: not through the fighting but because of the climate and disease found in Burma. After almost two years of service in Burma, Lieutenant Colonel Auchinleck contracted pernicious anaemia which caused him to retire prematurely at the age of 55 as a full colonel, having served in the British army for thirty-five years. He returned to the UK during the autumn of 1890 and was reunited with his family who had already made the trip back home. However, his return home was to be short-lived as Colonel Auchinleck died prematurely at the age of only 57 just after Christmas 1892.[1] His widow was only aged 43 and was left to live on a small army pension of £40 per year. There was a legacy left to Mrs Auchinleck in February 1893 which it is always claimed was small, but to many people it surely would have represented a fortune. Nevertheless, the lady began to plead poverty and a life more austere than the one to which she had been accustomed. It seemed needless but still, there we are.

The priority of Mrs Auchinleck was to settle down to life and ensure that her children did not notice the apparent discomfort of the straitened financial situation perceived by their mother. The children really did not know their father as he was always away, and of course Victorian children were brought up as 'seen and not heard'; there was little 'hands-on' childcare at that time. So the children with their mother settled down in a smaller house while receiving financial aid from the family as well as living off the small pension. It must be said that Mrs Auchinleck was a splendid mother as her illustrious son, when he was able to in later life, treated his mother and sister to small luxuries and holidays.

At the age of 10, Claude was sent to a nearby preparatory school from which many boys were intended to go to nearby Wellington College. The school seemed to have been quite grim and nasty and the young Claude did not flourish there but did make it to Wellington and finally, after much sweat and due to his weakness in mathematics, dropped his original intention of being an artillery officer like his father and instead decided to become an infantry officer and head eventually towards Sandhurst.

At the time of Auchinleck's arrival at Sandhurst in January 1902, the British military had been undergoing various changes during the previous twenty years or so as there had been sundry reforms to how the army should be administered as well as a far-reaching change in how officers should be promoted. A blatant absurdity was the ability to purchase rank in the British army prior to the 1870s except for the Royal Artillery and the Royal Engineers where only talent and intelligence counted. Auchinleck's father had been an artillery officer and so had earned his rank, but plenty of infantry officers and cavalry officers did not, instead relying on the fortunes of their families to buy their careers. Wealth was all in the Victorian army, and to a certain extent the Edwardian army, but at least promotion was earned. A further problem with the British army was that it was small and only intended for home defence and the defence of India, the major asset of the British Empire. The UK had been involved in several colonial wars and when Auchinleck entered Sandhurst the British army was just about to defeat the Boers in the Second Anglo-Boer War (1899–1902) but had hardly covered itself with glory and had largely relied on the harassing of civilians and concentration camps to bring the Boer fighters to heel, while a previous adventure in southern Africa had seen the British defeated by a Zulu army and a Boer army. Wars in the 1850s including the Crimean War and the Indian Mutiny had done little to convince people of the strength of the British army; the UK's real force rested with the Royal Navy.

Auchinleck arrived at Sandhurst in the middle of January 1902. He had already made up his mind that he wanted to join the Indian army as he could not afford to serve in the British army. Expenses not necessarily related to the work itself where clothes and sporting activities were part of a busy social life in the home British army were a serious financial burden on a young officer who was not from a wealthy family with access to independent means. The Indian army attracted a higher salary, while the cost of living in India was much lower than in the UK. However, entry into the Indian army was competitive and was dependent on how well a candidate did in his exams at Sandhurst. Before 1906, those who gained the top forty to fifty places were guaranteed a place in the Indian army, but after 1906 this was restricted to the top thirty to thirty-five.

Service in the Indian army was not unattractive because it was better paid with fewer expenses and there was also a real chance of seeing active service on the North-West Frontier. There were other opportunities such as those for exploration, mountain-climbing, big game-hunting, pig-sticking (boar-hunting) and duck-shooting. The expensive sport of polo was also possible, even for junior officers. There appeared to have been an absence of snobbishness in India, but that was more likely a sense of unity against the native Indians. Even at Sandhurst, Auchinleck found that his lack of independent funds curtailed his social life, yet he managed to complete the course and was commissioned.

Auchinleck was commissioned as an unattached second lieutenant in the Indian army on 21 January 1903 and joined the 62nd Punjabis in April 1904. Auchinleck took to India, quickly learned several Indian languages and was soon able to speak several fluently with his soldiers. He also absorbed Indian life and its rich culture, taking note of local dialects and customs. This made a great and lasting impression on Indian troops and their families and ensured a mutual respect which was furthered by his own personality. Auchinleck was promoted to lieutenant on 21 April 1905. He then spent the next two years in Tibet and Sikkim before moving to Benares in 1907 where he had the misfortune of catching diphtheria. He had a brief return to Aldershot, serving with the Royal Inniskilling Fusiliers before returning to Benares in 1909 and becoming adjutant of the 62nd Punjabis, promoted to captain on 21 January 1912.

To put detail on Auchinleck's early days in India it should be noted that he was perhaps fortunate in his first posting. He joined the 2nd Battalion of the King's Shropshire Light Infantry (85th KSLI) who had recently arrived in India from the war in South Africa. He was part of a small contingent of six junior officers posted to this unit. Auchinleck found himself stationed at Ranikhet which was 6,000ft up in the Himalayan Mountains. This made for splendid views and clean air and was about 80 miles from Tibet and 60 miles from Nepal; all very beautiful but not ideal for acclimatizing to India or for field exercises. Nevertheless, there were advantages as Ranikhet was an ideal field station for learning drill, weapon training and exercises in frontier warfare. It was also a good place to learn Urdu, the language of the Indian army. It took Auchinleck more than seven days to travel the 2,000-plus miles from Bombay (Mumbai) to Ranikhet: the first four days by train to the railhead at the foot of the Himalayas and then a further three days by pony to the hill station. It was not a journey for the faint-hearted, even though on the train every possible comfort had been made available for the young officer.

Greenwood, Auchinleck's ADC in later years, observed that the young Auchinleck was fortunate in as much as his first regiment was tolerant of youth and immaturity while others were less so. Life initially was interesting but fairly routine. However, after a few weeks, at the height of summer, a cholera epidemic broke out among the civil population in Ranikhet, causing many deaths. The KSLI were ordered to go and live under canvas in the surrounding countryside, but away from their comfortable barracks. In September the epidemic was over and they were able to return to their quarters. On his return Auchinleck was confronted with a mundane but expensive side of military life: his mess bill. The billeting out in the hillsides around the Ranikhet area proved to have been an expensive exercise for Auchinleck as he had had to pay for his own field equipment as well as for the tent of his batman. The demand for immediate payment caused Auchinleck to go into the red with his bank and he was forced to ask for funds from his mother. As Greenwood writes, pay for an officer in the Indian army was sufficient but the lifestyle was grand and the KSLI was not even the most expensive regiment.[2]

After a year of being attached to the KSLI, Auchinleck finally joined an Indian regiment, the 62nd Punjabis. He was joining the Indian army at a time of change and reform. A major reform was that all regiments were to see action on the North-West Frontier, that difficult and wild area bordering India and Afghanistan. A major difference between the 62nd Punjabis and the KSLI was that the former had little if any combat experience. After getting to know his men and their customs and religions, Auchinleck began to train his men for combat and was grateful for having served with the KSLI as they had had recent experience of battle and even if Auchinleck had no combat experience himself, he drew on what he had learned in his time with the KSLI.

Auchinleck was in command of about 200 men as the usual company commander was in the UK on home leave. In addition to training his men for combat, Auchinleck learned more about managing men such as taking the weekly pay parade until he had learned the name of every man under his command. He also made close inspection of his men's feet after long marches as Indian troops went barefoot until they joined the army. Another thing that Auchinleck learned was to ensure that his men were fed first before he began to eat his own rations. Auchinleck's style of command was part of a way of building trust between him and his men, thus forming a team with complete trust in their officer. One cannot help but think that perhaps the twenty-first-century employer and politician should take note and perhaps learn something from this. In April 1905 Auchinleck received an official offer of a transfer to the 5th Royal Gurkhas, a distinguished regiment permanently posted on the North-West Frontier, but Auchinleck turned down the offer, citing that the financial cost would be too much for him. The real reason was that he had come to love being with the 62nd Punjabis and had become part of the regiment.

After two years of careful training the 62nd Punjabis were combat-fit, and the battalion was divided into two independent units each consisting of double companies. One half was sent to north-eastern Assam to the borders with Tibet and the other to the Sikkim border with Tibet and then divided into two further independent units. Auchinleck commanded one of these – a company of 100 men – with orders to establish a base at Gyantse (now renamed Chiang-tzu) over 150 miles inside Tibet and 12,000ft above sea level. The objective of these missions, which clearly involved an armed incursion into a sovereign state as Tibet was at the turn of the twentieth century, was to prevent Russian incursions into the same territory and protect India from the north. After just over a year in Tibet Auchinleck was sent to Sikkim, an independent kingdom under the protection of India at the time, to command a double company. It was in Sikkim that Auchinleck learned to fish, a pastime that he enjoyed for the rest of his life. At the end of 1907 the battalion returned to India, to Benares (now Varanasi), the holiest of all Hindu cities. No matter the spiritual side of the city, its climate was toxic as it was both hot and humid and soon Auchinleck contracted diphtheria. Once he had recovered and the doctors had pronounced him fit to travel, Auchinleck was granted home leave in the UK; an entitlement granted to Indian army officers who were granted six months' leave at home every three years. With sick leave attached to his home leave, Auchinleck was granted a total of eight months' leave in the UK.

This long leave was just too long for Auchinleck and by the end of his eight months the restless and bored young man was glad to return to India and went back to his battalion at Benares in the summer of 1909. On his return, he was appointed adjutant which was an excellent opportunity for such a junior officer and carried extra pay. For the next three years Auchinleck spent his time training. Before the First World War recruits were sent straight from their homes into the battalion as there were no training depots or centres. Auchinleck had to ensure that new recruits were properly absorbed into the regiment. However, his primary duty was to be an efficient staff officer to his commanding officer, which meant that much of his time was spent in administration.

It fell to Auchinleck to prepare training programmes, to organize weapon training cadres and ensure the overall drill and discipline of the battalion, with which he had to be discreet as the company commanders were very senior to him in rank and service. In 1911 Auchinleck had to choose and train the regimental detachment for the King-Emperor George V's Durbar (court) in New Delhi, the capital of India. In the same year the Commanding Officer, Lieutenant Colonel Drever, died from cholera and the battalion was left without a new CO for many months. This all added to Auchinleck's responsibilities and experience, which would stand him in good stead in Mesopotamia (Iraq) during the First World War.

In January 1912 Auchinleck was promoted to the rank of captain and six months later he was sent on home leave again. This time, no doubt to avoid the tedium of his last leave, Auchinleck got himself attached to the Royal Inniskilling Fusiliers, a regiment in which his cousin, Captain Daniel Auchinleck, was then serving. The regiment was stationed in Aldershot, but during the period of Auchinleck's attachment had moved to the training ground in Norfolk for large-scale manoeuvres. These war games failed to impress Auchinleck and he later admitted that he had learned nothing except that manoeuvres should never be carried out by units with only half their war establishment.

On his return to India Auchinleck was appointed an Assistant Recruiting Officer (ARO) in northern Punjab. Once more he was on his own and responsible for recruiting in an area the size of England and Wales. Auchinleck did this by moving from village to village on horseback accompanied only by a batman and a syce (a groom for horses). The Indian army recruited most of its men from families with army traditions, while regiments had their own tribes and areas from which they recruited. Soldiering was an honourable profession and the families concerned took great pride in it; as a result Auchinleck was well received wherever he visited. It was considered an honour to serve the Raj and the regiment and youngsters were already prepared to serve the family regiment. Auchinleck, being proficient in Urdu, Hindi and Pushto as well as competent in many Punjabi dialects, only increased his popularity. This period serving as an ARO was the happiest of his career. However, Auchinleck's period of happiness was rapidly ending as the world was sliding towards war and in August 1914 the First World War broke out.[3]

*Chapter Two*

# The First World War

The First World War was not seen coming and then, after the assassination of the Archduke Franz Ferdinand with his wife in Sarajevo on 28 June 1914, nobody saw that within weeks the world would be at war. The problem was that the archduke was the heir to the Austrian throne and the Austrians did not take it lightly that Bosnian terrorists, or more likely groomed schoolboys, had just murdered the heir apparent to the Hapsburg throne. Initially the fighting that began in late July and early August 1914 was restricted to Europe, but as alliances and imperial concerns kicked in, the war reached India and Auchinleck.

Auchinleck saw active service in the First World War in the Middle East, a theatre which is largely forgotten today with the focus being on the Western Front while the other theatres of operation of the 1914–18 war tend to be overlooked. Turkey, with its vast Middle Eastern empire, had entered the war on the side of Germany on 30 October 1914 and remained active until 30 October 1918. The great prize in the eyes of the Turks was Egypt and the Suez Canal which provided a shortcut into the Arabian Sea and on to India. Prior to the opening of the canal in 1869, the British had to sail around Africa to get to their so-called 'jewel in the crown' of the British Empire, India. Therefore the Suez Canal had to be defended as the highest priority of British interests in Egypt and soon Auchinleck was on his way to help in the defence of Egypt and the Suez Canal.

Even if not many had seen war coming in 1914, during June the Indian government had been consulted by Whitehall to try to establish to what extent Indian troops might be used in a war against a European power. The new commander-in-chief in India, General Sir Beauchamp Duff, had proposed a contingent, possibly two or even three infantry divisions and a cavalry brigade. Eventually the Indian army went to war with three infantry divisions and a cavalry division. One infantry division embarked from Karachi on 24 August 1914 and another followed on 28 September. This shows some degree of efficiency in how the Indian army was organized and prepared for mobilization.

The 62nd Punjabis were stationed in Cawnpore in the United Provinces when war was declared and were mobilized with the 22nd Indian Infantry Brigade which was part of the reserve division. On 28 October 1914 the battalion embarked from Bombay in two ships, the SS *Elysia* and SS *Glenitive* [*sic*, probably SS *Glenlivet*]. The strength of the division, its supplies and reinforcements eventually made up a convoy of about forty ships. It was necessary for a strong naval escort to be provided as the German battle-cruiser *Emden* was known to be roaming the Indian Ocean through which the convoy had to pass as it headed towards Egypt and, it was thought, eventually to France. However, as the convoy sailed, Turkey entered the war against the UK and France during the first week of sailing. As an ally of Germany, Turkey bombarded the Russian ports on the Black Sea. This changed the war for Auchinleck and his battalion as even though the Turkish actions were not confirmed at the time on the convoy, rumour had already reached the ships and it was considered that the reserve division would never see France. In the event, when the convoy reached Port Said on 16 November the 22nd Brigade disembarked and the rest of the convoy sailed on for France.

The British understanding of the situation in the Middle East following the Turkish involvement in the war was that from their vast Middle Eastern empire the Turks would move southwards from Syria and attempt to occupy the Suez Canal, closing the route to India and the Far East. At the time Egypt was a British Protectorate and the Turks thought that once they arrived on the Egyptian borders, the Egyptians would revolt against British rule and welcome the Turks as fellow Muslims. The 22nd Brigade was ordered to Ismailia with orders to defend the line of the Suez Canal from the north of Lake Timsah to the south of the Great Bitter Lakes, a line of about 35 miles. The battalion's HQ was at Serapeum and the rifle companies were deployed in a defensive line on the west bank of the canal with advance posts on the eastern bank, positioned there to give warning of an enemy attack as well as providing a bridgehead on that side if ever needed.

Captain Auchinleck was in command of the battalion's machine guns, both on detachment on the eastern side of the canal between milestones 49 and 50, virtually due east of Serapeum. On 25 January 1915 the Turks made a short raid on El Qantara to the north; this was driven off without difficulty. It was probably a reconnaissance expedition as soon afterwards British intelligence reported that a large Turkish force was concentrated on the east side of the Suez Canal opposite Ismailia. Pontoons for crossing water or the canal were reported as well as artillery, therefore it was concluded that a major enemy attack was imminent.

The Turks began their attack at 0330 hours in the morning of 3 February 1915 when they attempted to cross the canal using their pontoons. Within a few minutes machine guns and rifles opened fire along the whole front and Auchinleck, for the first time in his eleven years of military service, was experiencing combat. He was a captain in a first-class infantry regiment, but had never heard a shot fired in anger before. The Turks managed to get a pontoon across the canal, but Indian infantrymen charged down the bank with bayonets fixed and killed all the advancing Turks save one who, although wounded, survived his ordeal. Auchinleck recalled his first action and remembered automatically ducking at the sound of a bullet going over his head. When years later he was asked about his first battle, Auchinleck remarked simply that it had been 'exciting'.

After a break of about two hours the Turks attacked once more; again, using pontoons to cross the canal and again they were driven back, leaving many dead and wounded on the banks. The 62nd Punjabis then counter-attacked and Auchinleck's detachment took part in this operation and drove the enemy from their newly-dug positions. The Turks made a final attempt to cross the canal on the morning of 4 February, but again they were repulsed with heavy casualties. The 62nd Punjabis were ready to counter-attack this time and once more used fixed bayonets when the forward groups of the Turkish attack decided to surrender; 6 officers and almost 200 men were taken prisoner. The remaining Turks withdrew and headed eastwards into the Sinai desert. The 62nd Punjabis lost seven men who had been killed in the fighting, with two officers and eighteen men wounded. Two of the British officers were later awarded the Distinguished Service Order (DSO) for the fighting along this section of the Suez Canal.

The Turkish army had moved to the canal from Beersheba, about 200 miles to the east. The move had been the result of forced marches over soft desert sands using only mules and a few camels as transport. At that time there were no roads in the Sinai desert. The Turks had been ordered into battle with no rest or preparation for the offensive, while their lines of communication were long and unreliable. There was very little food and even less reserve ammunition. This more or less doomed the Turkish offensive against the Suez Canal. The 62nd Punjabis had made a creditable opening to their participation in the First World War and settled down to patrolling activity and training.

In the first week of July 1915, the 62nd Punjabis were ordered to Aden where the Turks had captured the town of Sheikh Othman and the main water supply for the important Aden base 8 miles to the south. The 62nd Punjabis joined the 28th (Punjab Frontier Force) Brigade and embarked for Aden from Port Said on 12 July. Four days later the brigade disembarked at Aden and on 21 July they had completed their operational task and driven the Turks from their positions. The Turks never again threatened Aden while the Turkish high command continued to fail to understand the need for a secure and manageable line of communication. The battle for Aden had taken place in one of the hottest areas of the Middle East during the height of summer. The 62nd Punjabis remained in Aden for the remainder of 1915, and apart from some patrol activities against hostile Arabs, most of the time was spent in training and keeping fit ready for further action against the Turks which seemed to be taking its time in coming.

During the summer of 1915 there were two major campaigns being waged by the allies against the Turks: Gallipoli, which ended in acrimonious disaster by the end of the year; and the campaign in Mesopotamia, which is today's Iraq. The Mesopotamian campaign looked as if it was going to end in a similar way. In November 1914 the 16th Indian Infantry Brigade, part of the 6th Indian Division (known as the Indian Expeditionary Force) had been dispatched to capture the port of Basra and so secure the approaches to the Anglo-Persian oilfields around Abadan. The same oilfields were to figure large in Auchinleck's strategy during the Second World War. The brigade was successful in securing their objectives and was later reinforced by the remainder of the division under the command of Major General Charles Townshend. The Turks, however, counter-attacked the defences around Basra in April 1915 but were repulsed at Shaiba about 12 miles south-west of Basra in the marshland of the combined rivers Euphrates and Tigris as they entered the Shatt-al-Arab. By this time there were three divisions in the area under the overall command of General Sir John Nixon with headquarters in Basra, so the force was then renamed the Mesopotamian Expeditionary Force (MEF). Operational orders, however, still came from General Sir Beauchamp Duff, Commander-in-Chief (C-in-C) in India. Duff demanded that Baghdad be taken as soon as possible.

Using river steamers, the 6th Indian Division moved up the Tigris and captured Amara on 2 June 1915 and the 12th Indian Division under the command of Major General George Gorringe advanced alongside the Euphrates and captured Nasiriyah on 25 July. There was further success on 28 September with the capture of Kut-al-Amara, despite 1,230 British and Indian casualties. Nixon sent word of his successes to India and was ordered to press on to Baghdad immediately. However, there were doubts if this was a good idea as Townshend, whose lines of communication were already overstretched, was not so confident, especially as Baghdad was over 500 miles from Basra. Even so, the advance towards Baghdad continued at the end of October, despite a lack of reinforcements, overstretched supply lines and unusually wet and cold weather conditions.

On 22 November Townshend attacked Turkish positions at Ctesiphon, a mere 18 miles from Baghdad. The ensuing battle lasted for four days and four nights with heavy casualties on both sides. However, Townshend lacked both ammunition and supplies and could not mount a final entry into Baghdad, while neither the Turks nor the British could support a stalemate at Ctesiphon. The only answer was that the Anglo-Indian force had to retreat to Kut, which was done by 3 December. Four days later Kut was surrounded by Turkish armed forces and nearly 10,400 British and Indian troops, many of whom were wounded, were totally besieged. Nixon immediately set about organizing a relief force to lift the siege at Kut, but reinforcements were already on their way from France as the 3rd and 7th Indian divisions were en route under the command of Lieutenant General Sir Fenton Aylmer VC. Aylmer made a rushed attempt with a collection of units, known as the Tigris Corps, to break through the Turkish siege at Kut on 6 January 1916, but this failed miserably.

Captain Auchinleck arrived with the 62nd Punjabis as part of the relief force at Basra on 31 December 1915. The battalion strength was 13 British officers, 22 Indian officers and 907 men. There was chaos at Basra owing to the weather and poor anchorage which meant that ships lay unloaded for more than a month while supplies rotted. The battalion on arrival embarked on a paddle-steamer and moved up the Tigris to join Aylmer's force at Hissah. On 7 January 1916 the 62nd Punjabis were ordered straight into patrol action at Sheikh Sa'ad in front of the Turkish positions. The next day Sheikh Sa'ad was taken by units of the 7th Indian Division under the command of Major General George Kemball, but the cost was high. Two days of fighting had cost almost 4,000 British and Indian casualties, while there was a complete lack of field ambulances and medical supplies. The 7th Indian Division had been ordered straight into action without their medical units which were still on their way to the Middle East and at the time of the fighting were in a convoy sailing from Marseilles.

Aylmer's plan had been to advance on both sides of the River Tigris simultaneously and then encircle the town from the north. The 62nd Punjabis were ordered to join the 35th Indian Infantry Brigade which was part of the 7th Indian Division. During the night of 12/13 January 1916 the attack was launched in terrible wet and cold weather. Most of the units only wore thin tropical khaki drill and so were very cold as the driving rain and keen wind bit into them, but the 62nd Punjabis were luckier as their commanding officer had ensured that thick serge uniforms were available, having been bought out of regimental funds when the battalion had been stationed at Cawnpore in October 1914 and it had been anticipated that the 62nd Punjabis were going to France. The 35th Brigade was kept in reserve and so was spared the real fighting of the day which saw the attack repulsed under machine-gun fire and more than 1,000 British and Indian troops were killed in the twenty-four-hour battle.

Aylmer's latest attack was to renew the offensive on the right bank of the Tigris and for this purpose the 9th Brigade was ordered to cross the river on the night of 17 January. Once the crossing-point was reached it was discovered that floods had washed away temporary bridges made up of boats like pontoons and so the brigade's advance was halted. Aylmer decided that the next best thing would be a frontal assault launched against Turkish positions at Hanna which was situated on the bend of the Tigris about 10 miles north-west of Sheikh Sa'ad. As the heavy rain was yet to abate, an advance was made over open ground deep in mud. The attack began at 0745 on 21 January with the 35th Brigade in the vanguard and the 9th Brigade in support. The 35th Brigade advancing in line only managed to make 200 yards before being forced back to their own trenches under heavy and accurate Turkish machine-gun and rifle fire from their heavily-entrenched positions. Casualties were high, with the dead and wounded left in the mud on the battlefield.

Meanwhile the 9th Brigade attempted to take over the attack but once more in line, with the 62nd Punjabis on the right, the 1/4th Hampshires on the left and the Connaught Rangers in a second line in the rear. Once more the Turks fired with deadly accuracy from their well-appointed positions, while the British floundered knee-deep in the mud over which they had been expected to advance. Many of the advancing infantrymen could not use their rifles as they became clogged and useless as they stumbled to the ground. Driving rain added to the chaos. Even so, the 62nd Punjabis got within 250 yards of the Turkish trenches but at great cost including the commanding officer Lieutenant Colonel Ewing Wrigley Grimshaw being killed. As the casualties mounted, communications failed and control was lost. Remnants of the units got mixed, while continuous and steady machine-gun fire from the Turkish positions prevented any further advance by the British.

At 1530 on 21 January 1916 General Younghusband ordered a withdrawal but Auchinleck's company, No.3 Double Company, did not receive this order until 0300 on 22 January. Auchinleck had managed to emerge from the fighting unscathed. Major C.H.B. Wright assumed command of what was left of the battalion and made Auchinleck acting adjutant. The next few hours were harrowing for the British as wounded men lay out in the mud drenched in the icy rain, dying from the cold and lack of attention. Medical recovery was hopeless and worse than useless while there were no Very lights with which to light up the darkness of the night. In the morning many sepoys (Indian troops) were found to have died of exposure without having received a single wound.

Aylmer was forced to make a six-hour truce with the Turks on the morning of 22 January to recover the wounded. During the truce, the body of Major Skeen, senior double commander, was found and was later buried behind the British positions. The next day Lieutenant Colonel Grimshaw's body was found. It had been stripped completely naked by Arabs. Grimshaw's body was later buried alongside that of Skeen. The 62nd Punjabis had lost 30 dead, 15 men were missing and 327 wounded. Many of the wounded had to remain unattended for days owing to the complete lack of medical aid, which left maggots and gangrene to take hold and cause further deaths.

Major Wright reorganized the battalion into just two double companies and then for the next three weeks they remained on outpost duties as they strengthened their defensive positions while struggling with beetles and scorpions. On 14 February the 62nd Punjabis were sent to join the 36th Indian Brigade, then in reserve. By this time, the Mesopotamian campaign was being conducted from Whitehall and not from India, which meant that strategic operational orders came directly from the new Chief of Imperial General Staff (CIGS) General Sir William Robertson.

At the end of February 1916, Lieutenant Colonel Herbert Hastings Harington arrived to take command of the 62nd Punjabis. Curiously he was a distinguished ornithologist, but had spent twenty years of his army service in Burma. Within seven days he was leading the 62nd Punjabis, in line as ever, towards Turkish guns. On the morning of 8 March after an hour's artillery barrage against the Turks, the 62nd Punjabis moved against the Turks at 0945 but the Turks knew that they were coming. The 62nd Punjabis moved straight into Turkish gunfire but by 1130 had reached their objective. They were then ordered to support further attacks in the same sector; it was during this fighting that Colonel Harington was badly wounded and he died later the same day. In six weeks the 62nd Punjabis had lost two commanding officers. Captain Auchinleck then assumed command of the few survivors and withdrew them to the rear of the firing line. Once darkness fell, Auchinleck took his men to join No.2 Double Company under Major Wright, who once again assumed command of the battalion.

At midnight orders came from Aylmer's HQ for a general withdrawal to prepared positions at Ora about 2.5 miles to the east. The strength of the 62nd Punjabis was down to 12 British and Indian officers with 235 other ranks. They arrived at their bivouacs which were close to the Tigris at 1100 on 9 March, hungry and thirsty and completely exhausted. They had had no sleep for more than forty hours and had been shelled by the Turks for much of their withdrawal. Once again, a major attempt to relieve the British garrison at Kut had failed miserably. However, at Basra there were 12,000 men with artillery and animal transport which could not be brought into the operational area due to the lack of shipping. On 11 March news was received that Aylmer had been replaced by Lieutenant General Sir George Gorringe who had been commanding the 12th Indian Division and had just been promoted to corps commander. Years later Auchinleck blamed Aylmer for his stupidity in mounting such costly frontal attacks which he described as 'absolute murder' and 'bad generalship'. The problem was that Aylmer was not suited to modern warfare as it was in 1916 and had never previously commanded a large formation such as a corps in combat conditions; in March 1916 he was dismissed.

Throughout April 1916 General Gorringe mounted a series of attacks on the Turkish positions besieging Kut. The rains continued relentlessly and men continued to die. In Kut itself starvation began to take hold, costing on average twenty men a day. Meanwhile reinforcements continued to pile up in Basra; close to 30,000 men with more than thirty artillery pieces but no river transport to move them the 250 miles to Kut. On 26 April the CIGS signalled from London that negotiations should be started with the Turks to try to prevent the entire garrison from dying through starvation. On 29 April Kut was surrendered to the Turks. Townshend had ordered the destruction of all guns, ammunition and military stores. More than 9,000 prisoners were taken, of which 5,000 later disappeared without trace. The 62nd Punjabis had lost more than half of their original strength, while more than 23,000 casualties were suffered by the forces trying to relieve Kut. It was a lamentable episode of the First World War.

Auchinleck survived the fighting for Kut and in June 1916 was lucky enough to get ten days' leave. This was spent in a wooden hut in the British hospital compound at Amara. There he spent his time eating, swimming and sleeping. After this somewhat unorthodox leave, Auchinleck returned to his battalion refreshed and fit. His decision to do nothing on leave was wise as he was exhausted after the fighting in which he had been involved and needed to recharge his body, both physically and mentally. On his return to his battalion he was given command of a double company with the acting rank of major. In August 1916 Auchinleck was lucky enough to get more leave, this time a whole month in India. It was during this leave, which he spent in Simla, the summer capital of the British administration of India as well as the HQ of the Indian army, that he met his cousin Hugh Beaver and learned that his younger brother 'Tiny' had been killed fighting on the Somme. Auchinleck was able to catch up with news of the Indian army, but by the end of his leave was keen to return to his regiment. Even though the Mesopotamian campaign was horrific, the regiment was his home.

Auchinleck returned to the 62nd Punjabis in September 1916 and the climate was cooler than it had been when he had left on his leave. There were also changes in the military there. Auchinleck's battalion had been brought up to full strength and had a new CO, Lieutenant Colonel George Mortimer Morris. A new C-in-C in Mesopotamia, Lieutenant General Sir Stanley Maude, had also been appointed. Maude had commanded the 14th Division in the Relief Force. Auchinleck had huge respect for Maude, who could be bothered to visit those troops under his command which made him universally popular. Sadly, Maude died of dysentery on active service in 1917 aged only 53. However, during his time in Mesopotamia Maude many changes in how the army and administration was handled in the area. His priority was to strengthen the lines of communication to the forward areas and to do this he needed to make the port of Basra into an efficient base. He altered priorities to strengthening road and river transportation to the front. This allowed for a major offensive to capture Kut to begin on 13 December 1916.

The 62nd Punjabis were still part of the 36th Brigade which was by then part of the 14th Division, but in reserve. Maude's plan was one of encirclement which required a river crossing in force while each move forward was to be thoroughly reinforced before advancing. The following battle was fierce and both sides suffered heavy casualties, but this time the British were better prepared and had adequate medical facilities including evacuation. The 62nd Punjabis went into action at the end of January 1917 and in three days of fighting lost one company commander and another British officer killed and 191 ORs killed or wounded. Colonel Morris was ordered to hand his battalion's sector over to a reserve battalion but refused, saying that the 62nd Punjabis could still hold their positions as planned. Maude replied in a signal on 4 February and said: 'How much I admire not only your excellent work yesterday, but also the splendid spirit which has prompted you to ask to carry on.' Morris was awarded the DSO soon afterwards.

On 8 February 1917 Colonel Morris assumed temporary command of the 36th Brigade and Major Auchinleck took over command of the battalion. On 24 February he was promoted to acting lieutenant colonel. Meanwhile, he led the battalion forward to capture the last Turkish stronghold on the south bank of the River Tigris. Supporting units then advanced north, crossing the Tigris in an outflanking movement. Early on 23 February the 1/9th Gurkhas were ferried across the river with the objective of holding back the enemy while a pontoon bridge was erected. Later that afternoon Auchinleck and his men relieved the Gurkhas and established a secure bridgehead. The Punjabis occupied the trenches dug by the Gurkhas, but had to spend the night enlarging them given the difference in size between the diminutive Gurkhas and the tall Punjabis.

The following morning the 62nd Punjabis led the final attack on Kut. It had to be another frontal attack which meant advancing over more than 1,000 yards of open desert with no cover at all before getting to grips with the Turks. The 36th Brigade was deployed with their British battalion on the left, the 62nd Punjabis in the centre and the 82nd Punjabis on the right. Auchinleck fully expected high casualties, but this time he was in command and he ordered the advance to be by sections in file, the section commander leading his five or six men advancing with wide gaps between each section. There was far more control using this method instead of the usual extended line; only eight were killed and fifty-eight wounded compared with the 82nd Punjabis who advanced in line and suffered five times the casualties of the 62nd Punjabis. The British battalion also experienced severe losses.

During the final few yards of the advance the Turks abandoned their positions and moved back, fearing encirclement. The 62nd Punjabis occupied the now empty Turkish trenches. For the remainder of the day there were mopping-up operations which brought in many Turkish prisoners and two field guns abandoned by their Austrian and German crews. By 25 February the Turks were in full retreat and Maude decided to pursue the enemy with the objective of capturing Baghdad as soon as possible. The Royal Flying Corps (RFC) had been strengthened with both pilots and aircraft, which meant that Maude was able to receive valuable air reconnaissance as well as aerial support with which enemy columns retreating northwards could be harried. Over the next ten days both the 62nd and 82nd Punjabis were in hot pursuit of the enemy on both sides of the Tigris. The Turks tried delaying tactics which were unsuccessful. Auchinleck described this period of being 'a little fighting, long marches, no paths, plenty of lice, bit of good spirit'. The 62nd Punjabis were the first troops to enter Baghdad on 8 March 1917 and they met with little resistance when they entered the city. From aerial reconnaissance it was obvious that most of the Turkish force was making for Kirkuk, 150 miles further to the north.

On 12 March 1917 Auchinleck relinquished his temporary command to Colonel Morris and reverted to the rank of major and second-in-command of the battalion. At the end of May 1917 the 62nd Punjabis were sent to Baguba on the River Diyala about 40 miles north of Baghdad. Once there, the battalion dug trenches and dugouts and then settled down to general garrison life. At the end of August Auchinleck learned that he had been awarded the DSO for his service commanding the 62nd Punjabis on the outskirts of Baghdad in March. At the same time, it was announced that he had also been mentioned in dispatches.

In mid-September 1917 Auchinleck was posted to the 52nd Indian Infantry Brigade as brigade major. This brigade was a part of the new 17th Indian Division stationed near Baghdad. Auchinleck was not happy to leave his regiment which he still saw as his home, but the appointment to brigade major or 'BM' was a splendid recognition of Auchinleck's work and he was still a relatively young officer. His work as the temporary commander of the 62nd Punjabis had not gone unnoticed. Auchinleck by now had a lot of active service experience under his belt and as the 52nd

Brigade was busy receiving new soldiers from India, Auchinleck as BM was in an ideal position to share his knowledge of fighting the Turks and the conditions that could be expected in Mesopotamia.

Even though the 52nd Brigade was sent closer to the front, it never got involved in any of the serious fighting of the remainder of the Mesopotamian campaign and in the summer of 1918 Auchinleck applied for another leave which he spent in Sri Lanka. When he returned from this leave in August 1918, preparations were being made to advance into Kurdistan. Then on 2 November 1918 the Turks sued for an armistice, just nine days before the end of the First World War. In January 1919 Auchinleck was awarded the OBE for his outstanding work as brigade major of the 52nd Indian Brigade. Somehow, after four years of campaigning against the Turks, Auchinleck had emerged without a scratch. His contemporaries and future field marshals, Montgomery and Wavell, had also survived the First World War, but Montgomery was wounded several times as was Wavell who had been wounded in France and lost an eye. The UK was to be at peace for the next twenty years and Auchinleck returned to India.[1]

## *Chapter Three*

# A Return to India

Auchinleck did not immediately return to India after the war's end in November 1918 but for the following six months was stationed at the divisional garrison at Mosul where he had been appointed GSO2 (Ops); basically, a Grade 2 staff officer concerned with operations. Mosul was the northern capital of Mesopotamia and was situated on the banks of the River Tigris opposite the site of the ancient city of Nineveh. This was a site that Auchinleck never tired of exploring in his leisure time while his staff duties were not really exacting. In May 1919 Auchinleck was appointed GSO1 to a division ordered to pacify areas of Kurdistan. He was promoted to temporary lieutenant colonel and moved to his new divisional HQ at Sulaimaniyah in the mountains east of Kirkuk. This new area of operations had come about as local Kurds, after ridding themselves of 300 years of Turkish rule, were refusing to accept Arab rule, so had revolted and law and order had totally broken down. Major General Theodore Fraser, Auchinleck's new commanding officer, told Auchinleck of his ideas on how to restore order in the area but left Auchinleck with a free hand. Later Auchinleck admitted that he loved this appointment; the rest of the divisional staff were young and inexperienced and so Auchinleck did most of the staff work himself while instructing others as he went along. Auchinleck was also awarded another medal: the silver General Service Medal, together with the clasp 'KURDISTAN'. Fraser totally appreciated Auchinleck's work and recommended him for a 'Mentioned in Dispatches' and swift promotion.

In November 1919 Auchinleck was promoted to the rank of brevet lieutenant colonel, a rank that was only given to outstanding officers but carried no extra pay. At the same time Auchinleck was told that he had been nominated for a vacancy at the Staff College at Quetta. In 1919 there were no examinations to pass before entering the Staff College if the officer had a nomination. One-third of the vacancies on the course were allotted to officers with nominations; the remainder had to pass competitive entrance exams. Auchinleck had not seen his mother or the UK for more than seven years, but without hesitation he accepted the nomination to Quetta. The Staff College was the way forward to high command in the army and Auchinleck was still ambitious. The college was 3,000ft above sea level and therefore relatively cool for India, even in mid-summer. Its remoteness also ensured that its students were not distracted by the 'bright lights' of big cities and popular hill stations. Auchinleck found that he was quite often older than many of the instructors, let alone his fellow students, and certainly had more combat experience than the majority of both students and instructors. Auchinleck enjoyed his time at Quetta, but was critical of the syllabus which he considered to be too theoretical and academic. Little importance was placed on administration, especially the problems of supply and transport, some of which he had suffered first-hand in Mesopotamia during the campaign there. The staff course lasted for one year and Auchinleck passed out in the top ten. This gave him the distinction of being able to have the important letters 'psc' (Passed Staff College) after his name in the Army List. He was then granted twelve months' leave in the UK. His last home leave had been in 1912 and it was now 1921.

Auchinleck decided to pay for a holiday in the south of France for his mother and his unmarried sister Ruth. For the first time in his life he felt rich, having saved much of his pay during nearly five years of war. In that period, he had not had to meet any of the usual expenses of a British officer. Auchinleck arranged to meet his mother and sister in Marseilles at the end of February 1921 and from there they would travel to a resort at Hyères near Toulon. It was then that a major change in Auchinleck's life occurred as it was here that he met Jessie Stewart, a young woman 21 years of age and single; Auchinleck met her almost by chance as the young Jessie, after being told by her maid that a handsome war hero and single colonel was on the premises, went directly down to breakfast to seek out her quarry and collided with him in the entrance hall of the breakfast room. Auchinleck might have been confused and embarrassed by the incident. He was also smitten by and fell in love with Jessie Stewart; it was love at first sight. Auchinleck had had little to do with women; his career and the war had prevented this. Within a fortnight he had proposed to Jessie; he was immediately accepted but her mother Mrs Stewart, a widow, insisted that they should not marry for six months. Part of her objection was the difference in ages between Auchinleck and Jessie who was sixteen years younger than him. Reluctantly they both agreed, but during the summer Auchinleck was invited to stay at the Stewart home at Kinloch Rannoch in Perthshire. Eventually the marriage took place in London on 28 September 1921.

Even though Auchinleck was a brevet lieutenant colonel, he was posted to a major's appointment as deputy assistant quartermaster general (DAQMG) to Army HQ in Simla. It was to this hill station on the borders of Kashmir in northern India that Auchinleck took Jessie at the end of 1921. The quartermaster general (QMG) was a gunner of the British army, Lieutenant General Sir George MacMunn, who had for a brief period after the 1914–18 war been C-in-C in Mesopotamia. He was also a distinguished author, specializing in Indian history, religions and customs. Auchinleck got on well with MacMunn and enjoyed the work, even if it was to do with reducing the size and the structure of the army to pre-1914 levels. The new C-in-C in India was General Lord Rawlinson and he was reorganizing the regimental formations of the Indian army, which was to be more than just altering the names and designations of units. The 62nd Punjabis were about to become the 1st Battalion of the 1st Punjab Regiment, the senior regiment of the Indian infantry.

Auchinleck made further connections which were to be useful in the future as in early 1923 another DAQMG arrived; there were three in the establishment. This was Major Hastings Ismay, a cavalry officer of the Punjab Frontier Force, and he came direct from the Staff College at Quetta. Like Auchinleck, Ismay had also married recently and the Auchinlecks and the Ismays quickly became close friends. Ismay was an important friend to make as in the Second World War he was to become the British wartime Prime Minister Winston Churchill's chief of staff. After four years on the staff, Auchinleck was posted back to his regiment as second-in-command (2ic). The 62nd Punjabis had been renamed the 1st/1st Punjab regiment and was stationed at Peshawar on the North-West Frontier.

Unusually, in 1925 the North-West Frontier was quiet, but overall India was not. In the larger cities such as Mumbai, Kolkata, Karachi (now in modern Pakistan) and Madras, there was much nationalist ferment as Indians began to press for the British to leave India. Auchinleck was quite happy at this time as he was delighted to be back with his parent regiment and as he had passed his language exam in Pushto – the language of the Pathans before the outbreak of war in 1914 – Auchinleck could now put into practice his skills on the locals along the North-West Frontier as well as his own men. Very soon after Auchinleck's arrival his regiment was sent to Jamrud, halfway between Peshawar and Landi Kotal on the way to the Khyber Pass. The fort at Jamrud consisted of two separate two-storey buildings which stood astride the road leading to the mountains of Afghanistan. It is claimed that the mountains and the Muslim way of life made an impact on Auchinleck that decades later led him to retire to the Atlas Mountains in Morocco and to die there.

During his short return to his regiment as second-in-command Auchinleck was required to act as GSO2 to the Peshawar District commander, Major General Sir Robert Cassels. They had known each other from the Mesopotamian campaign and the fighting around Kut. The two men got on well and were to become firm friends. Fifteen years later Auchinleck took over from General Cassels as C-in-C in India. At the end of 1926 he was due six months' leave and so after five years of married life he and Jessie returned to her family home in Scotland. During this period of home leave Auchinleck met his two brothers-in-law for the first time. Early in 1927 while staying with more of Jessie's relatives, this time in the West Country, Auchinleck learned that he was to represent the Indian army, with Colonel Eric de Burgh, on the first course of the new Imperial Defence College in London. The college was intended for senior officers of all three services as well as a few civil servants who had been earmarked for the highest appointments of their professions. Successful completion of the course, which lasted a year, meant the addition of the letters 'idc' (Imperial Defence College) after their names in the Service Lists. It was and remains an honour to be nominated for this course. However, for Auchinleck it was something of a disaster financially as for the previous seven years he had held the rank of brevet lieutenant colonel but was only paid as a major. He had been married for five years to a wife who had no dowry and he had been on an expensive leave in the UK. Now he was about to lose much of his Indian army allowance and must live in London, which was and still is very expensive. Even so, Auchinleck chose to attend the course, telling his friends that it would save a fare from India.

While at the college Auchinleck made several important acquaintances and friends both from instructors and students which were to be of use later during the dark days of the Second World War, including Major General John Dill, the chief instructor and later CIGS, and the future Field Marshal Viscount Alanbrooke. Auchinleck got on particularly well with John Dill and in 1940 was able to use this friendship. Auchinleck, after passing his course, returned to India in early 1928 and was once more second-in-command of his regiment. He was stationed this time close to the regimental centre at Jhelum within sight of the Kashmir Mountains. His CO was Lieutenant Colonel G.E.C. Underhill with whom Auchinleck had served throughout the 1914–18 war in the Middle East in the same rank. The area around Jhelum was brilliant for battalion training and in the vicinity were three Indian battalions and a single British battalion.

Soon after Auchinleck's arrival, the district was visited by the C-in-C Field Marshal Sir William Birdwood, a veteran of the Gallipoli campaign having commanded Australian forces there. Birdwood was very curious about Auchinleck's experience of the Imperial Defence College. Birdwood had never attended any staff college and certainly could not see the point of mixing the three services together. It was around this time that Auchinleck was beginning to stall in his career. He had been an officer for twenty-five years and was by now 44 years of age but still only a major. Ten years earlier he had held the rank of temporary lieutenant colonel and had been paid as such. Auchinleck considered it unfair that as a brevet lieutenant colonel he was expected to live the part including the lifestyle but only received the pay of a major. On guest nights in the officers' mess it was expected that senior officers should 'treat' guests, a practice officially frowned upon but carried out according to social convention. This caused Auchinleck some financial strain, but he bore it stoically.

It had been hoped that Birdwood might put in a word regarding Auchinleck's future, but he did not and seemed more interested in the past rather than the future. Auchinleck decided to continue, saying nothing and hoping that something might turn up. He knew that he had been recommended several times for accelerated promotion but it was the wrong time for any such hope: 1928 was not a good year for the military as no one could foresee war while Ramsay MacDonald, soon to be prime minister for the second time, was demanding further cuts in military spending and so Auchinleck would have to wait for a long time for any promotion. However, patience was rewarded when in December 1928 Lieutenant Colonel Underhill, who had suffered for years with a leg wound, retired prematurely. On 21 January 1929 Auchinleck realized his ambition, and that of every officer, to command his own regiment; many are content to do this and often retire at the end of their period of command. Auchinleck was finally promoted to the full rank of lieutenant colonel exactly twenty-six years after his original commissioning as an officer. He, as with all commanding officers (COs), for the first time in his career had the opportunity of demonstrating his own ideas of leadership to both the officers and men under his command; he was completely in charge and the battalion often reflected the strengths and weaknesses of its CO.

Auchinleck set about training his battalion. He had spent much of his life with the people of Punjab but now he had the opportunity to mould them in the way that he wished them to be. Not only did Auchinleck get to know his men but he also met their families, visiting them in their homes. He had a mixture of the different representations of the Indian people in his battalion, but overall those serving under Auchinleck were Punjabi Muslims and he got along with them. During the summer of 1929 he was away from the battalion for a little over a month as Birdwood had remembered his conversation with Auchinleck and requested him to run a course for all three services for officers struggling to pass their promotion examinations. This cramming course was to last for two weeks at Murree, a hill station about 100 miles north of Jhelum. Auchinleck enjoyed the experience; he could teach, and he was in his element. There were no members of the Royal Navy or the RAF, which was not surprising as the syllabus for promotional exams in each service was quite different from their counterparts. After the course had been taught, Auchinleck returned to his battalion and to Jessie and continued the normal round of domestic and garrison duties. These were happy days but shortly before

Christmas 1929 he learned that he was to go back to the Staff College at Quetta as an instructor. The appointment was GSO1 with the rank of a full colonel. Auchinleck considered that Birdwood had been instrumental in this promotion and was grateful but unsettled as it meant leaving his battalion after so many years. When he came to leave in the New Year the entire battalion turned out for him and his loaded car was towed by his officers to the railway station as a mark of respect to him. Auchinleck was moved by this gesture and this showed when his train pulled out of the station for Lahore en route for Quetta.

Auchinleck's appointment and promotion began on 1 February 1930 and at last his bank could be satisfied with his earnings as he not only had the salary of a full colonel, but he also got a bonus for being a staff officer and for the first time he was free of financial constraints. He was also to shake up some of the teaching at Quetta. Auchinleck, instead of allowing the previous practice of exercises that bore no relation to the previous one or the next, insisted that each exercise was relevant to the previous and to the next and so installed a sense of fluidity, while the problems of frontier warfare, which were so relevant to the Indian army, were taken out of the general syllabus and taught as a separate study.

Auchinleck found that in teaching he was also learning, and his natural inquisitive nature and open mind were to stand him in good stead during the Second World War. Auchinleck enjoyed his time at the Quetta Staff College, but in April 1933 his time was up and he went on home leave to the UK. During this leave, in which he spent much of his time organizing his aged mother into a more comfortable home in Surrey, he learned about his next posting. Further promotion was pending, and he had landed a 'plum job' of the peacetime Indian army in his estimation, that of commander of the Peshawar Brigade. Auchinleck was ecstatic and could not wait to return to India even before his period of leave had expired. He arrived at Peshawar on 1 July 1933 and was promoted to temporary brigadier. The Peshawar Brigade was a large formation and consisted of four Indian infantry battalions, one British battalion, one cavalry regiment, three Royal Artillery mountain batteries and elements of engineer and signals units together with a field ambulance and four animal transport companies. The brigade was responsible for occupying frontier posts along the Afridi border right up to the Khyber Pass.

Almost as soon as Auchinleck arrived he was ordered out on a punitive expedition against tribesmen who were coming over from the Afghan border and raiding villages in British India. It was not an infrequent occurrence as these insurgents, often up to 15,000 in number, swarmed into the largely peaceful villages of northern India, causing trouble and looting the area before melting away back into Afghanistan. These raids were largely of nuisance value to the British but horrific to local Indians and the British needed to stamp them out before the raids became bolder and something more. The events of the Indian mutiny no doubt still exercised the minds of the ruling British and their Indian collaborators; therefore the C-in-C Field Marshal Sir Philip Chetwode (future father-in-law of the poet John Betjeman) felt that it was necessary to impose law and order by military intervention. The Peshawar Brigade was mobilized during July, the hottest part of the year. For the remainder of the summer the brigade skirmished with marauding tribesmen, but by the end of September the brigade was recalled to Peshawar for the winter training period which began at the end of October.

During early January 1935 another revolt started among the Muslim population in British India. This time it was far more serious and led by a strong and dangerous extremist, the Haji Sahib Turangzai. Tribesmen began to loot the plains continuously before retreating to their mountain hideouts. The GOC Peshawar District, Major General S.F. Muspratt, was on leave in the UK and so it fell to his deputy, Brigadier Auchinleck, who was acting as district commander as well as commanding the Peshawar Brigade, to step into the breach. Field Marshal Chetwode was quick to order an immediate expedition into tribal territory, with the objective of occupying the centre of the trouble at Kamalai. Auchinleck was put in command of the expedition which was named 'Mohforce' and consisted of two infantry brigades, the 18th KEO Cavalry, 2nd Light Tank Company and a section of the 8th Armoured Car Company of the Royal Tank Corps. These were supported by the 4th Field Brigade Royal Artillery and five companies of the KGO Bengal sappers and miners. No. 20 Squadron RAF was also used in the operation.

The operation began in earnest in August 1935 when the Peshawar Brigade and the Nowshera Brigade, commanded by Brigadier the Honourable Harold Alexander, advanced into the mountains. Brigadier

Alexander was to also make his name in North Africa during the Second World War. Auchinleck ordered his Vickers light tanks to lead the way. The tanks were armed with a 47mm gun and a Vickers machine gun and had a top speed of 22 mph. The tanks operated in pairs and this was the first time that tanks were used in India. The British advanced cautiously into tribal areas and by the middle of August Mohforce reached a major obstacle known as the Nahakki Pass which controls the entrance to Kamalai. A road had to be built and the sappers and miners were kept busy for the next three weeks while Mohforce increased its strength to four brigades. The tanks continued to operate, even if their supplies had to be brought up by camel as the hills were too steep for lorries.

During this period the Faqir of Alinjar joined the Haji Sahib Turangzai and so strengthened the rebellion. On 1 September Alexander went down with malaria and did not return to his brigade until mid-October. Meanwhile, Mohforce increased security at its main camp and pickets were sent out to scout the enemy positions at night, while in the daytime, infantry supported by tanks went out to fight tribesmen and to dominate the approaches to the Nahakki Pass. Finally, Auchinleck organized a night operation involving three brigades to secure all the heights around the pass itself. The operation was an immediate success and in the morning the cavalry advanced through the pass and into the plains beyond. Then the sappers and miners came forward to extend the road, protected by an advance mobile force of about brigade strength. It was during this period that the future Field Marshal Montgomery met Auchinleck for the first time. Montgomery was then GSO1 at the Quetta Staff College and was on tour to learn about the campaign. Later he remarked to Captain Patrick Burge of his regiment that 'a chap called Auchinleck was the best man' he had met on the frontier.

Throughout 1937 Auchinleck pursued his career, and he was often lonely as even though he loved Jessie, there were problems in the marriage. The age difference was certainly showing, as were their different temperaments. Jessie loved to entertain more lavishly than Auchinleck felt comfortable with, while the realization that they would never have children was a burden to be borne. Auchinleck buried himself in his work, much of which was to try to incorporate Indians into the Indian army as officers. Sadly, there were a great number of shameful racist practices in India which reduced Indians to second-class citizens in their own land, while the British were given the role of overlords. The situation was absurd in as much as Pandit Nehru, a future prime minister of India, was denied entry at the Lahore Club in 1935 as he was to join Brigadier Harold Alexander as his guest, even though they had attended Harrow together. It was a situation that allowed certain ignorant British people to lord it over sophisticated and well-educated Indians purely on the basis of skin colour. Auchinleck certainly disliked this form of apartheid. Nevertheless, during the 1930s there was a programme afoot for the 'Indianisation of the Army' or basically the replacement of British officers with suitable Indian officers, but it was considered that this might take many years to achieve.[1]

Auchinleck was not an officer to be tied to a desk, even though he was brilliant at administrative affairs and training in general. Therefore when there was further tribal unrest he made for Waziristan, the scene of an uprising led by the Faqir of Ipi, who was a fanatical religious leader and, according to Greenwood, a sexual pervert. This faqir had the support of the Mahsud and Wazir tribesmen and had led them to violence which was not to be tolerated by the government of India. A full-scale campaign was launched in 1936 to subdue this rebellion, with the operation lasting until the end of 1937 before the revolt was put down.

Once the revolt had been dealt with and Auchinleck was back to administrative and training duties, the year was 1938 and the situation in Europe was looking bad as Germany, under the tyrannical rule of Adolf Hitler and the Nazi Party, was beginning to look for and demand territories outside of Germany and it was clear to the astute that war was coming once more. During the years 1938 and 1939 Auchinleck was involved in advising those with no knowledge of India how that country might well be defended in the event of war and of the role of the Indian army. It was during this period, during May 1938, that Auchinleck met a man who was to become very important in his life; this was Brigadier Eric Dorman-Smith (who later changed his name to Dorman O'Gowan). Dorman-Smith had been appointed Director of Training; he was an Irishman from County Cavan and eleven years younger than Auchinleck. Commissioned into the Northumberland Fusiliers, he had never served in India but was a brilliant staff officer and had received three brevet ranks in six years, rising from captain to his present rank in that period. Auchinleck found that he and Dorman-Smith had a lot in common: both were early risers and enjoyed long walks. Despite the difference in their ages and ranks, they became firm friends. Auchinleck was to describe Dorman-Smith as very intelligent, very imaginative and very valuable to talk to. After Auchinleck's work in India was complete and the British government's financial contribution to the Indian army was increased by 25 per cent, Auchinleck came to the UK with Jessie on home leave as well as visiting relatives in the USA. During a stay in Aldershot he participated in a Higher Commanders' Course with Lord Mountbatten who was to be so important later in his career.[2] However, it was in Scotland that they learned that war had been declared on Germany on 3 September 1939.[3]

*Chapter Four*

# Norway and War

The British declaration of war against Germany was not unexpected except by Hitler who had refused to believe, perhaps misled by his Foreign Minister von Ribbentrop, that the UK would indeed honour its commitment to Poland and go to war against Germany which it did on 3 September 1939. The Poles were no doubt staggered by the lack of British and French action, which was not surprising given that Poland was already considered lost but would be recovered later. However, what was totally unexpected was the Soviet invasion of Poland on 17 September 1939. Auchinleck was unimpressed with arrangements in India when he arrived back there shortly after the outbreak of war in Europe. In India there was no sense of urgency and life continued as if nothing had happened in Europe. This time his stay in India was short; some fleeting three months before he found himself on a civilian Sunderland flying boat from Bombay back to the UK.

Auchinleck had been chosen to command the British IV Corps with the rank of lieutenant general. This was an unusual command for an officer of the Indian army, but was probably the result of a conversation between the new CIGS, General Sir Edmund Ironside, and Admiral of the Fleet Lord Chatfield in which Ironside bemoaned the dearth of young generals suitable for higher command. Chatfield suggested that Auchinleck might be a suitable candidate. This was an excellent suggestion as Ironside knew Auchinleck and had met him several times in India and so Auchinleck received orders to make his way, with all speed, to London. On 25 January 1940 Auchinleck arrived safely in London via Marseilles. He reported to Ironside the next day and his promotion to lieutenant general took effect from 1 February 1940. He was the youngest lieutenant general in the Indian army, of which there were only three in any case, and the youngest in the British army; by then Auchinleck was 55 years of age.

Auchinleck was charged with having to form and train IV Corps ready for movement to France by June 1940. His HQ was initially at The

Grange in Alresford, near Alton, Hampshire and Auchinleck moved into the Swan Hotel nearby. The original divisions of the corps were spread well apart – one in Dorset, the other in Scotland – and their supporting arms and services were spread around England. Most of Auchinleck's troops were reservists from the Territorial army who had trained overall without weapons and instead had used dummy machine guns, rattles and a great deal of imagination. As IV Corps was due to be sent to France in June, Auchinleck made a brief trip there in early April 1940 with his BGS. Together they flew to the BEF HQ at Arras where they met General Viscount Gort and later the British corps commanders General Sir John Dill and Lieutenant General Alanbrooke. They then visited the area allotted to IV Corps near Lille. What he saw there failed to impress Auchinleck as it was obvious the Allies seemed oblivious to the danger that the Germans posed to Western Europe. However, just after his brief visit to France and his return to IV Corps HQ, the Germans invaded Denmark and Norway. Denmark was invaded on 9 April 1940 and swiftly overrun. Norway, however, was a very different problem owing to its size compared with Denmark and its geography as much of the land lay within the Arctic Circle and more than half of its land was mountainous. Even so, within twenty-four hours the Germans had occupied the capital Oslo and the principal ports of Bergen, Narvik, Stavanger and Trondheim. War really had come to the West and the so-called 'Phoney War' was over.

A war in Norway had long been coming in the heads of the British and French planners as well as in the German high command. German naval chiefs had been impressed by the fact that in the 1914–18 war Germany had failed to even consider attacking and occupying Norway and as a result had denied themselves the Norwegian coast from which German warships and submarines operating from Norwegian fjords might have caused havoc across the North Sea. The British and French were mainly concerned with the Norwegian port of Narvik which had the advantage of being ice-free even during the harshest of winters and so allowed for the continued supply of Swedish iron ore via Narvik.

Winston Churchill, who at the outbreak of war was made First Lord of the Admiralty, was virtually obsessed with an intervention against Norway. As Hitler was being briefed by senior naval staff of the merits of invading and occupying Norway, taking Denmark as well, Churchill and his staff were also briefing the British War Cabinet of the necessity of intervening in Norway to ensure that Germany was denied the continuous supply of Swedish iron ore, the loss of which would have crippled the German war machine as its war industries were dependent on it. The problem for both Germany and the UK was that Norway was a neutral country. That didn't bother Nazi Germany too much, while even the British government sought a pretext for violating Norwegian sovereignty to secure their objectives in that quarter.

The British had no desire to invade and occupy Norway but, using its maritime supremacy, was willing to interfere at sea including the use of mines in Norwegian waters. There were also concerns that the Soviet Union might invade Norway via the Arctic, as by November 1939 the Soviet Union had attacked Finland but had become stuck there. Even so, Scandinavia remained quite defenceless in the face of overwhelming aggression. These were the problems facing the Allies until the Germans declared their hand and invaded Denmark and Norway. The Soviets had been fought to a standstill by the Finns who did sue for peace in March 1940, but were unbowed as they had illustrated the shortcomings of the Red Army as the miniscule but well-trained Finnish army had prevented the Soviet Union from annexing their country, so an armistice was declared.

The poor showing of the Red Army in the Winter War of 1939–40 against Finland caused German planners to think that the Soviet Union could be easily defeated and therefore coloured the planning of the 1941 German invasion of the Soviet Union which was to end so disastrously for Germany and her allies. There were plans for an Allied intervention in Norway, but the Allies were unlikely to commit themselves to naked aggression. The Germans and the Soviets had already given up any pretence of behaving in anything like a civilized manner, but were still willing to try to present themselves to the world as decent people, even if their records showed something quite different. The French gave the Germans an excuse when they mentioned in Sweden that the Allies were planning to interfere in Norway. The question of British interference into Norwegian affairs was one that split the British War Cabinet down the middle and that is not surprising as it was led by the uninspiring Neville Chamberlain who lacked all the leadership qualities necessary for the office of prime minister of the UK. However, on 1 April 1940 it was agreed with a plan from the Chiefs of Staff (COS) that allowed for the seizure and securing of Narvik if the Germans did attack Norway after the British had mined Norwegian waters. This plan was far-reaching and allowed for the seizure of several towns and airfields to prevent the Germans receiving iron ore from Sweden. Even so, the British would not act without the co-operation of the Norwegian government as the British government did not want the UK cast in the role of aggressor.

Churchill was always suspicious of the Norwegians. As we shall see, he had good reason to be and he was also cautious towards his own colleagues as it was obvious that not all of them were committed to a war against Germany. It was against this uncertain and unreliable background that Auchinleck was sent out to Norway to take command of the Allied force there and to try to rescue the situation. His reports were not always what the war planners wanted to read, but he was honest, reading the situation as a professional soldier and making his reports accordingly.

The initial Allied response was very disappointing to the Allied planners and General Staff still in their capital cities and not ready for modern warfare, far less that calling for ski troops and winter warfare tactics; something for which the Germans were prepared and had indeed planned for, even down to seeking out Norwegian-speaking Germans and Austrians of which there were many. The plentiful supply of these Norwegian-speakers had resulted from Norwegians who had, during the 1920s when Germany had been in a state of chaos, fostered German children who had been sent to Norway until such time that Germany returned to some form of order. Unfortunately, it was the Nazis who restored this so-called state of order and the children who had been taught to ski and speak Norwegian as well as being fed and clothed and treated as if they were family by charitable Norwegians returned as aggressors and invaded their former host country. Such ingratitude should be noted.

Therefore the Germans had carefully planned their operations and had the correct troops, but the same could not be said of the Allies who did not really have troops trained for winter warfare. There were French troops trained for mountain warfare and the Poles claimed that they had mountain troops, but this was mostly an illusion; the Polish army had been scattered after the German and Soviet invasions of Poland during the autumn of 1939. Thousands of Polish troops made it to France where an émigré Polish army and government were formed, but it was top-heavy with officers and quite often men that might be too elderly to be of any value on the battlefield. The dearth of suitable men for the Polish army led to the conscription of Polish civilians living in France into the Polish army. This led to the so-called Polish Highlanders, the Podhalians, being sent to Norway in 1940, even though many of their members were not trained mountain troops and were scarcely soldiers but civilians in uniform.

The soldier-citizen was to become a norm in the Anglo-American armies. Such men would not normally have considered the armed forces, and certainly not the army, to be a worthy occupation but conscription and the need to defeat Nazi Germany caused millions of men and women to serve and defeat the Germans and the Japanese. Even so the Poles, under inspired leadership, acquitted themselves well in Norway, as did the other Allied units that fought there. It transpired that the only troops genuinely equipped for Arctic warfare were the Norwegian and German armies. The Germans had the edge as the Norwegians were too few, lacked modern weapons and at times some of the loyalties of Norwegian officers was extremely dubious. The British sent a mixed bag of mountaineers and other troops, but nothing like the force that the Germans had assembled for the invasion of Norway. The weather in the Norwegian Arctic was worse than usual and so it seemed that only the Norwegians and the Germans were prepared to fight in the atrocious conditions that were met in Norway; even the hardy French mountain troops were not prepared for such terrible conditions.

The most bitter of the enemies found in Norway was snow, according to Major General P.J. Mackesy, commander of the Allied expedition to Norway or 'Rupertforce' as the expedition was known, who wrote so in a letter to the Permanent Under Secretary of State to the War Office. In his letter, Mackesy noted that even though it was spring throughout much of Europe, it remained winter in the high north of Norway. Mackesy wrote that much of the terrain to be covered in Norway lay under 4ft of snow, even at sea level. To add to the travails of the Allied troops, blizzards frequently blew up in addition to very heavy snowstorms, strong winds and very low night temperatures. The conditions were so severe that even the hardy French mountain troops, *Chasseurs Alpins*, suffered from snow blindness until the middle of May. Allied troops also had no skis or snow shoes and so were confined as to how they could operate in Norway. Mackesy became convinced that the terrain favoured defence, not only because of the weather but also the lack of equipment as Mackesy was not provided with landing craft or tanks while the artillery supplied was inadequate to support a landing and there was no anti-aircraft artillery (AAA) or aerial support coordination. Nevertheless, Mackesy planned landings but the very thing planned was frustrated by the severe weather including 'a real Arctic blizzard' that blew into northern Norway with a week's snowfall. This allowed the Germans to reinforce their positions while the Allies remained static.[1]

Auchinleck was also to remark on the weather conditions found in Norway. On 2 May he wrote that generally the snow at Narvik melted in the first week of April, but in 1940 winter did not finish until mid-May. Auchinleck also considered the hours of daylight in the Norwegian Arctic; in wintertime the hours of daylight were precious few, while in the summer there was almost perpetual daylight especially in the far north. Auchinleck stated that operations in Norway, especially in the north, were only possible between April and October; any other time was impossible. He also called for specialist clothing to be made available for Arctic operations.[2] However, Auchinleck was not convinced of the viability of operations in Norway and could only see success if the weather changed. The Allies remained put wherever they had landed while German ski-troops posed a threat to them. Auchinleck feared that Allied troops, including those using modern transport, would be confined to using mountain tracks even between April and October, and so he considered that the Allied troops needed to be more mobile and that decent ski troops should be provided for the Norwegian campaign.[3]

Auchinleck had other observations to make, especially on Narvik itself. Even if Narvik was captured by Allied forces on 1 June 1940, it would be of little value until 1 December 1940.[4] The port at Narvik would first have to be cleared of the wrecks of German warships that had been sunk by the Royal Navy during April and were now blocking the harbour. Auchinleck also noted that to hold Narvik by land would demand a lot of troops, especially between April and October. Auchinleck saw Narvik as a defended naval anchorage and a base for further operations against German positions in northern Norway. He also considered the overall objective of the Norwegian campaign: to prevent the Germans from obtaining iron ore from Sweden was going to be very difficult.

If there was any attempt to capture the ore areas at Kiruna (100 miles away) or Gällivare (160 miles away), there would have to be several ground bases established and air bases at Luleå and Bodø and the Allies would also have to achieve overwhelming air cover or the entire enterprise would not be feasible. Auchinleck also considered how he might best work with the Swedes and found that there was little that he could use. However, he did consider that he might try to establish a base in anticipation of future operations, perhaps in Sweden or at least towards the east of Narvik and perhaps help the Swedes should an 'opportunity occur'. In conclusion Auchinleck, writing at a time when the Germans were destroying Narvik, suggested that an alternative position for operations in Norway should be found as he was not convinced that Narvik was ideal.[5]

Even though events in Norway were not going brilliantly for the Allies, it was decided that they must still press on with the operation as at least they were fighting the Germans on land and were at least frustrating the enemy while the British naval victory appeared to have been overlooked by everybody. The main objective of the coming operation was to eject the Germans from Norway and it went ahead despite the lack of decent air cover for the Allied troops involved in the operation. Part of the preparation for this operation saw the appointment of Auchinleck as commander of Anglo-French Forces in Narvik designate. He was told by General Sir John Dill that the overall intention of the British government was that he should become the overall commander of the Anglo-French forces once the government decided to end the current system of command in which there was a shared command between Mackesy and Admiral of the Fleet Lord Cork which saw Mackesy technically subordinate to Cork. Once Auchinleck arrived in Norway, he was to link the naval and army commands and liaise with the RAF and then try to bring the three services together operationally.

Before he left London, Auchinleck tried to get abreast of the situation in northern Norway. He told the CIGS that the main objective in northern Norway was the establishment of airfields there. Auchinleck considered that an airfield should be established at Bardufoss, another in neighbouring Harstad and possibly a third at Bodø. All, according to Auchinleck, should receive adequate AAA defences. He also looked at naval defences and identified that a suitable naval base was needed with suitable anchorage, but one that could be defended 'economically' against all attacks ranging through surface, submarine and land attacks. He also said that AAA should be installed at any such base, as well as observing that any such place chosen should not only be defended from the above threats but was also to be developed so that a force of about three divisions (30,000 men) could be supplied through the port at Narvik and the railway line to Luleå. He also gave notice of his requirements for the conclusion of a successful campaign in Norway which probably dismayed the War Office. The CIGS received Auchinleck's requirements which did not include Air Force personnel or troops required for administrative purposes. In Auchinleck's estimation, a force to eject the Germans from Norway would require twelve infantry battalions, one or two machine-gun battalions, a regiment of mechanized cavalry and the 'due proportions of artillery and engineer units'. His AAA requirements were a gross of 3.7in guns and 112 Bofors light guns.

Auchinleck left for Norway with an advanced HQ from Leith in Scotland on the Polish liner *Chrobry* on 7 May 1940 and landed at Harstad on 11 May. He met with Mackesy and Colonel Dowler, an officer from Mackesy's General Staff, on Cork's flagship which was positioned off Skaanland. Auchinleck was quickly brought up to speed about the operations in Norway by Mackesy and Dowler. Immediately he learned of French landings taking place at Bjerkvik at the head of the Herjangs Fjord which were being directed personally by Lord Cork. Auchinleck left for Skaanland with Brigadier Gammell from his own General Staff to meet with Cork. By the time Auchinleck arrived at Skaanland, the French landings had taken place in wet and cloudy weather during the early hours of 13 May 1940. The landings had been supported by naval fire from the Allied fleet anchored offshore.

The French landings were successful, despite the lack of darkness to mask their moves and heavy enemy machine-gun fire from the shore. The Germans were ejected from the north and east of Herjangs Fjord, which allowed French troops to join up with their comrades advancing from the direction of Gratangen in the north; also the countryside down to Oijord, immediately across the Rombaken Fjord which was across from Narvik, was cleared. The French operation impressed Auchinleck and he expressed his admiration for the troops of the French Foreign Legion (FFL), who had been largely responsible for the success of the operation. It was noted though that the French operation had not been hampered by enemy aircraft as the weather had not permitted them to operate. At this point the Allies had no airfields in Norway and it was noted by Auchinleck that if the Germans had been able to get their aircraft into the air, the Allies would not have been able to respond and an enemy aerial bombing raid might have well turned the operation from success to failure.[6]

Auchinleck's words were extremely relevant as it was only poor weather and a fierce naval bombardment that had prevented the Germans from taking effective countermeasures which would have ensured the failure of the French landings. It was to be a few years before the Allies learned how to undertake successful amphibious landings in the face of strong enemy resistance. It was clear that future landings should have sufficient air cover, overwhelming naval support and ensure that effective numbers of troops were being landed. There was a further and very important observation made by Auchinleck: that of the poor relationship between Mackesy and Cork. A major problem was that Mackesy refused to see the significance of close co-operation between land and naval forces and so Auchinleck decided to sack him. Auchinleck told Cork of his decision and, not surprisingly, Cork agreed with him.[7]

It seems that Churchill already had a problem with Mackesy as on 22 April, prior to Auchinleck going to Norway, Churchill had sent a wire to Cork with this strong yet strange message: 'If this officer [General Mackesy] appears to be spreading a bad spirit through the highest ranks of the land force, do not hesitate to relieve him or place him under arrest.'[8] As this was a personal message to Cork, it cannot be said that this was official Admiralty policy, but it does give rise to evidence that Mackesy was not co-operating from the very outset of operations in Norway. Auchinleck later considered that perhaps Mackesy had some form of breakdown. Auchinleck, in a letter to General John Dill, Vice Chief of the Imperial General Staff, made it quite clear that he considered Mackesy was not fit to command troops and claimed that the latter was too timid in his approach towards Norway. According to Auchinleck, Mackesy was more concerned with how the world would view him and that Mackesy's 'cleverness and cynicism completely outweighed his reason'.[9] Auchinleck's main thesis was that the Allies would be better advised to begin a counter-offensive sooner rather than later to prevent the enemy from being able to reinforce their garrison in Norway. Auchinleck considered that Mackesy was too worried about the future to be of any further use in Norway and that was the main reason for his dismissal.

On 13 May 1940 the situation in northern Norway was reviewed and found to be wanting. There was little coordination between the Allied forces in the area; even if Mackesy and his staff had tried to organize inter-Allied co-operation via diplomatic channels, nothing had come of it. Auchinleck sought to rectify this matter and on 16 May had a 'cordial and satisfactory' interview at his HQ with Norwegian generals Ruge, C-in-C Norwegian army, and Fleischer, commander of the 6th Norwegian Infantry Division which had been working closely with French forces to the north of Rombaken Fjord. Ruge and Fleischer insisted that both Mo and Bodø should be protected and prevented from falling into German hands. They also stressed the need to go from the defensive, move over to the offensive and recapture Mosjøen.

Auchinleck's local initiative was reinforced by international diplomacy as the Allies sought to unify their offensive in Norway. On 15 May, the head of the British military mission, Colonel R.C.G. Pollock, MC, set out to assist Auchinleck's HQ to maintain a close relationship with the Norwegian government. Sir Cecil Dormer, the British minister in Norway, had recently returned to Norway from the UK. Dormer met with Auchinleck and Cork to discuss the situation in Norway before taking up his diplomatic post and meeting the Norwegian king, Haakon VII, and the Norwegian government. Cork and Auchinleck took the opportunity in their meeting with Dormer to emphasize the urgent need for closer control of the civilian population in military-controlled areas.

On 23 May Lord Cork flew to Tromsø and discussed the situation in Norway with King Haakon and his government. The result of this meeting and of Dormer's relationship with the king was that relationships between British armed forces in Norway and the Norwegian authorities began to take on a more businesslike and realistic attitude, especially regarding the establishment of a base at Tromsø, something to which the Norwegians had previously objected. The Norwegians had feared that a British presence in Tromsø would provoke enemy aerial attacks and even when the Norwegian government agreed to the establishment of a British base at Tromsø it was stipulated that adequate AAA protection had to be put in place. One assumes that the British would have done this in any event anyway. Even so, Auchinleck did complain that his already meagre supply of AAA was to be diverted and the War Office was not allowing him any further guns.

On 16 May Auchinleck sent a complete report to the British chiefs of staff in which he stated that not much had changed since his last report. He noted that serious aggression was developing from the Soviet Union via Finland and from Germany via Sweden. Even so, Auchinleck considered that the positions already held by the Allies in Norway could be maintained subject to the supply of demands he was to submit in his report. Auchinleck was also in favour of a limited offensive designed to deny the enemy the air base at Mosjøen. However, his list of requirements sent back to Whitehall was quite substantial. For the Royal Navy he requested 4 cruisers, 6 destroyers, 4 escort vessels, 12 anti-submarine vessels and 2 submarines, as well as auxiliary vessels. For his land forces Auchinleck demanded 1 division of cavalry, 1 squadron of armoured cars, 1 mounted infantry unit (Lovat Scouts), 5 batteries of field artillery, 2 batteries of medium artillery, 13 batteries (104 guns) of heavy AAA, 8 batteries (96 guns) of light AAA, 5 companies of engineers, 17 infantry battalions and 1 machine-gun battalion. He also requested two squadrons of Hurricane fighter planes, one bomber squadron and an army co-operation squadron; a very long list indeed.

Auchinleck's primary objective was the denial of iron ore to Germany via the port at Narvik. This had been accomplished owing to the destruction at Narvik by the Royal Navy as well as the sinking of much of the German surface fleet in the waters around Narvik, again the work of the Royal Navy. The secondary objective was the denial of iron ore to Germany via Luleå, but this was not practical unless the Swedes co-operated and this was highly unlikely to happen. The third objective, the maintenance of the integrity of northern Norway, seemed to be the only one of the three objectives that could be immediately considered.

To try to achieve the third objective meant that both Tromsø and Harstad had to be taken and held as bases for Allied forces. However, the problems for the Norway campaign were just about to begin in earnest and become more complicated as on 10 May 1940 the Germans finally began their drive westwards, sweeping through Holland and Belgium and advancing towards France. This meant that Auchinleck's shopping list for Norway was reduced as illustrated by a telegram dated 17 May from COS to Auchinleck. The German westward advance meant that Auchinleck's force was to be limited to twelve French and three British battalions and ten independent companies. This force was to receive the appropriate artillery, engineers and services for those numbers and not what Auchinleck had requested or needed. In addition, forty-eight heavy and sixty light AAA guns were to be sent to Norway, while provision for air cover was reduced to a single Hurricane squadron, a single Gladiator squadron and a possible army co-operation flight. This telegram also stated that the objectives of operations in Norway were to be the denial of iron ore through Narvik to Germany and the preservation of northern Norway. It was suggested that a base needed to be maintained in Narvik to try to deny the Germans iron ore via Luleå, but this was not seen as a priority at that time. Auchinleck's views regarding the retention of Narvik were sought by the COS.

After consultations with Cork and Group Captain Moore RAF, Auchinleck sent his reply on 21 May. He considered that land forces might be able to manage with some additions, but AAA provision was unlikely to be adequate in the face of heavy and determined enemy aerial attacks. Auchinleck maintained that his original air estimates were necessary for a successful campaign and could not be altered and that he still required two Hurricane fighter squadrons, the Gladiator bomber squadron and one squadron from army co-operation and that nothing less would do. Even so, Auchinleck made the best of the situation including the poor provision of AAA guns.[10]

The worsening situation in France as the Germans relentlessly pushed on towards Paris failed to halt operations in Norway. Part of the preparations for a major offensive in Norway included the reinforcement of Bodø which in turn was linked with the holding of Harstad and its surrounding area; on all of this hung the chance of Allied success in Norway. Holding Bodø was essential in Auchinleck's opinion as it provided depth to his defences and was the only port available to the Allies that could be used as an advance base as Mo was already threatened by the enemy. An adequate force needed to be established in the area and so British troops were sent to Bodø. The French, assisted by Norwegian troops, continued to maintain pressure on German forces in the Narvik area. On 14 May Auchinleck ordered French forces under General Béthouart, in relation to operations in the Narvik area, to destroy enemy forces in that area and capture Narvik.

The capture of Narvik was to be the high point of the Allied campaign in Norway. Its capture would have not only denied Germany its supply of iron ore from Sweden, but it would have been a political success and illustrated that Germany was not an all-conquering military power. After the Norwegian campaign had played itself out, Auchinleck gave an account of it to the British government. He began his narrative by stressing the importance of the clearing of the Oijord Peninsula which had been the consequence of a succession of successful landings near Bjerkvik and subsequent operations which had cleared the Oijord Peninsula north of the Rombaken Fjord as far east as Lilleberget. Auchinleck linked these feats to Béthouart's plans for the capture of Narvik.

In his narrative Auchinleck noted that until the ground north of the eastern entrance of the Rombaken Fjord had been cleared, an assault on Narvik would have to be launched onto difficult beaches which the enemy defended using machine-gun posts. Any element of a surprise attack from the sea on Narvik was not possible as all craft necessary for such an assault would have been forced to muster in Oijord in full view of the enemy. The capture of the northern shore of Rombaken Fjord widened the front from which an Allied attack could be made on Narvik and allowed for French field artillery support which had been established north of Oijord. Great secrecy was necessary for a successful Allied attack on Narvik and so the first wave of troops and their landing craft were assembled in secret in the cover of Oijordneset point. The plan was that this hidden force would be able to emerge less than a mile from Narvik, behind a naval bombardment once the Allies began their assault against Narvik town and its harbour.

After careful reconnaissance, Béthouart decided that it would be best to land the first wave of troops on a beach east of Oijordneset. Three battalions of infantry including a Norwegian battalion were transferred by motor landing craft (MLC) across the Rombaken Fjord from Oijord. Once ashore this force, having first blocked the approach of enemy reinforcements from Sildvik by establishing a position astride the railway line in the area, would advance across the peninsula and be able to take Narvik town from the rear. The assault on Narvik was to be accompanied by an attack towards Beisfjord undertaken by Polish troops already on the Ankenes Peninsula. The Poles were to contain German troops in the operational area as well as threaten the enemy line of retreat from Narvik along the road which ran along the northern shore of Beisfjord.

The proposed landing was made particularly dangerous as there were few landing craft to be used in the operation. Owing to enemy action and mechanical breakdowns there were only three amphibious landing craft (ALC) and two MLCs to be had. This limited the number of men who could take part in the initial landing party; only 290 could be taken. This weakness caused great anxiety to both Auchinleck and Béthouart. The original attack against Narvik had been pencilled in for the night of 24/25 May 1940, but at a conference between Auchinleck and Béthouart on 23 May it was decided to delay the attack. There were several reasons for this. One was the weather, as usual, but the conditions were so foul that the two commanders considered an operation undertaken in such conditions would be an 'unjustifiable risk'. Another factor was the lack of air cover. Even if the operation went ahead, it could have been so easily wrecked by German aerial bombing raids as there was only a single fighter squadron available to the Allies to fend off enemy attack. In view of this it was decided that the operation should be delayed until the arrival of a Hurricane fighter squadron which was due on 27 May. Lord Cork agreed with this decision.

Just after this agreement had been reached, news of the British government's decision to evacuate northern Norway was received. Clearly this altered everything in Norway and Auchinleck and Béthouart held another meeting, and after referring to Lord Cork decided that Narvik was still to be attacked during the night of 27/28 May 1940. Regarding the operation against Narvik, Auchinleck wrote:

> In doing so I considered that apart from the desirability of making sure whether the facilities for shipping ore from Narvik had, in fact, been destroyed as thoroughly as had been reported, the chances that a successful attack would do much to conceal our intention to evacuate the country in the immediate future would outweigh the possible disadvantages involved in extending air commitments by establishing troops in close contact with the enemy on the Narvik Peninsula where his main forces were thought to be located.[11]

Auchinleck's intelligence, professional training and nerve were revealed in this incident.

Operations against Narvik began at 2340 hours on 27 May 1940 when three cruisers and five destroyers steamed into position at the mouth of Rombaken Fjord and began to bombard German positions there. Admiral Lord Cork flew his flag on HMS *Cairo*, aboard which were Auchinleck, Béthouart and his staff. The naval bombardment against the Narvik Peninsula was across a wide front with selected targets such as mouths of tunnels as well as suspected enemy machine-gun and artillery positions. The naval gunfire and that of field artillery was heavy and accurate, but close support of the attacking Allied troops was hampered by the terrain which made accurate observation of shell-fall difficult.

The initial landings were quite successful with little opposition and achieved with few casualties. This ensured that the first wave of Allied troops was able to establish a beachhead on the shore at Narvik. However, for a short period further movement was hampered by a small artillery gun firing further to the east of the south shore. This gun caused casualties until it was silenced by naval gunfire. By 0330 hours, a battalion from the FFL and the Narvik Battalion of the Norwegian army were ashore on the peninsula. The enemy managed to launch a counter-attack from the east, which meant that Allied troops in advanced positions had to fight hard to maintain their positions while the landing beaches came under German fire. Eventually the Allies were able to counter-attack the German counteroffensive and begin to advance once more. It was during this period of intensive fighting that HMS *Cairo* was hit twice by bombs and thirty men were killed or wounded. By 2200 hours, the entire peninsula west of a line from Fagernes to Forsneset was in French hands and about 200 Germans had been taken prisoner. Polish troops, after an initial setback, had advanced along the Ankenes Peninsula and had established themselves on high ground overlooking Beisfjord.

Auchinleck considered that the entire operation against Narvik had been carried out with the 'barest margin of safety' and might well have ended in disaster. The first echelon of men, which numbered no more than 290, had had to support itself for forty-five minutes and if the enemy had counter-attacked for a second time, the entire Allied operation at Narvik would have been crushed. Auchinleck took two lessons away from the experience. The first was that adequate landing craft had to be made available for the first wave of troops landing on a hostile shore to ensure large numbers of troops could be landed and reinforced by a second wave of troops. The second observation made by Auchinleck was the lack of bomber aircraft available to the Allies, but overall he considered that the risk run at Narvik had been justified.[12]

Even though the Allies had met with success at Narvik, it was for nought as the Germans had advanced deep into France and that country was on the verge of collapse. The British government decided in view of the catastrophic events unfolding in Europe that all British weaponry and men should be removed from Europe and be prepared for the defence of the UK against a feared German invasion. This, of course, meant that Norway had to be evacuated. The action had to be conducted in secrecy and meant that the British and French commanders in Norway had to deceive their Norwegian counterparts for a while at least regarding Allied activity in Norway. This naturally made relations difficult and relations with Colonel Finne, the Norwegian liaison officer to Auchinleck's HQ, became quite fraught after the Allied evacuation at Bodø. Even General Fleischer was kept ignorant of the intentions of the British government, even though his forces were fighting in the Narvik region. Béthouart was extremely uncomfortable about having to deceive his Norwegian allies, especially as French troops were fighting alongside the Norwegians.[13]

Even though the Germans were running rampant across Europe, it seems extraordinary that events surrounding the Norwegian campaign illustrated that the western Allies were still uncertain as to who the enemy really was: Nazi Germany or the Soviet Union. An amusing side of British caution was that Auchinleck spoke, via telephone, to Pollock in Hindi as a security measure while briefing him, but it was General Ruge who revealed Norwegian thinking when he met Pollock at noon on 4 June. Ruge told Pollock that the Norwegians feared a Soviet invasion of Norway, very much in the manner that the Soviets had invaded Finland during November 1939. Consequently, the Norwegian government was considering inviting the Germans through Sweden to stabilize a frontier around Narvik and the Norwegian position in the north, while using all their resources to combat the Soviet Union.

To compound its staggering naivety, the Norwegian government thought that its idea would be acceptable to the German government as they had commitments elsewhere (the invasion of France perhaps!). Nevertheless, the Norwegian government was not inviting the Germans to take over Norway but even so, it was preferable to having the Soviet Union annexing the country. In the event of a Soviet invasion, the Norwegian government would be evacuated and the Norwegian army would surrender to the Germans. The Norwegian government hoped that if the Soviet Union was to endanger Norway and the Germans were willing to defend it, that the British would leave lorries and other materials which could be used against the Red Army. In the same meeting Ruge admitted that the Norwegian government would like to see the British leave Norway. The Allies continued to proceed with their evacuation plans and considered that any delay would be dangerous.[14]

As late as 26 May it was still considered that perhaps any evacuation of Norway could be put on hold for a short while at least. There were several considerations for this, the main one being how Allied morale and prestige might be affected if Norway was abandoned. It was also noted that the Allies in Norway were holding down German forces there while the use of the Royal Navy to evacuate Norway would tie up ships that were needed for service in the North Sea. There was also talk that perhaps Auchinleck might have been wrong in his estimation that it would take six months to clear the harbour at Narvik and that it would not take long to repair the wrecked railway line between Narvik and the Swedish frontier. It was considered that the Germans had unlimited resources and would swiftly effect the necessary repairs. There was also a fear that a large proportion of Allied stores, including ammunition, would be lost in any evacuation. What was suggested was the rapid capture of Narvik and a defensive line, formed by the Allies, in northern Norway. It was also thought that to supply an Allied garrison in Norway would not require many destroyers if they were used properly to bring supplies as well as troops to reinforce the garrison. There was also a warning that the destroyers were not to be used exclusively as troop carriers. British planners thought that the use of railway tunnels would be extremely useful for protection as well as the hiding of supplies of men and stores from enemy aerial attacks.[15]

Even so, the arguments being put forward to maintain an Allied garrison in Norway were doomed and had been since 24 May when the British government realized that it was about to fight for the very existence of the UK in the face of German aggression and a signal was sent to the flag officer at Narvik. This signal read as follows:

> His Majesty's government has decided that your forces are to evacuate Northern Norway at the earliest moment. The reason for this is that the troops, ships, guns and certain equipment are urgently needed for the defence of the United Kingdom. We understand that from a military point of view operation of evacuation will be facilitated if the enemy's forces are largely destroyed or captured. Moreover, the destruction of the railway and Narvik port facilities make its capture highly desirable. Nevertheless, the speed of evacuation once begun should be the primary consideration to limit the duration of a maximum naval effort. Two officers will be sent out from the United Kingdom to concert the evacuation plan with you and General Auchinleck. Evacuation of all equipment, vehicles and stores will clearly take too long. The following are required to be evacuated in order of importance for the point of view of the defence of the United Kingdom: personnel, light AA guns and ammunition, 25-pounder field guns, heavy AA guns and ammunition. Tactical conditions must rule but so far as they permit plans which should be formed accordingly. The Norwegian government have not, repeat not, yet been informed and great secrecy should be observed.[16]

The need for secrecy was obvious as there was an element in Norwegian society that had sympathy for Germany, while the French security system was not as good as it might have been.

Despite security concerns, the British government, after only a single day after deciding to evacuate Norway, informed the French government of its intentions. The flag officer at Narvik suggested that he should inform the local French commander of the unfolding situation rather than the French government doing so and that he would ensure the need for secrecy locally about British intentions in Norway.[17] The problem with the Narvik campaign was that it could only be deemed a failure despite its apparent success – the German surface fleet had largely been sunk by the Royal Navy which had blocked the waters off Narvik and its harbour and then later, the town and harbour and surrounding areas were captured by the Allies – but the tempo and pace of the fighting in Europe in 1940 were being set by the success of the German advance into France.

The main failing at Narvik was timidity, as prior to the arrival of Auchinleck, Allied commanders, as Churchill observed, refused to go where the Germans did. An example was the road between Namsos and Mosjøen which had been declared by British and French commanders as impassable, but the Germans passed along it in seven days.[18] The Germans were better prepared for the invasion of Norway, of course, but this still didn't explain why Allied commanders behaved as they did until the arrival of Auchinleck, and Churchill was not shy about this in his criticism of the early day of the Norwegian campaign. Churchill's point was that the German plan for the occupation of Norway was ruthless and well-executed, using air power to perfection. Churchill also noted that at Narvik 6,000 German troops had held 20,000 Allied troops at bay for six weeks. He wrote that even though the Royal Navy had opened the Narvik attack 'so brilliantly', it was paralysed by the refusal of the military commander to take what Churchill admitted was 'a desperate risk'.[19] Of course, he was referring to General Mackesy.

An evacuation of northern Norway had always been a prospect even before Narvik had been captured, but the fall of France meant that the evacuation was speeded up to prevent a German conquest of the UK and a Nazi domination of Europe. The matter of secrecy later led to recriminations as it was alleged by some that there had not been enough effort to safeguard equipment and that more might have been brought back from Norway ready for the defence of the UK. Colonel Graham at Base Command, Tromsø was told on 1 June by NWEF HQ that an evacuation was imminent, and it was stressed that all service personnel including the British Military Mission at Tromsø were to be evacuated; an overall figure of 350 men to be lifted out of Tromsø. Graham was given a comprehensive list of what to do and what to expect during the evacuation. The FO Narvik had already instructed the captain of HMS *Devonshire* to contact Colonel Graham and make the necessary arrangements for removing him and his men from Tromsø on or before 6 June 1940.

It was noted that not all equipment could be saved from Tromsø save for personal arms and such equipment that might be possible to move onto HMS *Devonshire*. Secret papers that could not be taken aboard the ship were of course to be destroyed. Interestingly, the matter of finances was strictly controlled, as part of the instructions issued by Auchinleck's HQ was as follows:

> You will hand over to the British consul sufficient money to meet all known liabilities and withdraw the balance from the Bank and take it with you. If this, for any reason, is not practicable you will transfer your credit to the account of the Consul. You should keep a record of your financial action.[20]

In other words, the British needed to try to keep the accounts up to date and squared up!

Colonel Graham's instructions were based on the least amount of people knowing what was happening in Norway and included a pretence of an advanced base being established in Narvik to explain why Tromsø was being evacuated.[21] The RAF at least was given clearer operational orders relating to the evacuation and how it was to support it. Orders revealed that the NWEF was to be re-embarked (evacuated) over a five-day period beginning at 2200 on 2 June 1940. The method of embarkation was to transfer troops via small boats called 'puffers' or from the quays to waiting destroyers in the four main areas of Harstad, Skaanland, Ofotfjord Sørreisa and Salangsverket. Later, the evacuated troops were to be transferred from the destroyers to transport ships that were lying about 60 miles to the west of the evacuation points.

The re-embarkation of the NWEF was not to be a continuous process but had to be undertaken at varying points in each twenty-four-hour period. The main task of the RAF was to provide air cover for the evacuation. The FO Narvik arranged for Swordfish aircraft, operating from aircraft carriers, to carry out reconnaissance patrols to try to discover enemy movements between Sorfolla and Tysfjord. The RAF was also to bomb, every day, the German HQ at Hundalen as well as other bombing raids in the Hundalen area as and when necessary. Later a pair of Swordfish was to be sent to Bardufoss to guide Gladiator fighter-bombers from 243 Squadron RAF to naval carriers which were to take them back to the UK.

Lord Cork had been informed that forces and equipment being evacuated from Norway were needed for the defence of the UK and that the most important element to be evacuated was manpower. If equipment could be brought back, so much the better, but logistically this was going to prove to be difficult and therefore various pieces of equipment had to be prioritized. After men, the next most important items to be loaded onto ships were light AAA guns and their ammunition; then 25-pounder field guns and finally heavy AAA guns. After the evacuation Cork was criticized for the lack of war matériel returned from Norway, especially AAA guns, as out of a possible forty-eight heavy AAA guns, only six were returned.[22] The summer of 1940 was a time of great unease and fear for the British, especially the service chiefs as they sought a response to German aggression and success across Europe, so it is not surprising that tempers became frayed and unfair accusations were made.

Cork was not slow in responding to the criticism of his actions in Norway; he was particularly angered by the charge of not bringing enough heavy AAA guns back from Norway. He responded to the accusations by asking how he was expected to defend the embarkation points without AAA guns as the Allies had never established air supremacy throughout the Norwegian campaign. Without the heavy AAA guns, ships being loaded would have been extremely vulnerable to enemy aerial attacks. Another point made by Cork was the absolute need for secrecy as many local Norwegians, including military commanders, could not be trusted, which served to make the task of Allied commanders that much harder.

During July 1940 Cork robustly defended himself against his critics who had not been in Norway and were ignorant of the situation there during the campaign, but this did not prevent them maintaining their views from the safety of a desk in Whitehall. Cork was blunt as he criticized the Norwegian campaign from the view of someone who had served there. He said that the embarkation points were unsafe, as had been the entire campaign in Norway, but then war is never safe. Part of this lack of safety was that despite there being a need for secrecy, how could secrecy be maintained? Cork gave Harstad as an example of what he meant: the Germans made daily aerial reconnaissance flights over the area and could see clearly what might be happening there. The trick was to deceive the enemy and not allow the Germans to discover what was really taking place. As Cork observed, if the Allies had removed the AAA defences at Harstad during the last week of May 1940, the Germans would have realized that they were planning to abandon Norway as during the previous week much effort had been spent in installing the same defences. This was the very reason that the dismantling of AAA defences at Harstad did not begin until 2 June, the day that the evacuations were to commence. On the same day Cork took the initiative of informing the Norwegian government that the Allies were about to begin evacuation from Norway. Returning to the question of the low numbers of AAA guns being returned to the UK, Cork observed that as many of the embarkation points were on open beaches and subject to enemy aerial attacks, he needed AAA defences until the very end of the embarkation period and that was the reason why few such guns were returned to the UK.[23]

Auchinleck was appalled to hear the criticism of Lord Cork coming from Whitehall regarding the question of the AAA guns and considered that this was due to ignorance on the behalf of the Admiralty. On 7 July 1940 he wrote to Cork:

> As you know on 24 May, the Bodø situation was critical and unless Gubbins could have been reinforced, he would have probably been pushed into the sea, as happened at Namsos and Åndalsnes, or would have been surrounded. As you know, we had reinforcements actually embarked and ready to go down; if the order for evacuation had not

> come, these reinforcements would have been sent. Similarly, if the general evacuation had been appreciably delayed or postponed, these reinforcements would have had to go, as Bodø could not be evacuated too far in advance of the evacuation of Harstad, for the reason that the enemy pushing up the coast (as they did) would have seriously compromised the latter operation. In actual fact, the period between the evacuation of Bodø and the final evacuation of Harstad-Narvik was only just long enough as you will remember. If Bodø had had to be reinforced and a delaying action fought around it, the withdrawal from that area would have been definitely more complicated and difficult and might well have become another Åndalsnes or a minor Dunkirk. As it was, owing to the lack of suitable ships and port facilities, the four field guns and two Bofors had to be abandoned there (the other two Bofors were left at Mo as you will remember).[24]

Auchinleck's letter to Cork illustrated just how difficult it was to evacuate Norway. As with many military evacuations, it was planned in haste and plans set often have to be compromised to get personnel away while some equipment had to be abandoned often owing to lack of facilities to remove or transport them. In the case of Norway, the AAA guns were being used until the last possible moment; both Auchinleck and Cork knew this but had difficulty trying to explain what had happened in Norway to those who had not served in that campaign. The main point though, was that despite enemy aerial attacks at the embarkation points and fighting on the high seas between the Royal Navy and the German navy, the evacuation from Norway was successful, returned to the UK and the British campaign in Norway was ended.

*Chapter Five*

# Return to England: Southern Command, 1940 A Short Interlude and then India Once More

When Auchinleck returned to the UK in June 1940 he found a very changed country. The British people expected to be invaded by the Germans and were ready to fight for their homeland. Instead of the dithering and near traitorous clique that had surrounded Neville Chamberlain, Churchill's predecessor at Number 10, a new government under the premiership of Winston Churchill was preparing the nation to defend the UK against the expected German invasion. Churchill was much more warlike and hostile towards Germany and knew who the enemy was: Germany. He knew that you could not negotiate with the Nazis, something that some of the effete British upper classes thought they could do. They were more concerned with the Bolshevik threat from the Soviet Union as it threatened their way of life, while they considered that Nazi Germany could well be beneficial to them. As Greenwood writes: 'A new defiant spirit was abroad.'[1] This sentiment was echoed in Field Marshal Ironside's diary as he wrote on 4 June 1940: 'More than ever I feel that we must get men who can fight. The namby-pamby people that have grown up in late years are not to be trusted in this emergency. Character and guts. That is what is wanted.'[2]

The emergency to which Ironside refers is of course the evacuation of the BEF from France via the beaches at Dunkirk. He was right; guts and character were necessary during the summer of 1940 and so many of the political elites in the UK could not be trusted owing to their pro-German sympathies. Churchill would sort this group out and have them imprisoned. It takes character to imprison your friends to preserve one's country from a foe. Auchinleck made an observation when he gave his report on the Norwegian campaign. He made a comparison between French and British troops and wrote that the British troops lacked training and experience; he used words like 'callow' and 'effeminate' to describe them, while claiming that the French were 'real soldiers'. Auchinleck did not blame the men but the previous decade. This report was badly received by the War Cabinet and he was criticized for being so direct. Some said that as Auchinleck had spent so much time in India, he did not really understand the situation in Europe. However, many knew that he was correct, and training methods from that time on became more rigorous.[3] Auchinleck became quite frustrated by talk of a 'Dunkirk medal' being struck.[4] Dunkirk, of course, was the British withdrawal from mainland Europe, and one does not win wars by making withdrawals. Dunkirk was the third major defeat of the Allies. First the Poles had been driven from their own country and across Europe to France. Prior to Dunkirk, there had been the Norwegian campaign, which had seen the Allies abandon Norway as troops and equipment were needed to defend the UK after the fall of France, the retreat to Dunkirk and the British withdrawal from the beaches there. It is not surprising that Auchinleck could not conceive why anyone would want to remember Dunkirk and the humiliation of having to withdraw from Europe.

The year of 1940 was a wretched one for the UK as it saw its armies driven from Europe, not necessarily defeated as Norway had shown, but certainly in France and if the British could make the winter of that year, there was an opportunity to regroup and to rethink. As history records, the Germans did not invade the UK as the Luftwaffe failed to gain air superiority, which would have been necessary to support the German army as it made an amphibious assault against British beaches. Furthermore, as already narrated, the Royal Navy had sunk most of the German surface fleet. If the Germans had gone ahead with their plans to invade the UK, warships from the Royal Navy would have caused havoc with the German invasion barges as they tried to make their way across the English Channel.

It was in this frantic atmosphere that Auchinleck was to take command of V Corps and very quickly found himself in command of Southern Command from where he was expected to defend the realm from Bognor Regis to Bristol. Years later, Auchinleck remarked that this task was 'quite hopeless really'.[5] Nevertheless, he took his work very seriously and issued specific orders ensuring that there were no unguarded moments and that all sentries and guards covered one another. He also ensured that there was no concept of being off-duty and that everyone under arms would be ready at a moment's notice. There was little chance of leave unless in exceptional circumstances. Auchinleck ensured that all commanders from the most senior to the most junior platoon commander were aware that the area of V Corps, Southern Command was the front line, a forward position and that they must make all the men and women under their command well aware of this. Auchinleck knew from his active service on the North-West Frontier that a sentry who gave away his position was quickly picked off and that when danger threatened, it was likely that an attack could come from any direction and often from the least likely. Auchinleck's father would have recalled that the Indian Mutiny began with an attack on a church parade when the rebel Indian troops knew that the British would not be carrying their weapons.[6] These were the very reasons why Auchinleck gave such strict and some might have said draconian orders, but his recent service in Norway had also suggested to him that troops must be ready at all times, the Germans were likely to launch surprise attacks and civilians should not be trusted.

Despite this air of being almost helpless in the face of a determined German invasion of the UK, plans were being drawn up of how such an invasion might be stopped. On 9 July 1940 Auchinleck held a conference for his divisional commanders and senior staff officers. It was during this meeting that it was decided the Germans must be stopped on the beaches before they could land any of their heavy equipment. This was in full agreement with Lieutenant General Sir Alan Brooke, who was Auchinleck's immediate superior. Three days later on 12 July, Auchinleck was invited by Churchill to dine and spend the night at Chequers, the official country home of British prime ministers, in Buckinghamshire. Once there Auchinleck met with Major General Bernard Paget and Major Duncan Sandys, who was also a Member of Parliament and both were veterans of the Norway campaign. Auchinleck was also delighted to meet his old friend, Major General Ismay of the Indian army.

At dinner Auchinleck was seated next to Mrs Churchill who, even though there had been heavy Luftwaffe attacks on the south coast two days earlier, including in Auchinleck's area of command, did not discuss the war with him. However, once the ladies withdrew after dinner, Auchinleck considered himself to be under the microscope as Churchill more or less monopolized the conversation with his view of the expected invasion. What is interesting is that Churchill did not consider that an invasion would happen, but it would be best to be prepared for it and that the invasion scare did not harm the country at all as it united the people. Churchill kept his generals until one o'clock in the morning studying maps and possible invasion tactics. Auchinleck and Paget made observations on the tactics used by the Germans in Norway as well as the enemy tactics used in Western Europe during the summer, such as paratroopers and gliders, but there was little opportunity owing to Churchill dominating the conversation such as it was. After lunch the next day, Auchinleck returned to London with Ismay who told him that Churchill was about to make some command changes which would benefit Auchinleck.

On 19 July 1940 Auchinleck accompanied General Brooke on a tour of the Isle of Wight defences. During this time while they were having a picnic lunch, their peace and quiet was disturbed by the arrival of a dispatch rider who handed an urgent message to Brooke; he was being summoned back to London to report immediately to the Secretary of State for War. Later that evening Brooke was told that he was to take over from General Ironside as C-in-C Home Forces with the acting rank of general. Ironside had been promoted to field marshal and been given a peerage. Auchinleck was to take over as GOC Southern Command and the then unknown Major General Bernard Law Montgomery was to take over V Corps from Auchinleck and become the youngest lieutenant general in the British army at the age of 52. Montgomery, or 'Monty' as he was more popularly known until very recently, now seems to have been forgotten by many but remains an interesting and controversial figure among military historians and was a thorn in the side of Auchinleck.

The summer of 1940 was fraught as the British fully anticipated being invaded by Germany and were prepared to defend the UK but luckily Churchill's resolve to defend the British Isles to the last was never tested as the RAF and its allies were able to defeat the Luftwaffe. Auchinleck was charged with the defence of much of the south coast of the UK where the Germans were expected to land; he took his work very seriously, even if he considered the task to be largely quite impossible. He sought to make the best of his allotted task and developed strongpoints which would be used to delay or defeat any German advance into the UK as well as looking at the personnel at his disposal. He also took the Home Guard very seriously, realizing their potential, not as the comic old men of *Dad's Army*, that popular oft-repeated BBC sitcom but as a locally raised force that could use their knowledge of the immediate locality to ambush and delay advancing Germans. It has to be admitted that at this time there was little knowledge of the atrocities of the SS who no doubt would have punished such activities, while there was still a naïve assumption about the German army being honourable. One only needs to view the record of the German army on the Russian Front to see that the German army's record was atrocious and murderous. However, Auchinleck seems to have spent much of his summer dealing with Monty's huge appetite for self-importance and vanity.

Montgomery and Auchinleck each had their own ways of training men. Auchinleck at one time would visit V Corps and attend some of Monty's lectures, with the following comments: 'No coughing, no smoking, runs before breakfast – all very aspiring and made me feel quite inadequate. But I doubt if runs before breakfast really produce battle-winners, of necessity. However, we got on, though we had one row.'[7] This was how Auchinleck, many years later, recalled his summer with Monty while Greenwood, citing a number of letters, observes that there was more than one row between Montgomery and Auchinleck. Not only did they view training differently as Auchinleck was not so warm towards PT and drill as Montgomery, but Auchinleck resented the way that Monty tried to obtain the best officers for V Corps and wasn't too fussy about how he did it. In early August in a formal letter to Montgomery Auchinleck cautioned him against trying to recruit officers with BEF experience (experience of fighting in France in May–June 1940) by using underhand tactics which dismayed Auchinleck. Montgomery had an unpleasant habit of bypassing the normal route to securing officers for his command and went behind Auchinleck's back by dealing directly with the War Office and not going via Auchinleck, who was Montgomery's superior officer, and requesting certain officers to be sent to V Corps. Auchinleck wrote to Montgomery during October 1940 and demanded that he follow the chain of command whenever he was seeking to recruit officers for his own unit.[8] On the same day Auchinleck, in another letter, explained to the adjutant general at the

War Office, Lieutenant General Sir Henry Wemyss, why he was so vexed with Monty. Auchinleck told Wemyss that Monty was causing 'friction' by his actions and that he had written to him about this and hoped that Montgomery would cease the practice of circumventing procedure in an attempt to get his own way.[9] Greenwood notes that there were no written replies to Auchinleck's letters to Montgomery.[10]

While Auchinleck attempted to fight his personal war against Montgomery, the Germans still threatened invasion but by the autumn of 1940 this threat had receded. On 11 October Anthony Eden, the Secretary of State for War, visited Auchinleck at his Command HQ and stayed for lunch. Afterwards as they walked in the gardens, Eden told Auchinleck that the government wanted him to return to India as commander-in-chief. Auchinleck was not officially notified of this posting until 21 November 1940 when the CIGS informed him, and it was another ten days before notice of his new appointment was officially posted. On 12 December Auchinleck handed over Southern Command to his old friend Lieutenant General the Honourable Harold Alexander, and then set off for Scotland to spend some leave there with Jessie. Christmas 1940 was very busy for Auchinleck as on Christmas Eve, in a private ceremony at Buckingham Palace, he was knighted by King George VI with the Knight Grand Commander of the Most Eminent Order of the Indian Empire (GCIE) and on Boxing Day was promoted to the rank of full general. Auchinleck was 56 years old and the youngest general in the British army.

The route to India taken by Auchinleck was long and dangerous. Flying in the 1940s was dangerous anyway but with the added hazards of war it was extremely dangerous as aircraft from both the belligerent sides were forced to fly via neutral or friendly air space and this took some planning. Since the fall of France and the entry of Italy into the war, the Mediterranean had become a war zone, thus cutting off the shortest route to India. As the Auchinleck party was to fly over neutral territory, it was necessary for military personnel to wear civilian clothes and carry false passports. After several delays they flew from Southampton Water in a Sunderland flying boat on 27 December 1940. The first leg of the flight involved flying about 400 miles from Land's End over the Atlantic Ocean to avoid enemy fighter planes operating from France. Once it had been decided it was safe to do so, Auchinleck's aircraft headed towards neutral Portugal. After a stopover in Estoril in Portugal, the next leg was to Las Palmas in the Canary Islands and then on to Freetown in Sierra Leone and Port Harcourt in Nigeria, both British possessions in West Africa. Once in Nigeria, the party changed for a small aircraft that took them to Kano, a military station in the hills of northern Nigeria. This was followed by another leg of the journey, this time finishing in Khartoum, the capital of the Sudan, yet another British possession. While he was in the Sudan, Auchinleck stayed at the residence of the Governor General Major General Hubert Huddleston. During his stay, Auchinleck took the opportunity to visit the 4th and 5th Indian divisions who were due to invade Italian Eritrea.

The next stage of this epic journey was to Cairo where Auchinleck took the chance to familiarize himself with the war situation in the Middle East as he visited the C-in-C there, General Sir Archibald Wavell. Even though British armed forces were chasing the Italian army across Cyrenaica in Libya, there was pressure on Wavell to release some of his troops so that they might be sent to Greece to reinforce the Greek army. Indeed, during Auchinleck's stay in Egypt, Wavell went to Athens for talks with the Greek government and General Papagos, C-in-C of the Greek army. Finally, after many demands, mainly social ones on the time of the Auchinlecks, they left Cairo on 18 January 1941, flying to New Delhi via Habbaniya in Iraq and then Karachi. Auchinleck's party arrived safely in New Delhi after an air journey that had lasted for twenty-five days.

Auchinleck formally took over from General Sir Robert Cassels as C-in-C India on 27 January 1941. With this appointment went the extra political duties as War Member to the Defence Department of the Government of India. This meant that Auchinleck was a member of the Viceroy's Executive Council as well as a nominated member of the Council of State. However, Auchinleck was not impressed with what he found in India in 1941. The main source of his dismay was the lack of sense of urgency and purpose in India; it seemed that life continued as before, even though the British Empire was at war. Auchinleck sought to disrupt the sense of peace and normality that he found in India. He was too late to prevent the prepared move of the army HQ to Simla, but he did other things to try to impress the fact that the British and Indian armies were at war with Germany and Italy, while there was also a definite Japanese threat against the British colonial possessions in Asia including India. There was also a German threat against India as it was feared that the Germans might intervene in Iraq and Persia (Iran) which were stepping-stones towards India, while the North-West Frontier could flare up at any given time. Indeed the situation in Iraq was to deteriorate, even though initially Iraq appeared to be pro-British. The problem lay with the ruling structure. In September 1939, the king of Iraq was only 4 years old and so his uncle Amir Abdul Illah ruled in his stead as regent. The Iraqis did break off diplomatic relations with Germany, but in June 1940 failed to do this with Italy, so the Italian legation in Baghdad became the centre of Arab nationalism and anti-British agitation. Axis prestige was at a record high owing to German victories in the West and the arrival of the Italian Armistice Commission in Syria. At the same time, British prestige was at an all-time low.

The situation in Iraq was becoming critical and there had been talk of sending British troops to Basra to protect Anglo-Iranian oilfields, something that the government of India had long been committed to, but it was thought that sending British troops into Iraq would inflame an already difficult position there. However, by the end of September 1940 the situation was causing renewed anxiety in London. The Iraqi Prime Minister Rashid Ali al-Gaylani was quite pro-Italian, while the Grand Mufti of Jerusalem, who was very anti-British and exiled from Palestine, was clearly intriguing with the Germans. Furthermore, most of the Iraqi officer corps were pro-Axis. It was clear that measures had to be taken with Iraq before the atmosphere of anti-British and pro-Axis went any further and got out of control. Limited measures were approved by the British War Cabinet on 7 November 1940. The situation continued to worsen in Iraq with the British looking ineffective.

By the end of January 1941 there had been a political crisis in Iraq which threatened civil war. Rashid Ali resigned his post as prime minister and was replaced by Taha al-Hashimi. This was of no help as al-Hashimi was a committed Pan-Arabist and was suspected of working with Rashid Ali. The British tried to compel the Iraqi government to break off diplomatic relations with Italy but failed. On 31 March, the Iraqi regent learned of a plot to arrest him, so he fled Baghdad and made his way to the British Air Force base at Habbaniya in Iraq. From there he was flown to

Basra and given refuge on HMS *Cockchafer*, a British minelayer nearby. Rashid Ali, with the support of four prominent Iraqi army and Air Force officers known as the 'Golden Square', seized power on 3 April 1941 and proclaimed himself Chief of the National Defence Government. The new British ambassador, Sir Kinahan Cornwallis, arrived on the previous day, straight into the lion's den that was Iraq.[11] As we shall see, events in Iraq began to spiral out of control and required Allied intervention as Iraq was critical to the Allied supply line to the Middle East and thus needed to be defended against any attempt by Germany to gain a foothold there and endanger several fronts including the Russian front and the Middle East as well as India and South-East Asia as Japanese aggression, prior to the attack on Pearl Harbor, was apparent. Meanwhile, Auchinleck had to take up his new post in India.

To try to get a sense of the urgency of the world situation Auchinleck was limited in what he could actually do, but he made some minor adjustments to the nonchalant atmosphere found in India. The most outward sign that things were different was that he ordered officers to wear their uniforms whenever they were on duty and that their mess uniforms were to be put away for the duration of the war, and he renamed the army HQ as GHQ. It made the situation sound somewhat more belligerent, but it was only tinkering at the edges and until there was an obvious threat to India there was little that Auchinleck could do in practical terms.

In North Africa the situation was beyond hostile as the British and Italian armies clashed in Libya with the Italians being driven from the Libyan province of Cyrenaica and the port city of Benghazi falling on 6 February 1941 to the Eastern Desert Corps commanded by Lieutenant General Richard O'Connor. The Italians lost thousands of men taken prisoner by the British. Within a week the German General Erwin Rommel, fresh from his victories in France, arrived in Tripoli. Under Rommel, the Italians were replaced by German troops and the war in North Africa altered. The Germans had reluctantly gone to Africa. Hitler did not want an Italian military collapse that might turn into a political collapse. Indeed, the German general staff did not understand why the British had not pressed their advantage against the Italians and captured Tripoli in February 1941.[12]

On 22 February 1941, Anthony Eden, now British Foreign Secretary, together with CIGS General Dill and accompanied by the C-in-C Middle East General Wavell flew to Greece to consult over the dispatch of 60,000 trained men from the Middle East to Greece. This meant that men who were about to be deployed to the Middle East were instead sent to support the Greek army in Greece. This proved to be a mistake as British successes in Libya were reversed by Axis troops under the command of Rommel and indeed O'Connor was captured in the desert while operations in Greece were a disaster and so the Allies were defeated there with heavy losses on the Greek island of Crete. There was a need to rethink the course of the war if the Allies were to defeat Germany. After the war Field Marshal Lord Alanbrooke, writing a reflection in his wartime diaries, said of the Greek campaign: 'I have…always considered from the very start that our participation in the operations in Greece was a definite strategic blunder. Our hands were more than full at that time in the Middle East, and Greece could only result in the most dangerous dispersal of force.'[13] Clearly there was little joined-up thinking in British operational planning in 1941 and they were still engaged in what could be described as fire-fighting in as much as the British, understandably, tried to fight the Germans wherever there was an opportunity but failed to look at the bigger picture. It could be argued that if the British had not been involved in Greece, the North African campaign might well have been shorter, but that is conjecture and not history.

Auchinleck's primary task in India was to expand the Indian army ready to face any external threats to British interests in the Middle East and its Asian possessions including India. As already mentioned, there were two main threats: the Germans stirring mischief in Iraq and Persia with a possibility of landing troops in Iraq, perhaps coming through Syria, while Japan had been expanding its own empire through south-east Asia and was beginning to threaten British possessions such as Hong Kong, Singapore and Malaya. Auchinleck in a letter to the Secretary of State for India, Leopold Amery, dated 17 March 1941, discussed his problems in trying to prepare the Indian army for war and its lack of modern equipment. He considered that it might not be long before he would be required to send troops to settle unrest in Iraq and if necessary fight the Iraqi army. However, this meant that the line of communication

(L of C) might well run from India to Syria via Basra, Baghdad, Mosul and Aleppo and might well become an extremely important L of C before the war became much older.[14] Such a line, of course, is staggering in length even today, but in the 1940s it was colossal, while the cities mentioned are, sadly, all too familiar to the twenty-first-century reader owing to wars and unrest continuing in the region since 2003.

In March 1941, even though the Japanese were threatening the peace of South-East Asia, it was Iraq that most concerned Auchinleck. On 13 March, he received a letter from CIGS General Sir John Dill who informed him that the situation in Iraq was bad and that the Iraqi army was politicized.[15] Auchinleck had already decided that any operations in or against Iraq should be planned and controlled from India; something to which Wavell had agreed on 8 March as an initial step which was also agreed by the Chiefs of Staff in London. On 10 March, Auchinleck informed Major General Edward Quinan, GOC Western District at Quetta, that he had been selected to command the Iraqi force which was to consist of three divisions (30,000 men). On 15 March Auchinleck sent his Chief of General Staff, Lieutenant General Thomas Hutton with Quinan to Cairo to coordinate the planning for operations in Iraq. Auchinleck made certain that Hutton understood the need to ensure that the Middle East Staff realized the urgency of the situation in Iraq. He considered that the British should obtain a firm grip in Iraq and quickly, and that it was important that the Euphrates tribes were got onto the side of the British as the tribes and their territories bestrode the L of C to British-controlled Palestine and the Suez Canal.

During the first week of April 1941 the successful British campaign in North Africa was unravelling as the Germans, better known as the Afrika Korps or DAK under the command of Rommel, had counter-attacked and had advanced as far as Benghazi. German troops had also invaded Greece, while at the same time Rashid Ali al-Gaylani, with the help of senior army officers, seized control of Iraq. Rashid Ali was very pro-German and an extreme Iraqi nationalist. On 3 April the Foreign Office was briefed by the British ambassador in Baghdad, Sir Kinahan Cornwallis, on the unfolding situation there. Rashid Ali made an explanation of his position to an advisor of the Iraqi Minister of the Interior. Taha al-Hashimi, the Iraqi prime minister, had resigned and refused to carry on until a new government had been formed. However, the Iraqi regent had disappeared, so no new government could be formed constitutionally. In these circumstances the Iraqi army as a de facto source of authority had asked Rashid Ali to take over the country temporarily and to ensure public security pending the formation of a constitutional government.

Rashid Ali affirmed what he called his 'fidelity to the Anglo-Iraq alliance' and stated that his actions in taking over Iraq were inspired solely by his consideration for the welfare of Iraq and its people. Rashid Ali claimed that he had consulted all available ex-ministers who had unanimously urged him to take control. However, a different view was related by the Iraqi Foreign Minister Tawfiq al-Suwaidi, who claimed that it was Rashid Ali and his friends in the Iraqi military who had made it impossible for the late Iraqi government to continue or to even carry on after the prime minister's resignation until another government could be formed. Moreover, it was Rashid Ali who had devised the plan that he should govern as a mandate for the Iraqi army and had insisted on carrying out this plan in spite of appeals of responsible men in public including Naji al-Suwaidi, the former Minister of Finance. Rashid Ali's intention was to extort from the regent a decree that would have made him prime minister or, failing that, force the regent to resign. It was considered that Rashid Ali would be unlikely to succeed in his intentions as it was clear that the regent had already planned a course of action that would deny Rashid Ali from being able to carry out his plan.[16]

Even so, Rashid Ali was consolidating his control over Iraq and, as Greenwood suggests, was doing it in the manner of Hitler and Mussolini by informing the world that these actions were to preserve peace and not hinder it. He also informed the Iraqi Senate that his coup d'état was not connected to the Axis powers and that the Anglo-Iraqi Treaty would be upheld by him. This was unlikely, but a further problem for the British was that Cornwallis had only been in post for a fortnight and had been brought out of retirement as he had previously been for many years an advisor to the Iraqi government but could not be considered a professionally-experienced diplomat. Cornwallis advised that Rashid Ali would keep his word.[17] This was naïve.

Cornwallis sent an immediate signal to the Foreign Office to the effect that he would inform the Iraqi government that the military situation in the Middle East required the urgent passage of troops from India through Iraq and onward to Palestine and that, depending on advice from London, paratroopers from Shaiba near Basra in southern Iraq would remain in India. The result of this signal was that Amery, with suggestions from the Chiefs of Staff, considered that the convoy that had already left Karachi should be held up in Bahrain or some other port en route and that the dispatch of paratroopers should be delayed. Auchinleck totally disagreed with the above decisions and in a letter to Sir Gilbert Laithwaite, private secretary to the viceroy, dated 12 April 1941, listed the shortcomings of the proposed actions, especially the delay in landing paratroopers on Iraqi soil.

Auchinleck considered that any delay in getting to Basra could mean that the British might not get the port area at all and that a base in the Basra area was essential for success in the Middle East. Auchinleck urged the possession of Basra rather than delay as in his opinion the time for diplomacy was over and any delay might mean that Rashid Ali would use such a time to consolidate his own position in Iraq. Auchinleck also feared that Rashid Ali would try to get German aid for Iraq which might have taken the form of aircraft and airborne troops. He considered that the British, in order to maintain their position in the Middle East and to prevent a deterioration there, needed to show some resolve and use force if only to overawe countries such as Turkey, Iran, Iraq and Saudi Arabia.

Auchinleck's view was accepted and on 17 April, British troops began to land in Iraq at Basra, taking Rashid Ali and the Iraqi army by surprise, and the landings went unopposed. However, very soon the Iraqi government requested that restrictions should be placed on British troop movements and concentrations in Iraq. Churchill, as ever, refused to consider this and pressed his Chiefs of Staff to speed up the build-up of the 10th Indian Division in the Basra area. Auchinleck and Churchill were both right not to trust Rashid Ali and when he received notice of further British landings in Iraq, he took the notice as an ultimatum. Rashid Ali refused to accept any further British landings in Iraq but incredibly, at the same time, he made sure that the British knew of a secret treaty that he had recently signed with the Axis powers.

Using military manoeuvres as an excuse, units from the Iraqi army occupied the long low plateau which overlooked Habbaniya, the British RAF base. Habbaniya was roughly halfway between Basra and Palestine and lay between the River Euphrates and Lake Habbaniya, a large lake about 20 miles from Baghdad. It was designed rather like the standard British cantonment as found in India, but a large iron fence surrounded the entire base including its airfield for No. 4 Service Flying Training School with ancillary units and a base hospital. It was quite a large base. There were about eighty obsolete aircraft used for training, and about 1,000 airmen. The civilian population, mainly Indian and Assyrian, were about 9,000 in number. The AOC, Air Vice Marshal H.G. Smart, had just received six Gladiator fighters and eighteen RAF armoured cars as reinforcements. Three companies from the 1st KORR had been flown in from Shaiba under the command of Lieutenant Colonel Ouvry Roberts, the GSO1 of the 10th Indian Division.

Early on 30 April 1941, Smart received an ultimatum from the commander of the Iraqi forces in the Habbaniya area. Smart was told that he was to stop all flying and other movements in and out of the British cantonment. If the British flew aircraft out of the base or allowed armoured cars to leave, they would be shelled by Iraqi artillery. Smart replied that the ultimatum was in direct contravention of the Anglo-Iraqi Treaty and he would ignore it. Furthermore, if Iraqi forces did interfere with British forces, he would consider it an act of war. The same afternoon Auchinleck signalled the WO, GHQ Middle East, the British ambassador in Iraq and Force HQ, Basra: 'We consider air action should be taken immediately against Iraqi forces threatening Habbaniya.'[18] A message from the Air Force HQ in Iraq to HQ RAF Middle East told of the position at Habbaniya which was that Habbaniya was surrounded by Iraqi troops supported by tanks and armoured cars that had their guns trained on the British cantonment. The Iraqi commander accused the British of breaking the Anglo-Iraqi Treaty.[19] Auchinleck was supported by Churchill, who sent him a message stating that if he must strike Iraqi forces, he should do it hard and resolutely.

The next day, Smart sent his ultimatum to the Iraqi commander telling him to withdraw his forces immediately or British aerial attacks would follow. This was ignored and so Smart ordered every aircraft possible to attack the Iraqi positions in an attempt to drive them beyond artillery range. As soon as the British bombing began, the Iraqis replied by shelling the cantonment. The fighting lasted throughout the day. Five aircraft from the Flying School were lost and thirteen people, mainly civilians, were killed in the cantonment. The next morning, 3 May, Smart changed his tactics and ordered his aircraft to attack the Iraqi Air Force landing fields and the road links from Fallujah and Baghdad. Smart's aerial force was reinforced by a squadron of Blenheim bombers and Hurricane fighters from the Middle East Air Force during the afternoon. These aircraft attacked the Iraqi airfield at Mosul where it had been reported that there was a Luftwaffe presence. During the night of 5/6 May, patrols of the KORR attacked Iraqi forward positions and as a result the Iraqis began to withdraw from the plateau in the early morning of 6 May. At first light the Flying School aircraft began to harass the entire retreating Iraqi force. Soon afterwards the KORR began to collect prisoners in large numbers; 12 officers and about 300 soldiers had surrendered before daylight had broken properly. Throughout the day Smart's aircraft pursued the Iraqis along the routes to Baghdad and Fallujah, destroying lorries and ammunition trucks as well as killing soldiers. More prisoners were taken, and the total number taken by the end of the day exceeded the strength of the KORR.

The situation in Iraq remained confused, but Auchinleck seemed to be in control and issued directives to Quinan. However, he emphasized to Quinan that he, Auchinleck, remained in command regarding the situation in Iraq which was still under the control of the India command and therefore Auchinleck as C-in-C India. On 3 May, one day after Auchinleck had been in contact with Quinan, the British Chiefs of Staff sent a signal to Auchinleck stating that as the situation in Iraq had changed from what had been anticipated when it had originally been given to the India command, the Iraq command should fall temporarily to that of the Middle East unless Auchinleck had deep-seated objections to this decision.

Auchinleck certainly did have some tactical objections to the plan of removing Iraq from India and placing it under Middle East command and voiced them in a telegram to the CIGS on 3 May 1941. Auchinleck wrote that if Egypt, including the port city of Alexandria and the Suez

Canal, was lost to the British it would not be a major disaster but all efforts should be made to hold these positions. Auchinleck considered that if Egypt was lost, the fight could continue from Sudan and so deny the enemy the Red Sea. Auchinleck saw the Middle East as being part of Asia (which it is) and so considered that any defence of Asia began with ensuring that countries such as Turkey, Syria, the British possession of Palestine and Iraq were held and that these countries might well become primary strategic objectives in the near future. Auchinleck saw that Iraq and especially Basra were extremely important for operations including those in the Middle East and he urged the development of Basra and of communications leading from there to the north and north-west which had become an urgent requirement. He agreed that something needed to be done about Iraq and by force if necessary in order to consolidate the British position there but at that time Auchinleck considered that only India had the necessary troops for an occupation of Iraq. However, these troops could not undertake the task unless they were equipped with modern weapons and aircraft which could not be provided by India and so the provision of such equipment was extremely urgent.[20] Auchinleck's views were certainly unorthodox, especially his views on the possibility of the loss of Egypt, but with consideration they made sense. It was just that officials caught up in the blast of war in London were studying their maps from the wrong side – that is, from the West – and did not really consider the advantages of the East.

Wavell also sent a telegram to the Chiefs of Staff protesting the proposal of placing Iraq under his Middle East command. Wavell's objection was that it would further stretch his already overburdened command and that Iraq should fall under the India command. Auchinleck's and Wavell's objections were ignored by COS who refused to alter their decision. However, they had not reckoned with the influence of Winston Churchill, who was not only prime minister but also Minister of Defence and understood India and Asia relatively well, as well as being another unconventional thinker. On 6 May Churchill, after looking at the arguments of Wavell and Auchinleck, sent an urgent minute to General Ismay in which he expressed his support for Auchinleck, as well as expressing his doubts about Wavell's ability to continue to command in the Middle East. Churchill wrote: 'He gives me the impression of being tired out.'[21]

Churchill continued his support for Auchinleck and his planning for Iraq and a possible British occupation of that country. On 14 May Churchill signalled Auchinleck praising him for meeting with Wavell in Basra in the near future. This had been an initiative taken by Auchinleck who had told Wavell that he was willing to meet wherever and whenever was suitable for Wavell. This turned out to be Basra. Churchill suggested that Wavell might well tell him of two upcoming operations for North Africa: TIGER and SCORCHER. In Churchill's mind, a British victory in Libya would change the German and Iraqi minds about the situation in Iraq. Churchill wanted a British-friendly regime installed in Iraq and thought that perhaps there might be a tightening-up of the situation in Syria as it was feared the Germans might get a foothold there. Even so, Churchill was more than willing to allow the Free French to retain Syria as it was a French-administrated country. The meeting between the two commanders took place on 24 May 1941 and it was successful in every way. A major success was that Wavell agreed with Auchinleck concerning the India command retaining Iraq for the reasons that Auchinleck had advocated, rather than Wavell maintaining that it was too much for the Middle East command.

On his way back to India Auchinleck wrote to the CIGS in London appraising him of the meeting between himself and Wavell. Auchinleck said that Wavell had agreed, owing to Auchinleck's arguments about Iraq and its position regarding Asian defence, and had agreed that 'bold action' should be taken in Iraq. Uppermost in Auchinleck's mind was preventing the Germans from infiltrating the country, so not only had Baghdad to be taken and held, but also key points in the north of Iraq such as Mosul, Kirkuk and Erbil. Auchinleck knew that taking these objectives involved great risks, but he considered that the risks were worth taking, including the maintenance of a supply line from Turkey.

While in Basra, Auchinleck met Jamal Madfai who was a prominent supporter of the Iraqi regent as well as an ex-prime minister of Iraq. Madfai was clear with Auchinleck and told him that in order to establish an Iraqi government friendly towards the British and under the auspices of the regent, the British would need to physically support the Iraqi army to hold important Iraqi towns and areas. Madfai considered that the Iraqi army could be re-established but needed British support. Auchinleck emphasized that the UK had no interest in permanently occupying Iraq, so the meeting ended amicably. Auchinleck had done some sterling work; the meetings in Basra had been his idea and they had gone well.[22]

The result of the Basra meetings, probably because of Churchill's earlier intervention, was that on 30 May, the COS approved the recommendations of Wavell and Auchinleck. However, by this time British troops had surrounded Baghdad and Rashid Ali had fled to Iran accompanied by several senior Iraqi officers and most of the German staff officers who had recently arrived in Iraq. On 31 May an armistice was signed, the regent of Iraq was reinstated, and Jamal Madfai became prime minister with a new government. Iraqi intrigue was over for now. The next stage was to sort out the situation in North Africa and, as already indicated, Churchill had already considered that Wavell was too tired for the task and so on 21 June 1941, Auchinleck's 57th birthday, Churchill wrote to the viceroy of India informing him of his intention to replace Wavell with Auchinleck. On 23 June Auchinleck acknowledged this new posting and, in a signal, thanked Churchill for his trust in him. In the same message he informed Churchill that he intended to be in Cairo by 30 June, travelling by air from India, and that he was maintaining the strictest secrecy regarding this matter.[23] It should be noted that on arriving in the Middle East and meeting with Wavell, Auchinleck did not agree with Churchill's assumption that Wavell was tired, and wrote of him: 'Wavell showed no signs of tiredness at all. He was always the same. I think he was first-class; in spite of his silences, he made a tremendous impact on the troops. I have a very great admiration for him…but he was given impossible tasks.'[24]

*Chapter Six*

# North Africa

On the day that Auchinleck took up his command in the Middle East, Churchill sent him a message:

> You took up your command at a period of crisis. After all of the facts had been laid before you it will be for you to decide whether to renew the offensive in the WESTERN DESERT and if so when. You should have regard especially to the situation at TOBRUK, the process of enemy reinforcement in LIBYA and temporary German preoccupation in their invasion of RUSSIA. You should also consider vexatious dangers of operation in SYRIA flagging and need for a decision on one or both these fronts. You will decide whether and how these operations can be fitted together. The urgency of these issues will naturally impress itself upon you. We shall be glad to hear from you at your earliest convenience.[1]

From Churchill's note to Auchinleck it is quite clear that there were two immediate tasks that the latter needed to confront: the war in North Africa, and the pressing problem with Syria where the Allies feared German infiltration as the Germans sought to obtain bases there to further their North African campaign or indeed progress across Asia towards India. Auchinleck considered the Syrian problem to be the most immediate danger to the Allies. On 2 July 1941 he sent a personal message to the CIGS regarding the French, Syria and the Free French leader, General Charles de Gaulle.

The French had a strong interest in the case of Syria and of Lebanon, which were territories acquired by France after the First World War. The French acquisition followed the collapse of the Ottoman Empire after its military defeat in 1918. The Turks had previously ruled Syria and Lebanon and they passed into French hands following a subsequent peace treaty which concluded the war between the Allies and post-1918 the defunct Turkish Empire. Nobody seemed to have consulted the Syrians or Lebanese at the time. In 1941, de Gaulle was considered to be the leader of all Free French who had managed to escape France for the UK or to French imperial territories outside of German occupation.

Of de Gaulle, Auchinleck wrote that there were many problems with him as the French leader did not liaise with the British if there was discussion relating to French concerns in the Middle East at this time; Auchinleck was referring to Syria and Lebanon. He also considered that General Edward Spears, a French specialist who worked closely with de Gaulle, was part of this bypassing of official procedure.[2] The problem with French overseas possessions was just who was to administer them? During the summer of 1940 the invading Germans had divided France into a northern occupied zone and a southern unoccupied zone administered from the spa town of Vichy which gave rise to the name of the collaborator French regime, the Vichy regime or Vichy government. Syria had initially been governed by a pro-Vichy regime, but in July 1941 Free French forces supported by British troops landed in Syria and occupied it. Auchinleck, in his missive to the CIGS, considered that the Free French would inherit all the problems of the Vichy government's rule in Syria. In his opinion, the attitude of de Gaulle and the Free French might endanger Allied operations in the region. The problem was that de Gaulle was not willing to compromise French integrity at all. He was perfectly willing to grant the UK military, naval and air facilities in Syria, but anything that interfered with the Free French political or economic situations was denied to the British.

A further consideration was that de Gaulle and his comrades denied there was an Arab question or problem at all and he failed to see that the French were unpopular all the time they remained in Syria and the Lebanon, commonly known as the Levant. In the Levant, Arab nationalism was gaining ground along with a strong call for independence for both Syria and the Lebanon. This was a call that de Gaulle and the Free French considered could wait until the war was over, but local Arabs thought the opposite. Auchinleck reported that a note handed to General Wilson by General Catroux, the first paragraph of which had been drafted by de Gaulle, stated that France remained the sovereign power in the Levant and that all her power was exercised through the Free French, and the Allies in going to Syria were not occupying the territory of an enemy but that of an ally, Free France. Auchinleck feared that if the Free French were given a free hand in the Levant, it might well lead to an Arab revolt throughout the Middle East on the grounds that promises made to the Arabs had been broken again and it seemed unlikely that they could be reconciled.[3]

Auchinleck certainly did not see that much could be done in the Middle East until the situation in Syria had been addressed. On 4 July 1941 he told Churchill that there was little point in a further offensive in the Western Desert until the situation in Syria had been resolved, which meant an Allied occupation and the securing of Cyprus from enemy attack, ensuring that it could be used as a base for operations in North Africa. Therefore Auchinleck demanded that the Vichy French should be immediately ejected from Syria, as well as the completion of all necessary security measures in Cyprus. He reported to Churchill that an offensive in Syria was already under way and being prosecuted with the utmost vigour but was hampered by a shortage of mechanical transport, while forces from Iraq were giving all possible assistance to the Syrian campaign. Auchinleck considered the needs for the defence of Cyprus and concluded that it would take at least a division to ensure the island's safety and plans were being drawn up to that end.

However, Auchinleck then returned to his thesis preceding this particular signal to Churchill, the issue being that before any further offensives could be carried out in the Western Desert, Iraq and Syria had to be secured by the Allies to prevent the Germans landing in these territories and attacking North Africa, notably Egypt and the Suez Canal, from the east. Once this had been accomplished, Auchinleck thought that was when an offensive in the Western Desert could be considered. For any such campaign he suggested that the bare minimum force needed for success would be at least two armoured divisions and a motorized division and this was the first essential, while the final objective was the clearing of the enemy from North Africa. Such an operation would be done in stages, with the first stage being the clearing of Cyrenaica, which again would have to be completed in stages.

Auchinleck then turned to how he saw the operations and the first thing he made clear was that even well-trained infantry would be of no use against enemy armoured forces. Infantry divisions would be used to hold defended areas and to capture enemy positions, but only after enemy armoured forces had been defeated and removed. The main offensive, according to Auchinleck, had to be undertaken by motorized formations. Having served in the Middle East during the First World War, Auchinleck was acutely aware of the vast distances and lack of provisions there and that troops had to be carried by transport and could not really be expected to march under a broiling heat across many miles of empty desert and then fight; it simply wasn't on. The second essential that Auchinleck required was sufficient air support that was to be at the disposal of the army. His demands on the Air Force were wide-ranging, from fighter to medium bombers as well as tactical reconnaissance squadrons and close air support on the battlefield. The third essential of Auchinleck was naval support, which meant of course harrying enemy sea communications and ensuring that the enemy was denied supply by sea as far as possible as well as giving close support to army operations. Overall, Auchinleck was looking for inter-service co-operation in North Africa. He also cautioned against trying to conduct operations in Syria and the Western Desert simultaneously as he felt that both would fail, but that Syria had to be secured before operations could commence in North Africa.[4]

Churchill concurred with Auchinleck and agreed that Syria had to be secured first, as well as Cyprus being held and if needs be recovered (in the event Cyprus was never taken from the British during the Second World War). Churchill considered the security of both Syria and Cyprus to be prerequisites for a successful campaign in the Western Desert. He also observed that a successful campaign in the Western Desert would make it an essential theatre for the autumn and a possible defence of the Nile valley. Churchill then went further and argued that it was only by retaking the lost airfields in East Cyrenaica that the RAF and the Fleet Air Arm (FAA) would begin to act effectively against enemy sea supplies. He agreed that armour was needed for any coming land offensive in North Africa.

Auchinleck was also briefed by Churchill on what intelligence had revealed. It had been learned that the Italians were still sending considerable reinforcements to North Africa, while the Germans were preoccupied with their invasion of the Soviet Union which had begun on 21 June 1941 and was sending few troops to aid their Italian allies in Africa. Churchill admitted that if the Soviet Union collapsed, this would have repercussions for the British as the UK mainland would once more be under threat of invasion and that the Germans would have troops to spare for North Africa. Churchill also pointed out the problems that lay before Auchinleck: the situation at the port city of Tobruk which was besieged by the enemy had not gone away and Churchill worried that the position there might even worsen and could lead to a 'serious invasion of Egypt'. Indeed, the British prime minister was quite the Jeremiah in his assessment of events in North Africa as he considered that the situation there might not be any better by mid-September 1941 and may well have worsened. There was only one piece of good news for Auchinleck coming from Churchill and that was that Australian reinforcements were on their way to the Middle East.[5]

It should be noted that both the Italian and German high commands considered the capture of Tobruk to be of great importance and as Playfair comments, its safety was only down to Major General L.J. Morshead's 9th Australian Division and attached troops who defended the port with great spirit and devotion. The initial enemy assault on Tobruk failed in May 1941 owing to the resolution of its defenders and the enemy offensive became a series of local actions including aggressive patrolling and the seeking of weaknesses of the enemy. The garrison became the virtual master of no man's land, but from which a large offensive could not come as it would have meant reinforcing Tobruk, something to which Auchinleck would not agree. Nevertheless, the 20th Australian Infantry Brigade made a series of night attacks to improve the position in the Ras el Medauar salient and the 24th Australian Infantry Brigade later tried unsuccessfully to retake the shoulders of the salient. After this, a series of aggressive defence moves became the rule.[6]

By mid-July Auchinleck, after being on the ground for a while, expressed some of his fears to Churchill. One was the reality facing him in terms of his armoured units: on paper he had 500 cruiser tanks available to him, but the truth was that the number was much smaller at 350. There were also concerns regarding Tobruk: Auchinleck doubted if the besieged garrison could hold out much past September, while he also feared for the future of the Egyptian town of Sidi Barrani on the Mediterranean coast. Fears about how long Tobruk could hold out had been on the mind of Auchinleck and his commanders since February. The retreat of the Eighth Army during January and February 1942 had stopped about 30 miles west of Tobruk. The new line ran inland from Gazala, where the coastal road passed through a narrow gap that was easily blocked. While the position held no real important tactical advantages, it did cover the tracks running east towards Acroma with the Trigh Capuzzo and Trigh el-Abd further to the south. At the beginning of February 1942 the line was weakly held but Auchinleck ordered it to be made as strong as possible in order to preserve Tobruk as a base for a new offensive. Even so, Auchinleck was not obsessed with Tobruk and even though he did his best to ensure the enemy should not capture the city, he was not so stubborn as to insist that the port be defended to the end if it was quite clear that the enemy was about to take the position. In that event, Tobruk was to be evacuated and destroyed as far as possible in order to deny the enemy its facilities, especially the docks. Auchinleck wasn't willing to lock up a single division in Tobruk as he always thought of the bigger picture with the Iran-Iraq-Syria front being uppermost in his mind.[7]

Realistically, Auchinleck feared that the enemy might capture the town which would reduce the fighter protection that could be supplied for ships to and from Tobruk.[8] It was only General John Dill who was able to send Auchinleck anything like good news as he observed that the Germans had become bogged down in the Soviet Union which meant that the UK was safe from invasion.[9] It seems 1941 would prove to be a mixed bag for the UK. The German invasion of the Soviet Union was the break that the British mainland needed; if the Germans were preoccupied with their venture in the Soviet Union, German resources were denied an invasion of the UK. The war in the Middle East ebbed and flowed but at the end of the year, Japan finally attacked the US forces at Pearl Harbor as well as attacking British and Dutch possessions in South-East Asia. The Japanese attack brought the Americans into the war, while the German declaration of war against the USA brought the Americans into Europe as men and supplies were sent there. American war materials kept the Red Army in the field until it finally defeated the German army in the east, while at the same time, millions of Americans landed in the UK in preparation for the day when the Allies could land in Europe once more. This is not to forget the Americans in the Pacific war against the Japanese and those American service personnel who served in North Africa and later in Italy. The year 1941 was a pivotal one for the course of the Second World War.

The American supply of war materials to the Soviet Union was essential as it ensured that the Germans and their allies were kept in the deadly morass of the Russians and denied the ability to supply other fronts including North Africa. Meanwhile, the British had to stop making mistakes and focus on what was needed to win the war and Auchinleck was such a man who could analyse what the problems were and how to remedy them. Greece was an obvious mistake and as already discussed, the sending of British troops there was wasteful and threatened the security of the Middle East.

Even so, the Syrian campaign was swiftly concluded, on which Leo Amery at the India Office congratulated Auchinleck. Amery's opinion was that the success of the Syrian campaign had secured the Middle East up to the Turkish and Iranian borders. He also noted that operations in Abyssinia (Ethiopia) had almost finished and now was the time to 'polish off Libya'. Amery considered that the British had to try to aid the Greeks but did regret that in doing so Wavell was denied the resources to have 'pushed on' to Tripoli after taking Benghazi and if that had happened there may well have been more supply routes available to North Africa and that a smaller force might have been able to hold the area. Amery had many ideas of what might have happened if there had not been a Greek expedition. Perhaps the Allies might have been able to take Tunis itself and that a larger Allied force might have been landed on the African Atlantic coast and brought by rail into North Africa and that area cleared once and for all, which would be 'an essential step towards final victory'. However, Amery did flag up a concern that had dogged the Middle East for decades: the Allied victory in Syria, in Amery's opinion, took the side of the Jews but at the expense of the Arabs.[10] Amery made several astute comments in his letter to Auchinleck. The note regarding Jewish-Arab relations was the most observant, but he wasn't probably aware of just how poisonous this relationship would become. However, Churchill, as ever, grasped the essentials of the situation, which was that the British needed to take full advantage of the German invasion of the Soviet Union to recover Cyrenaica.[11]

By the third week of July Auchinleck was still identifying himself as 'the new boy' but in a letter to General Dill, Auchinleck considered that he had grasped the overall situation in the area yet admitted that it remained a complex problem. Much of the issue which lay before Auchinleck was the chaos that had gone before him and he cited the disorganization and improvisation resulting from failed operations in Greece, Crete, Tobruk and recent fighting at Sollum, a port on the Egyptian coast. Auchinleck was optimistic about the future and considered that the mixed units he had inherited would be reorganized and made into useful formations. He also considered that Tobruk would only be abandoned as a last resort, but had decided that Cyprus would be retained. Auchinleck was perhaps the first British commander of the war to see it as a genuine global conflict as he told Dill that he saw his theatre of operations as a continuous line running from Afghanistan through Iran, Iraq, Syria and Palestine to Cyrenaica and all action along this line must be coordinated.[12]

By August 1941 Auchinleck was already planning for the next operation in the desert and he began this with changes at senior command level. Greenwood describes how both senior and junior officers in Egypt at the time of Auchinleck's arrival there thought of him 'as a breath of fresh air' who was able to get his ideas over to others swiftly and remain popular with those under his command. Yet he was not always on such good terms with Churchill who was always anxious that action against the enemy should be taken as soon as possible. Auchinleck was called to London to see Churchill almost as soon as he had taken up his command in the Middle East.[13]

Auchinleck headed back to the UK, taking the first flight available as at the time he didn't have his personal aircraft and so was squashed into a Sunderland flying boat once more with a group of ORs and naval ratings. It was an uncomfortable journey as well as a dangerous flight. Auchinleck took with him his ADC Tony Phillpotts and his Deputy Director of Plans

Colonel Charles Gairdner. They arrived on 30 July and Auchinleck went straight to Chequers to dine with Churchill. Auchinleck's appraisal of the situation in the Western Desert was probably not welcomed by Churchill, but Auchinleck impressed him all the same. He told Churchill that the situation in the desert had been mishandled not by the high command but strategically. He also cast doubts on the assertion that the Germans would remove an armoured division from Libya to Russia. Auchinleck also had a view on de Gaulle whom he considered to be unstable and consumed with personal ambition, meaning that de Gaulle cared little for British interests during the war but was handled well by Oliver Lyttelton, which kept him on message but only just. Auchinleck found the ten-day hiatus in London, meeting Churchill and senior politicians and military figures, quite tiring having been in meetings and conferences with them, most of them trying to persuade him to take actions that he knew were not possible. In a letter to his wife, Auchinleck was quite proud of how he had managed to withstand such pressure and considered that he had won people over with his arguments about operations in North Africa and how the Allied lines should be maintained there.[14]

However, Auchinleck was no politician and this was something that had worried General John Dill, who was still CIGS, at the time of Auchinleck's appointment. Dill had doubts about Auchinleck and his new post in the Mediterranean theatre as Dill was aware that this required not just military skills but also political adroitness. Auchinleck only saw a military scene from a military point of view; he never seemed to have taken on the demands that often pressed on civilian politicians. This even included Winston Churchill himself. During the Second World War it transpired that generals had to be something different. They needed to be able not only to inspire the soldiers that served under their commands but also do the same for civilians as they looked towards victory and eventually peace. At the same time, they also had to demoralize the enemy. From the outset Auchinleck knew that his new role was going to be difficult and he knew that Churchill would be on his case for much of the time. He didn't need Dill to warn him as he had already experienced Churchill's impatience during the Norway campaign. Churchill was a great man but also a difficult one, yet Auchinleck was not afraid of him.[15]

Roy Jenkins notes that Auchinleck did make a good impression on Churchill during this visit, which was something needed for the Cairo command because, as Jenkins observed, there was quite a gap between the early victories against the Italians in Africa and Montgomery's victory at El Alamein.[16] As ever, this is to completely ignore Auchinleck's victory in the First Battle of El Alamein which allowed for Montgomery's victory later in the same year. The British historian Correlli Barnett also comments on how the position of ignoring the First Battle of El Alamein went unchallenged for a number of years, especially with the publication of the history of the Second World War penned by Churchill, but once Montgomery published his memoirs in the 1950s, things began to change.[17] As we shall see, much of the defence of Auchinleck was led by Eric 'Chink' O'Gowan, originally Dorman-Smith, who was a close friend of Auchinleck as well as his chief of staff during the summer of 1942 in North Africa. Once Montgomery's memoirs were published O'Gowan was almost driven to ensure that Auchinleck and the First Battle of El Alamein was credited as the beginning of the overall success of the North African campaign because, as Barnett observed, one got the impression that before Montgomery's victory at the Second Battle of El Alamein, there had been nothing but failure and defeat.[18] However, of Auchinleck's visit to the UK in 1941, Churchill later wrote that 'He [Auchinleck] certainly shook my military advisors with all the detailed argument that he produced. I was myself unconvinced.'[19] That was the problem for the generals: Churchill and his stubborn and frequently wrong attitude.

On his return to Cairo, Auchinleck set about making changes to his command. The first change was that Major General Sir Alan Cunningham was appointed GOC-in-C Western Desert Force (about to be renamed Eighth Army) with an immediate temporary rank of lieutenant general. Cunningham had already made his name as GOC East Africa where he had been responsible for the defeat of the Italian Empire there. The nucleus of the Western Desert Force was to become XIII Corps under the command of Major General Alfred Godwin-Austen who had commanded the 8th Infantry Division in East Africa and Abyssinia (Ethiopia). A new corps, XXX Corps, was also being formed during this time. This corps was to have been made up of most of the armour available and should have been commanded by Major General Vyvyan Pope, Royal Tank

Regiment, an expert in tank warfare.[20] Pope was wanted by Auchinleck as a replacement for General Michael O'Moore Creagh, who had been in Egypt since December 1939 and had commanded the 7th Armoured Division since February 1940. Auchinleck had nothing against Creagh but considered that he had been too long in the desert.[21] Sadly, Pope was killed in an accident during October 1941 shortly after taking up his post and was succeeded by Major General Willoughby Norrie who had previously commanded the 1st Armoured Division.[22] As can be imagined, operations over the desert called for vehicles and, of course, armour. As Playfair noted in his history of the Second World War, the desert war was becoming one of stalemate as neither side had quite the edge to provide that killer blow. Large numbers of infantry were useful but could not provide the necessary victory; only armour could do that. The enemy had two modified German armoured divisions, a partially-armoured Italian division which was, according to Playfair, 'of doubtful value', one Italian motorized division and four infantry divisions. Auchinleck considered that he would need at least two if not three fully-equipped and trained armoured divisions if he was to capture Cyrenaica in its entirety. At the time he only had one such division, the 7th Armoured Division, as the other one, the 2nd Armoured Division, did not really exist following retreats from Greece and Benghazi.

The problem for Auchinleck was not only not having enough armour, but that what he had wasn't good enough. He had light tanks which were of no fighting value once pitched against German armour, but he did have 500 other tanks. However, half of these were of the heavy infantry type and again unsuitable for fighting German tanks. The British tanks were too slow and their radius of action too short, while their radios were not designed for the distances over which the fighting took place. For the above reasons, the infantry 'I' tanks were withdrawn from the 7th Armoured Brigade, leaving it with one armoured brigade of British cruisers, while the 4th Brigade did not have enough British cruisers and was to be gradually re-equipped with American Stuarts. They would remain below strength by the end of September.

The speed and mechanical reliability of the Stuart was impressive but the main gun ammunition that it used was scarce while the tank, overall, was unsuited to desert warfare. This meant delays as the tank was modified in preparation for desert warfare, which meant that there was a further wait as once the tanks were ready, the crews who were to fight from them had to be trained and become familiar with their new vehicles. The extra work thrown at the workshops in modifying the Stuarts caused major problems as there was already quite enough to be done owing to the current list of repairs and overhauls, and this caused Auchinleck to consider that he needed a reserve of 50 per cent to cover tanks in workshops and to provide a pool readily available to replace casualties. This programme of changing from one tank to another type which was very different from the previous one meant a heavy commitment to training. An added strain was that there was a need to maintain a reasonable state of readiness in case of an enemy attack.

In Auchinleck's opinion the importance of training could never be understated as previous battles, especially Operation BATTLEAXE, had shown that the present standard of training was insufficient and that mistake was not to be repeated. The problem was that it was not the training of the units belonging to the division but that each brigade and the division needed to train and learn how to work together as a single unit. At the end of September 1941 there was not a single fully-equipped and trained armoured division. By mid-October there would be one as well as an army tank brigade of 'I' tanks. Playfair notes that the Germans were struck by the poor standard of British training and often commented on it. Eventually the Defence Committee decided to send out the 22nd Armoured Brigade (1st Armoured Division) from the UK as soon as possible.

This brigade had been trained to defend the UK from a German invasion and so needed re-training on arrival and desert navigation was a good example of this training. They were equipped with British cruisers needing a few alterations for desert warfare, and this would all take time. It was hoped that the brigade would reach Egypt by mid-September and be ready for action by 1 November. It arrived on 4 October.[23] The Defence Committee, at the end of July 1941, had wanted, most strongly, an offensive in North Africa as soon as possible and preferably not later than September. Auchinleck wished to wait until November.[24] This was because he detected that there was an outside chance of a limited victory in October but a probable complete success in November.[25]

Later Churchill, in his own memoirs of the Second World War, was still complaining that Auchinleck's delay was a mistake. Playfair, looking at previous events in North Africa, tends to disagree with Churchill and come down on the side of Auchinleck waiting to ensure that he had adequate equipment and properly-trained troops before going onto the offensive.[26] As Playfair observed, Auchinleck had to wait to build up his force which he estimated would be ready by early November and that he was anxious it should not be later.[27] Churchill wasn't the only one looking at the calendar that year.

Auchinleck continued to plan for the forthcoming offensive in the Western Desert, but there were distractions. Part of the distraction was that Auchinleck considered officers should not enjoy undue luxuries in the field when these were perhaps denied to the other ranks. Therefore he sought to move GHQ out from Cairo where he considered there were too many attractions. The Egyptian capital was a problem as far as Auchinleck was concerned. There was no wartime atmosphere in Cairo, while society there did not appeal to Auchinleck who had not taken his own wife to Cairo. Auchinleck had, perhaps eccentrically, to force the staff of GHQ to sleep in tents in the desert and commute daily to their offices in Cairo. This plan didn't come to fruition as there was a problem with transport, but it does show that Auchinleck, like all humans, had quirks in his character and this was perhaps one, even if it was well intended. In the event Auchinleck had to be content with moving himself and his small staff out to the desert at Mena.

During July and August Churchill maintained his barrage of questions and statements to Auchinleck, so eventually Auchinleck sent his DMI, Brigadier John Shearer, to London to brief Churchill and the COS of his intentions. Shearer's visit was successful, but he was away for a month owing to enemy action and the limited availability of aircraft to return to Cairo. Ismay took advantage of Shearer's visit to give him a letter of advice to deliver to Auchinleck. The letter told Auchinleck of Churchill's visit to President Roosevelt and the signing of the Atlantic Charter. Ismay also advised Auchinleck to write letters to Churchill rather than telegrams or official letters. Churchill apparently could gauge more from a letter than an official script and it would be best to write 'long personal chatty letters' to the prime minister as they worked better for him, noting that

Churchill 'isn't a normal person (thank God) and these aren't normal times'.[28]

On 16 September Auchinleck did sent Churchill a lengthy and detailed letter concerning forthcoming operations, but not before a paper on Auchinleck was circulated in Whitehall intended only for the eyes of commanders-in-chief and written by Oliver Lyttelton, Minister of State for the Middle East. A major problem was that Auchinleck felt isolated as he was getting facts but no opinions from the commanders-in-chief. Auchinleck sought their opinions about operations as well as keeping him in the loop regarding operations outside of his area. It was agreed that liaison between London and Auchinleck was improving. The report considered that at the time of Auchinleck taking up his post in North Africa, it was thought that the Germans would have been successful with their invasion of the Soviet Union. This meant, at that time, that Allied planners considered that there was only a small window to succeed in North Africa while the German army was committed against the Soviet Union.

By September, it was clear that the enemy was being distracted in the east more than had been anticipated by the German planners. This caused some thought about what the Spanish or Vichy French might do regarding North Africa as both could launch operations against Allied interests there, while the Spanish might even invade the British colony of Gibraltar, which stood guard over the western Mediterranean and controlled shipping in and out to the Atlantic from the Mediterranean. Without doubt the Germans would have ideally wanted this British sentinel to fall into their hands in order to gain free access to the Atlantic Ocean and the Mediterranean Sea. There were also concerns about what the Germans might do in North Africa. It was wondered whether the enemy might withdraw from Cyrenaica and consolidate its forces further back, thus making the Allies use more men than they were comfortable with to eventually remove the Germans from Africa.

Then there were questions about whether Tripoli, the capital of Libya, was worth capturing. Did it have a worthwhile military value as opposed to other ideas such as a defensive line up to the south of Sirte, which was given as an example? A further discussion was that if Tripoli was deemed to be valuable and advantageous in being captured by the British, when could this be done as it seemed that Benghazi was a priority and just how long after the capture of the besieged Benghazi could an operation against Tripoli begin? Another question raised was that if the enemy did leave Cyrenaica, how long before the Allies could launch an operation to follow up on this and would all of this lead to operations against Italy? This question was initiated by Lyttelton himself.[29] Clearly operations in North Africa remained fluid, with much depending on how the Germans fared in the Soviet Union; if they got bogged down, as was the case, they would have fewer troops to spare for the North African campaign, while it was necessary for Allied commanders, especially Auchinleck, to get on top of the situation and begin to drive the Axis forces from North Africa.

Auchinleck replied to Lyttelton's paper within a few days. He agreed that the enemy should be hit very hard during the coming winter, but expected Tobruk to suffer further if it was not relieved soon. Auchinleck asserted that he did not fear an enemy land offensive in the Western Desert unless it was supported from the air. However, what he did fear was the loss of Malta which had been besieged since June 1940. Auchinleck noted that the loss of Malta would have been a disaster as it was the British base between Italy and Libya. His overall view was that the future of Allied war planning was to get back to Europe, gain a footing in Greece and invade Italy via Sicily.[30] Auchinleck was pretty much spot on with his analysis of the situation. Even so, he received a signal from the C-in-C, Mediterranean Station, which was pessimistic. Auchinleck was informed that if the Germans broke off their attack on the Soviet Union, it might lead to full-scale air attacks on the Red Sea ports which might not be able to be met; this would only serve the situation, given that both Tobruk and Malta were under full-scale attacks.[31] The situation in the autumn of 1941 remained unclear, but it was hoped by the British that the Soviets might well keep the Germans in the Soviet Union and not allow them to be able to turn westwards or reinforce the Afrika Korps.

Auchinleck outlined his forthcoming plans in his letter to Churchill of 16 September 1941. He described how he had prepared forward supply bases near Sidi Barrani and at Jarabub in the south. The plan was to remove the threat of an enemy attack against the landing grounds at Sidi Barrani which were vital to aerial operations over Tobruk that ensured the garrison's supply by sea. Auchinleck explained to Churchill that the preparation of two advanced bases so far apart gave flexibility and would enable the thrust of the British attack to alter if needed as well as confuse the enemy as to what was intended. As Auchinleck remarked to Churchill: 'We cannot conceal the existence of these advanced bases, but I hope we can conceal the direction and strength of our blow.'[32]

There were other changes made ready for the forthcoming operation. On 26 September the Western Desert Force was officially renamed the Eighth Army; Churchill preferred to call it 'The Army of the Nile'. Later Auchinleck said: 'We weren't anywhere near the Nile. It was pure romance. I don't think the army cared a twopenny damn what it was called; I didn't anyway.' Churchill was always a romantic when it came to history and had already instructed the Minister of Information to discourage the use of the name Iran for Persia. There was the argument that Iraq and Iran could be confused when used together, but Churchill preferred Persia anyway. The operation that Auchinleck was preparing was Operation CRUSADER.[33]

*Chapter Seven*

# Operation CRUSADER

Auchinleck had already charged Cunningham at the beginning of September with a directive 'to drive the enemy out of North Africa in two phases: first the capture of Cyrenaica; second, the capture of Tripolitania.' As Greenwood notes, there were two courses open to the Eighth Army: to use its main force on Jarabub and then advance via Jalo to cut off the enemy's retreat, or to attack from the coastal sector, south of the escarpment, and then to make a feint from the centre and south. This was Operation CRUSADER.

Cunningham was given XIII Corps (Lieutenant General Alfred Godwin-Austen) which consisted of the New Zealand Division (Major General Bernard Freyberg), the 4th Indian Division (Major General Frank Messervy) and the 1st Army Tank Brigade (Brigadier H.R.B. Watkins); XXX Corps (Lieutenant General Willoughby Norrie) which was made up of the 7th Armoured Division (Major General William Gott), the 4th Armoured Brigade Group (Brigadier Alexander Gatehouse) and two brigades of the 1st South African Division (Major General George Brink); plus the 22nd Guards (Motor) Brigade (Brigadier John Marriot). In addition to these, Cunningham had command of the Tobruk Garrison Force consisting of the 70th Division (Major General Ronald Scobie) and the Polish Carpathian Infantry Brigade Group (Major General Stanisław Kopański). Finally, he had a small force based on the southern oases around Siwa which consisted of the 6th South African Armoured Car Regiment and a battalion group from the 29th Indian Infantry Brigade (Brigadier Denys Reid). In reserve were the 2nd South Africans of two brigades under the command of Major General Isaac de Villiers. The whole force of the Eighth Army at that time consisted of about 120,000 officers and men. Cunningham had the use of 455 tanks; mostly Crusaders which were under-armed with a pea-shooter of a 2-pounder gun as its main defence, only effective at 500 yards or less. There were no anti-tank guns of any use but as Greenwood writes, there was an adequate supply of 3.7in AA guns that could have been used for anti-tank artillery but never were deployed as such.[1] Auchinleck had already considered that Rommel would probably concentrate his armour somewhere south of Fort Capuzzo and strike at Cunningham's force advancing towards Tobruk and adjusted his plans for the use of his own armoured units accordingly.[2]

An early problem for Auchinleck and Churchill was a political one when the New Zealand Prime Minister Peter Fraser claimed that Freyberg was unsuitable to command the New Zealand Division. This was blatant nonsense as Freyberg was a First World War veteran and had won the Victoria Cross and the Distinguished Service Order during that conflict. Freyberg continued to command New Zealand forces throughout the rest of the Second World War. Fraser never substantiated his claim that Freyberg was unfit for his command and so it can be largely ignored.

The next problem also came from 'down under' as the Australian Prime Minister Arthur Fadden demanded changes in the deployment of Australian armed forces serving in North Africa. Fadden was concerned that the 9th Australian Division was located at Tobruk and the Australian opposition parties demanded that all Australian forces should be concentrated into a single Australian corps under an Australian commander. This would have meant that the 9th Australian Division would have to leave Tobruk which would have been catastrophic. Fadden's problem was that he had a majority of only one in the Australian parliament. Churchill was being pressurized by Fadden to ensure that Auchinleck should acquiesce to Fadden's wishes, but Auchinleck told Churchill that this was impossible even if it might be politically desirable for Fadden; operationally, if the Australians left Tobruk, this might jeopardize coming offensives in the Western Desert, essentially CRUSADER. Fadden tried to ignore Auchinleck's military experience and continued to demand that the 9th Australian Division be removed from Tobruk.[3]

Churchill arrived at a decision and decided to agree with the Australian demands even though he and the British Chiefs of Staff agreed with Auchinleck's analysis of the situation in North Africa. In his communiqué to Auchinleck, Churchill said that he had to make 'great allowances' for a government with a majority of one whose opposition was 'bitter' and 'isolationists in sentiment'. Auchinleck was asked to put his personal (and professional) feelings aside, as had the British War Cabinet, and prevent 'an open dispute with the Australian Government'. Churchill continued by adding: 'Any public controversy would injure the foundations of the Empire and be disastrous to our general position in the war. Everything must be borne with patience and in the end, all will come right.'[4] The outcome of this was that during August, September and October, the Australians at Tobruk were replaced by the 70th British Division. During this three-month movement, three ships were sunk, four seriously damaged, and there was loss of life. Years later, Auchinleck said of the NATO command structure that he would not like to be the C-in-C of NATO because owing to its international construction there might well be undue influence and demands made by politicians citing their own national interests.[5] Even so, Auchinleck complied and wrote to Churchill, saying that he understood the need to dispel the myth that the fighting in the Middle East was being carried out using solely Dominion troops, as Australian and New Zealand units were known.[6] Later Churchill wrote to Auchinleck in relation to a previous request made by Auchinleck to postpone relieving the final Australians out from Tobruk until after CRUSADER. By this date, 14 October 1941, Fadden was no longer prime minister of Australia after losing a vote of confidence in the Australian parliament and so Churchill told Auchinleck that he had asked Fadden's successor, John Curtin, if he would agree that the remaining two Australian brigades could stay at Tobruk until CRUSADER had been decided.[7]

By the end of September 1941 Cunningham's plan was ready. It was to be a two-pronged assault with the majority of the armour from XXX Corps advancing north-west from Sidi Omar towards Tobruk. While this was happening the infantry of XIII Corps was to move along the coast to the area between Bardia and Tobruk. The final date of the attack was naturally a secret, but Auchinleck considered mid-November to be ideal and so planning was based around this date.[8] Churchill had already told Auchinleck that CRUSADER would affect the immediate outcome of the war, while Auchinleck had to consider what faced him. Greenwood notes that the Afrika Korps consisted of five infantry divisions, three armoured divisions and two motorized divisions, but the enemy was overwhelmingly Italian. The combined enemy strength was estimated to be about 100,000 all ranks and so the British were outnumbered by about 20,000 men and officers. The German armour consisted of about 250 Panzer III and Panzer IV tanks equipped with 4-pounder guns that quickly gained an awesome reputation, but the Germans had little by way of armoured reserves.[9]

September 1941 saw Churchill trying to interfere with Auchinleck's planning as the British prime minister was seeking an early offensive because he feared a Soviet collapse in the east and a renewed threat against the UK and the Middle East. Auchinleck stubbornly refused to name a date until his forces were ready to move onto the offensive. As part of this deception, encouraged by his DMI (Director of Military Intelligence) Brigadier Shearer, Auchinleck planned to confuse the enemy by the spread of false information that he would soon be sending some of his forces from Palestine and Syria to help the Soviets protect their oilfields. On 3 October, as part of this ruse, Auchinleck paid a quick visit to units in both Palestine and Syria.[10]

Throughout October, Churchill continued to badger Auchinleck for the coming offensive and once more reminded him that on CRUSADER hung the immediate outcome of the war. A successful campaign (and Churchill would only see such an eventuality) would cause, according to Churchill, Turkey, French North Africa and Spain to 'pick their steps accordingly'; basically either choose to remain neutral or join the war against the Axis powers. Another outcome of CRUSADER would be that the Soviet Union would feel that others were fighting the Germans. As Churchill noted, even British people thought that the UK was 'supine' compared with the Soviet Union. Churchill wrote to Auchinleck the following words:

> I am however fully in control of public opinion and of the House of Commons. Nevertheless, it seems to me, on military grounds alone, that everything should be thrown into this battle that can be made to play its part. This is also the view of the Defence Committee, both political and expert members. God granted us this long breathing space and I feel that if all is risked all may be won.

Churchill continued with his thoughts on CRUSADER and stated that there was a '...need to capitalise on any victory which may be granted – any delay pushing on from Cyrenaica to Tripoli would seem fatal to that extension of your plan.'

Churchill called for speed and a rapid advance into enemy-held areas of North Africa before the enemy could recover and bring in reinforcements to North Africa and Italy. As ever, Churchill was thinking all over the place as he considered that he might send an expedition to Norway; probably he let this gem slip as Auchinleck had served in Norway during the previous year. Then Churchill dragged himself back to events in North Africa and mused that a successful operation there might change the French General Weygand's attitude, who tried to keep the French Empire intact by denying everybody bases in French North Africa. Churchill considered that if the British were victorious with CRUSADER, then General Weygand might be persuaded to allow the British access to the port city of Casablanca or even join in operations against Sicily.[11] On 23 November, Churchill reminded Auchinleck that he was waiting for the moment to appeal to President Roosevelt to put pressure on Weygand to comply with the wishes of the Allies and that CRUSADER was part of the plan, but it was hard going for the operation by this point.[12]

During the third week of October Churchill and Auchinleck were still wrangling over the timing of the beginning of CRUSADER, which had a sequel named ACROBAT. Churchill's concerns were largely political. Auchinleck, writing to Churchill on 23 October 1941, said that he fully understood the need for speed and avoidance of delay but was unwilling to go onto the offensive at half-cock. Auchinleck observed that no advance could be made without adequate supplies of petrol, ammunition and other supplies to be accumulated and carried forward which took time, while noting that distances were great and means of transport scanty. He made it very clear that General Cunningham and all others concerned with the planning of CRUSADER were fully aware of the need for haste and for the need to improvise where necessary to overcome immediate shortages in some quarters.[13]

Clearly Auchinleck was refusing to kowtow to Churchill and was doing what was demanded of him professionally, ensuring that an operation was not about to go off badly owing to political concerns. Even so, despite Auchinleck's fears of shortages, the situation in North Africa was better than it had been as from July 1941 onwards the Red Sea was open to American shipping and supplies, especially munitions, began to flow into the Middle East, coming from the USA, the UK and the Dominions as their war production began to take off. By the end of October 1941 about 300 British cruiser tanks, 300 American Stuart light tanks, 170 'I' tanks, 34,000 lorries, 600 field guns, 80 heavy and 160 light anti-aircraft guns, 200 anti-tank guns and 900 mortars to name some of the equipment that was landed in North Africa. This list looks impressive but, as Playfair remarks, it was not enough to make up the losses and wastage sustained by that point in North Africa and certainly was nowhere enough to allow for a decent reserve of equipment to be built up. Nevertheless, the flow of armour into Egypt allowed the programme of re-equipping to near fulfilment. By early September the 1st Tank Army was equipped and the 4th Armoured Brigade was equipped by the end of the same month. However, the 7th Armoured Brigade was still short of its tanks. In mid-September the 32nd Army Tank Brigade was formed in Tobruk as a mixed force of cruisers and 'I' tanks. Finally, the 22nd Armoured Brigade, coming from the UK, was not disembarked until 4 October and it was discovered that its tanks required modification for the desert. This took treble the time normally spent by new arrivals in the base workshops. This work was not completed until 25 October and then the crews needed training.[14]

The political concerns had everything to do with the German offensive against the Soviet Union. There was exasperation with this as General Sir John Dill acknowledged in a private letter to Auchinleck. Dill knew that the situation for the Soviet Union was dire and that people, especially in the press, were clamouring that 'something must be done' [for the Soviet Union]. Dill considered that this might have been acceptable if the calls came from the tabloid press or 'yellow press' as he refers to it, suggesting that the stories were based on little or no research or facts – basically in today's post-truth parlance 'fake news' or more bluntly lies – and read by 'ignorant people' as Dill chose to refer to the readership of such unworthy journalism. However, as he observed, this lay with the fact that people who should know better were also agitating for aid to the

Soviet Union including Stalin and the Soviet ambassador to the UK, Ivan Maisky. Dill was well aware that certain journalists such as John Gordon, writing for either the *Evening Standard* or the *Sunday Express*, he wasn't sure which, considered that the 'Brass hats' (Chiefs of Staff) lacked imagination. On hoardings and walls Dill saw posters urging for an offensive in the West immediately to relieve the Soviet Union and divert German armed forces from that country. Dill informed Auchinleck that within the War Cabinet, Lord Beaverbrook, the Canadian press baron, was also urging that the West should do something and do it soon. Dill considered that Beaverbrook might well resign his position in the Cabinet or at least orchestrate his own resignation on the grounds that he could not continue to be a member of a government that 'so signally failed to help Russia'. Meanwhile, Dill confirmed that the Chiefs of Staff were looking at the problem from 'every possible angle'.[15]

Dill was quite right in his assessment of the situation in the UK regarding many people, but especially the working classes who saw a common alliance with their Soviet brethren and demanded that something be done. Maisky makes an interesting observation in his diary on 3 November 1941 regarding Beaverbrook. Given that Beaverbrook was a tycoon and not one given to the mores of the Soviet system which in turn should have been antagonistic towards him as a paid-up member of the capitalist class, it is odd to read Maisky's concern that the British government might be on the verge of a reshuffle and that Beaverbrook might be about to resign. Maisky wrote that '…Beaverbrook's resignation at present would be most inconvenient for us!'[16] It was an unlikely alliance, but so was the one between Rippentrop and Molotov that allowed Germany to invade Poland; war makes for odd bedfellows. Beaverbrook, however, had not told Maisky that he was in bad odour with the British War Cabinet following the Moscow conference during which he gave much away to the Soviet Union and did little, for example, for the Poles, either in the Soviet Union or in exile in the UK. He also briefed the Soviets against senior British figures, including the British ambassador, Sir Stafford Cripps.[17]

The sense of urgency to get CRUSADER going was growing elsewhere as General Wavell sent a cipher message to the CIGS on 30 October 1941, expressing his alarm at the German approaches towards the Caucasus

Mountains which were encroaching on British-held interests. Wavell was concerned with the weaknesses of Allied forces in Persia and Iraq.[18] This was a major fear of Auchinleck as well and this was reinforced by his message to the CIGS in which he re-stated his view that Iraq and Persia were vital for the defence of the Eastern bases.[19] Meanwhile, the veteran South African leader and Prime Minister Field Marshal Jan Smuts wrote to Auchinleck and said:

> ...success will be a vital matter for us, not only because of the present psychological moment in the war, but because it will be imperative to free ourselves of vast risks and commitments on both our right and left hands. The progress of the enemy towards the Caucasus makes a move in force against us from that quarter more than likely next spring, and we are lucky to have the opportunity to clear our other front this winter. The prospects and chances both for and against us this winter in your theatre are enormous, and the ultimate issue of war may well depend on the job that now lies before us.[20]

Smuts was a veteran of several wars including, as a young man, the Second Anglo-Boer War (1899–1902) which saw him fighting against the British. He was also an astute politician and a friend of Churchill, despite them having fought against one another at the turn of the twentieth century. His advice and analysis of the war was always valuable, as was this piece of advice given to Auchinleck.

There was a further postponement of CRUSADER on 8 November 1941 before finally the attack began on 18 November 1941. As Greenwood wrote, the enemy had been taken by surprise as the tanks from XXX Corps moved into Libya as no enemy opposition was met on the first day and the armoured brigades reached their planned positions around Gabr Saleh that evening, having arrived earlier than had been planned. It was then that Cunningham altered his original plan and split his strength. He ordered the 7th Armoured Division to destroy the Italian units guarding Bir el Gubi on the extreme left flank of XXX Corps. Following this they were to advance to Sidi Rezegh protected on their right flank by the 4th Armoured Brigade Group.

The enemy was not slow to react and the next day, 19 November, elements of the Afrika Korps were seen moving towards Gabr Saleh which had been vacated by XXX Corps. Both the British and the Germans somehow managed to avoid each other the following day and as the 7th Armoured Division approached Sidi Rezegh that night, 20 November, without any opposition, General Gott signalled to his army commander that it was time for the Tobruk garrison to break out and join up with XXX Corps. Cunningham agreed to this and once more the original plans were altered as it had been agreed that any break-out from Tobruk would only begin once all enemy armour had been destroyed.

Gott prepared to attack the enemy on the Sidi Rezegh ridge on 21 November. The 7th Armoured Division was to be supported by the 5th South African Brigade. The South Africans had been held up during the advance march as their troops were not sufficiently trained to keep their direction while marching across the desert at night. The Italians had put up stronger than expected resistance at Bir el Gubi, so coupled with the delay in receiving the South Africans, there was a lull before a concentrated attack could begin on Sidi Rezegh. By this time, Rommel had realized that the Eighth Army was on the offensive and that XXX Corps were not making reconnaissance in force as he had previously believed. The battle raged around Sidi Rezegh and soon descended into chaos as the British and Germans clashed. Armoured vehicles intermingled with tanks and communications broke down. Tanks were destroyed by anti-tank fire, while armoured cars ran out of fuel and were lost. The sands of the desert, smoke, fire and dust meant that entire units disappeared and then reappeared, broken down and bewildered.

While this carnage was going on, Eighth Army HQ at Maddalena was being fed with optimistic but misleading information and as a consequence Auchinleck was transmitting equally optimistic reports back to Churchill. The near capture of General Cunningham by Rommel illustrates perfectly the confusion of the fighting in the desert. Cunningham had spent the night of 20 November with General Norrie at XXX Corps HQ, was on his way back to Maddalena and had stopped to check his bearings. At the same time Rommel was up, as he often was, on the German forward positions, checking and had stopped in his command vehicle which was a captured British armoured command vehicle to which Rommel had taken a fancy, re-named it *Mammut* meaning 'elephant' and began to use it as his personal command vehicle. As soon as he stopped, Rommel, through his binoculars, saw two British staff cars and a small group of staff officers studying their maps. Rommel immediately called to his aides that it was General Cunningham and that they should go and get him, but before the Germans could react Rommel declared 'too late' and set off himself to capture Cunningham. The ensuing cloud of dust headed by Rommel as he led a group of staff cars and motorcycles naturally alerted Cunningham to his impending capture, but he sped off in his staff car and avoided capture.[21]

The confusion in the desert was total. As Greenwood relates, at one point Rommel arrived at a British field ambulance hospital where both British and German wounded were being treated. The commander of the British post was a young captain who thought that Rommel was a Polish general taking an interest, but it was Rommel who realized his mistake and so, making quick apologies, leaped into *Mammut* and sped off, leaving behind him a mystified group of medics. There were further incidents: General Norrie mislaid his Corps HQ, while elsewhere General Reid found no opposition when he captured the fort at Gialo where he found a group of Italian officers about to begin a formal dinner for a visiting staff officer.

Cunningham gave the order for XIII Corps to begin their advance along the coastal road on 21 November. The mainly infantry New Zealand Division led the advance. The Kiwis completed their march of seventeen hours and arrived on the outskirts of Bardia. En route, the fortresses at Capuzzo, Musaid and Sollum had been captured with little opposition. Then the confusion of desert warfare was fortuitous for XIII Corps as the New Zealanders suddenly arrived at the HQ of the Afrika Korps from which General Crüwell had only just left. After some close-combat fighting, the entire enemy HQ was overrun and all the staff captured. The next day, the 15th Panzer Division, moving south-east of Sidi Rezegh, chanced upon the HQ of the 4th Armoured Brigade who were totally unaware of the German presence in the vicinity. The brigade commander, Brigadier Alexander Gatehouse, was attending a conference with his divisional commander at the time but the rest of his entire HQ with 35 tanks and a number of assorted armoured cars and artillery pieces were captured as well as 17 officers and 150 other ranks being taken prisoner.

As Greenwood describes, the war in the desert was largely confusion and chance, mainly owing to the barren and featureless terrain spread over such a vast area; something that no European was used to. At times units of the Eighth Army were chasing the rear of the Afrika Korps, and then just as suddenly the reverse happened. On 23 November the Sidi Rezegh area was recaptured by the German 21st Panzer Group. Cunningham thought that the battle was lost, and he spoke to Brigade General Staff, Brigadier Alexander Galloway about withdrawing the Eighth Army back into Egypt. Galloway, having served in the ill-fated Greek campaign and having seen worse situations, was aghast at Cunningham's musing and telephoned his opposite number at GHQ, Brigadier John Whiteley, and suggested that a very senior officer should fly down immediately and see the situation. However, it was Cunningham who shortly phoned Auchinleck and requested that he should come and see what he considered to be a most desperate situation. Auchinleck, with Air Marshal Tedder, flew down to meet Cunningham on the same evening.[22] Cunningham was a very sick man and had been advised to stop smoking. He had been a chronic chain-smoker and had stopped, but he was back to smoking again when Auchinleck met him. The latter found Cunningham to be in a distressed state and was talking all the time about withdrawing east into an area where it might be possible to save Egypt.

Auchinleck reviewed the situation and decided that the British attack should continue; he considered that there was no alternative. He also felt that Rommel would soon over-extend his lines of communication and would be running short of fuel very soon. The next morning Auchinleck wrote a new directive to Cunningham and handed it personally to him prior to lunch that day. The new directive ordered Cunningham to continue to attack the enemy relentlessly, using all his resources down to the last tank. His main immediate objective was to continue to destroy enemy tank forces and the ultimate object remained the conquest of Cyrenaica and then to advance on Tripoli. At the same time Rommel was ordering Crüwell to cross into Egypt and totally destroy Eighth Army's communications and supply lines.[23] Auchinleck's intervention on 23 November was decisive. He acted on a hunch: he had looked beyond all the facts that had been laid before him and just knew that Rommel would soon outrun his supply line. A German staff officer wrote of Auchinleck's action that 'this was certainly one of the great decisions of the war: Auchinleck's fighting spirit and shrewd strategic insight had saved the CRUSADER battle and much else besides.' Churchill wrote: 'By his personal action Auchinleck thus saved the battle and proved his outstanding qualities as a commander in the field.'[24]

Auchinleck had been correct about Rommel and the state of his forces as on the evening of 23 November he was down to 100 tanks and his army was in a state of chaos. General Bayerlein wrote that 'the wide area south of Sidi Rezegh had become a sea of dust, haze and smoke.' With the coming of dusk 'hundreds of burning vehicles, tanks and guns lit up the field'. However, Rommel, like Auchinleck, was a great general and seemed to read the mind of Cunningham who faced him. Rommel led a counter-attack on the morning of 24 November and headed towards Egypt in a column 40 miles long. This route took Rommel through the headquarters of the 30th Corps, the 7th Armoured Division, the 1st South African Division, the 7th Support Group and the 7th Armoured Brigade, most of which were caught napping! The British were in full panic mode. Cunningham arrived back at Maddalena and met Auchinleck who handed him a directive which set out in detail Auchinleck's understanding of the situation and orders to continue the battle.

Auchinleck considered possession in strength of the Rezegh-Duda ridge by the 13th Corps and the Tobruk garrison to be key to the battle. The problem was that Cunningham was quite disturbed by the events of that morning and was further disheartened by an observation from the air of a tank battle which to Cunningham seemed to suggest that Rommel was sweeping all before him. Auchinleck was made of firmer stuff and said of Rommel's advance: 'He is making a desperate effort, but he will not get very far. That column of tanks simply cannot get supplies. I am sure of this.'

Auchinleck was correct, and the Afrika Korps moved around periodically throughout 24 and 25 November, hampered by a lack of fuel with its men foraging for petrol rather than fighting. The 4th Indian Division, in the Omars, beat off German attacks with heavy losses and then Rommel's counter-attack began to peter out. Auchinleck's presence with the Eighth Army had given it the sense of reassurance that it needed. There was a slight panic due to a scare that German tanks were moving towards Eighth Army HQ which alarmed Cunningham who was anxious to get Auchinleck, as C-in-C, away to safety. Auchinleck made it quite clear that Cunningham's only concern was for the safety of his chief, Auchinleck, and not for himself, Cunningham. Despite appearances, Auchinleck was impressed with the situation in North Africa, knew that Rommel would be defeated and so before flying back to Cairo left a message of support for the Eighth Army. However, it was all over for Cunningham and once Auchinleck returned to Cairo he was determined to relieve him as he could see that Cunningham had given his all and had nothing left to give.[25]

What was muddled through was the command of the war, both in the wastes of North Africa and from London as alterations were about to take place. The war was taking its toll on people and so Churchill decided to replace General Sir John Dill as CIGS. Dill had been ill with shingles for some time and was also suffering from nervous exhaustion. Dill, no doubt, was exhausted as he was expected to dine with Churchill, often at very short notice, twice or more a week. Over dinner Churchill would bombard Dill with questions and ideas, often until two or three in the morning. Then once or twice a month he was expected to be a guest at Chequers where once more Dill would be peppered with questions and ideas but this time in front of a mixed assortment of political guests. To replace Dill, Churchill chose the C-in-C Home Forces, General Sir Alan Brooke, who was expected to take up his new duties on 1 December; that is, within a week of his appointment.[26]

The other alteration was in the Middle East as Auchinleck reluctantly dismissed Cunningham who was sick and unable to do his job adequately. On 25 November, Auchinleck sent a letter of dismissal to Cunningham. The letter was couched in sympathetic terms, observing the positive aspects of Cunningham's late command of the Eighth Army. Auchinleck reflected on the recent battle and that Cunningham had asked that perhaps a withdrawal eastward might be considered and that after some thought Auchinleck had considered that it was best to press on, regardless of the possible losses. He noted that Cunningham had supported him in that decision and loyally accepted it and gave orders to best effect Auchinleck's directives. However, Auchinleck considered that Cunningham was by then thinking more of defence rather than offence and so Auchinleck was relieving him of his command. He informed Cunningham that he was going to replace him with Acting General N.M. Ritchie and that he was to hand over his command on receipt of Auchinleck's letter. Auchinleck then thanked Cunningham for his work to date.[27] He also sent Cunningham a more personal letter which began 'Dear Alan'. In this letter he wrote as a friend and urged Cunningham to go on the sick list and seek hospital treatment as it was clear that Cunningham was very ill and exhausted.[28]

Auchinleck also made a report to Churchill regarding the dismissal of Cunningham on the same day. He told the British prime minister that he had been on a two-day visit to the Advanced HQ Eighth Army and as a result of his visit did not believe that Cunningham was in any fit state to continue to command such an intensive offensive as CRUSADER. Therefore Cunningham was to hand over command to General Ritchie on 26 November 1941, while Ritchie was to be made local or acting lieutenant general for this role. Auchinleck was very clear about why he did as he did and told Churchill:

> This decision does not, rpt, not mean that operations have been mishandled up to date or that their successful issue has been in any way prejudiced. Cunningham most loyal but in my opinion had lost spirit of offensive and consequently I have lost confidence in him. Would have referred matter to you first but every hour counts at the moment.[29]

In addition, Auchinleck sent Churchill a report on the situation in the operational area. He wrote:

> Have just returned from HQ Eighth Army. Issue of battle is still in the balance, but I am convinced that we have only to persist to win. Enemy is thrusting here, there and everywhere in desperate attempt to throw us off our balance, disorganise our command and cause chaos in the ranks. He is showing great skill and determination. All the same he had little behind his effort and so far from all I have

> seen and heard has failed completely to shake the morale of our commanders and troops who are fighting magnificently. The enemy is trying desperately to regain the initiative. In this he has succeeded in part but locally and temporarily only. So long as we can maintain our pressure towards Tobruk, the real initiative is ours and we can disregard diversions towards Sollum and Maddalena or even further east temporarily inconvenient and unpleasant as they may be. Every effort is being devoted to the forwarding of the offensive by the New Zealand Division and other troops of 13th Corps towards Tobruk and I believe it is going well. While in the forward area I heard of no one who was not – repeat – not sure that we were going to win. There might be disquieting episodes, but the general situation should remain in our favour.[30]

It would seem that only Cunningham was having doubts and was therefore replaced.

Auchinleck also telegraphed the CIGS in London regarding the dismissal of Cunningham and explained the situation. Overall, as we have seen, Cunningham was unwell and owing to the large losses of tanks, he may well have become dispirited and begun to think of defence rather than continuing with the offensive. Auchinleck confirmed that he was doing his best to replace armoured cars and tanks lost in the fighting, while the Eighth Army was organizing defences against enemy raids in the rear areas such as Sidi Omar, Maddalena and the railhead. At the same time light forces to the south had been ordered to press forward relentlessly towards the enemy's line of communication which followed the line of Mechili, Benghazi and El Agheila and interrupt the traffic therein. Auchinleck also made it clear that he was aware of the importance of the early employment of the 1st Armoured Division and this was receiving the most urgent attention. He also heaped praise on the Royal Navy ships HMS *Aurora* and HMS *Penelope* which had been involved in the interception of an Axis convoy coming from the Aegean Sea, bound for Benghazi.[31] It was a great coup for the Royal Navy and a great relief for British forces fighting in North Africa as the enemy convoy had numbered 100 vessels packed with provisions.

The day of Cunningham's dismissal saw a number of messages between Auchinleck and Churchill, the bulk originating from Auchinleck. In one missive he reminded Churchill of trying to keep the publicity surrounding Cunningham's removal to the minimum possible.[32] As a sop to his prime minister, Auchinleck briefed Churchill on a message that he had sent to Cunningham:

> Before leaving 8th Army HQ I issued following message to General Cunningham for wide distribution to troops. It may interest you. Begins – During three days at your Advance HQ I have seen and heard enough to convince me though I did not need convincing that the determination to beat the enemy of your commanders and troops could NOT repeat NOT be greater and I have no doubt whatever that he will be beaten. His position is desperate, and he is trying by lashing out in all directions to distract us from our object which is to destroy him utterly. We will NOT rpt NOT be distracted and he will be destroyed. You have got your teeth into him. Hang on and bite deeper and hang on till he is finished. Give him no rest. The general situation in North Africa is excellent. There is only one order: ATTACK AND PURSUE. All out everybody.[33]

By the following day, 26 November, both Churchill and Auchinleck were over Cunningham's dismissal. Churchill sent a message to Auchinleck regarding the ongoing operation in North Africa. Churchill was musing on how Auchinleck was planning to move his reserves towards the battle zone. He asked Auchinleck the following:

> You are no doubt constantly considering movement forward of reserves towards battle zone. I am well aware this is conditioned by transport and how important it is for you to do the work with minimum mouths to feed. I should be glad however to know what you have in reserve; supposing you need another division, or two or three brigades, where would you get them from?

Churchill suggested that if necessary Auchinleck could bring back a brigade of the 50th Division from Baghdad.[34] As ever, Churchill was impatient for results and demanded to know how Auchinleck was to continue his campaign.

The next day Auchinleck sent Churchill a comprehensive reply:

> 8th Army had already arranged to concentrate 4 IND DIV (4th Indian Division) forward and so release New Zealand troops from Bardia area to join in main offensive towards El Adem. I hope that Tobruk garrison will from now on be able to apply increasing pressure from North and East on enemy investing it and may be able to provide mobile column for wider operations westward in co-operation with 7 Armd Div [7th Armoured Division] and New Zealand or South African troops. Royal Dragoons (Armoured Car Regiment) is moving from Syria to join 8th Army to provide fresh unit for pursuit. I am bringing one inf bde gp [infantry brigade group] and div recce unit [divisional reconnaissance unit] of 50 Div from Haifa to Amriya just west of Alexandria to be in GHQ Reserve. These units have to be re-equipped with transport before moving to Iraq and are not, repeat, not in any event due to move before 15 December. Other two bde groups of 50 Div are already on way to Iraq and I do not, repeat, not think that it is necessary or desirable to recall them.

Auchinleck added further detail:

> I am forming 38 Ind Inf Bde [38th Infantry Indian Brigade] from Welch Regiment and two Indian Battalions just due to arrive from Iraq and am putting it at Matruh also in GHQ Reserve. Am also holding 3 Indian BDE at Deir Ezor [*sic*] in readiness to come south should more motorized troops be needed. In addition, there are odd infantry, artillery and other units in (Nile) Delta available at short notice to fill gaps. I have orders for some time ago for several Indian and East African labour companies of good fighting material to be turned into armed units for L of C and garrison units and these will relieve regular units for active work. I am satisfied myself with situation but not complacent repeat not complacent and I am continually watching this aspect. Particularly wish to avoid giving

> impression that we are short of troops in Libya and all above activities are being suitably covered by plausible reasons. Arrival of 18 Div in January (1942) will ease the situation.[35]

This was the kind of reply that Churchill liked: to the point, plenty of movement and the British and their allies advancing and not even considering defence, just the offensive. The next day there was discussion about Cunningham and his immediate future.

Incredibly, given the kindness that Cunningham had received from Auchinleck at the time of his dismissal, he decided to play up. Auchinleck on 27 November wrote to the CIGS confirming that Cunningham did have problems with his eyes, but could not remain indefinitely in hospital 'incognito' and needed to be ordered home with the hope of employment later.[36] Cunningham had taken his sacking quite personally and no doubt was ashamed that he had been removed from his post which accounted for his staying in hospital incognito and not wanting to return to the UK as he would be unable to hide the fact that he was no longer in command of the Eighth Army. While considering the replacement for Cunningham which Auchinleck had already told Churchill, General Neil Ritchie, was to take over the command of Eighth Army, Churchill and the CIGS considered that perhaps Auchinleck should directly command that army as his presence on the spot 'will be an inspiration to all'.[37]

Auchinleck, despite Churchill's flattery, explained his reasoning for appointing Neil Ritchie. Auchinleck told Churchill that after he had realized that Cunningham was not well, he did consider that he might take over Cunningham's command of the Eighth Army but thought about this very carefully. Having mulled the question over, Auchinleck decided to appoint Ritchie as Cunningham's successor. Auchinleck told Churchill that in his view he would have been of little use overseeing a localized portion of the operation but was of more value seeing the entire operation in the round as much depended on the success of CRUSADER. Therefore, Auchinleck decided that his proper place was at his GHQ where he could see the whole picture and 'retain a proper sense of proportion'. Auchinleck confirmed his support for Ritchie, saying that he and Ritchie were at one with how the operation was going and to where it should go. Auchinleck observed to Churchill that he was at Churchill's disposal but said '...but my honest opinion is that for me to go now and supersede Ritchie might have BAD and not GOOD effect.'[38] The CIGS also tried to convince Auchinleck to take personal command of the Eighth Army when he wrote the following to Auchinleck:

> What I had in mind was that moment will come in fact may have already come when your drive and personality will be essential to reap fruits of victory. Troops will be dog tired, vehicles badly in need of an overhaul and petrol and water short. Everyone will say they cannot press on and with your drive will find they can go another hundred miles at least. Chetwode once told me how Allenby on one occasion drove him on when he was sure he had not another ounce in him.[39]

The references to Chetwode and Allenby reflect campaigning in the Middle East during the First World War against the Turks, while the positive views of Auchinleck by both Churchill and the CIGS must have been encouraging for Auchinleck; even so, he remained professional at all times and sought only what was good for the campaign in hand. Still, the problem of the chain of command continued following Cunningham's dismissal and his apparent bad reaction to it.

Auchinleck had learned from the doctors responsible for Cunningham's treatment that he was exhausted and needed two to three months to recover. It was recommended that he be sent straight home to the UK, by air if possible.[40] Cunningham wrote to Auchinleck protesting his sacking. He told Auchinleck that he was not happy to be replaced midway through the operation and that this had meant he was perceived negatively in both the UK and the USA. Cunningham refused to accept Auchinleck's opinion that Cunningham was beginning to think only of defence rather than maintaining the offensive as desired by Auchinleck. Cunningham claimed that the huge losses of British tanks during the fighting could not be ignored as the British superiority in numbers had been lost and that meant that the enemy might have been in a position to move around Cunningham's left flank and raid Egypt.[41] This may have been true, but the British were seeking a victory and had no time for any talk other than the offensive and victory in North Africa. Nevertheless,

Cunningham was to be sent home as he was without doubt over-tired, strained and suffering from eye problems, or so read his medical report on 30 November 1941.[42] Cunningham was a very sick man, physically and mentally, and had nothing to be ashamed of. He had done his duty and Auchinleck could see this and respected him but sadly, Cunningham, no doubt due to his physical and mental condition, could not.

The question of Cunningham's sacking and replacement was still a live issue in correspondence between Auchinleck, Churchill and CIGS General Sir John Dill, who was about to become field marshal. The promotion of General Ritchie was still something that puzzled Churchill and Dill. Churchill wrote to Auchinleck stating that he and the CIGS did not intend to suggest in any way that he should remove Ritchie and replace him with himself but that perhaps Auchinleck should visit the battlefield should any fresh 'impulse' be needed. Churchill's attitude was that Auchinleck, with his drive and full knowledge of the situation before them, could inspire and inject new vigour into the troops and all involved in operations in North Africa.[43]

On 1 December 1941 Auchinleck explained his logic regarding Cunningham's dismissal and the ongoing operation in North Africa. He told Churchill that he waited to reveal his change of command until he could see which way the campaign was going. He wanted to ensure that the fighting was running in favour of the British and that the enemy understood that it was on the defensive. Auchinleck had hoped that it might have been so by 1 December, but admitted that the latest information showed that the enemy was still attacking around Sidi Rezegh but the British were still hitting back hard. Therefore Auchinleck urged Churchill to keep the news regarding Cunningham quiet for a bit longer as the enemy did not know of the change of command, and if they did they might take advantage of this knowledge in their immediate planning. This was the very reason that Cunningham was in hospital incognito and very much against his will; the need for secrecy was paramount and it was clear to all that he was exhausted and mentally drained with this being confirmed by medical staff. Auchinleck was determined to be gentle with Cunningham and requested that Churchill should couch any announcement in view of Cunningham's work as commander of the Eighth Army along the following lines: 'General Cunningham, to whose brilliant planning and determined leadership the successful preparation and initiation of our present offensive in Libya were due became indisposed on 24 November and was admitted to hospital. His place was taken by Lieut-General N.M. Ritchie.'

Auchinleck stood up to Churchill as he was not comfortable about making the announcement of Cunningham's sacking along the lines that Churchill proposed. Auchinleck reminded Churchill that he had asked Cunningham to go sick 'for the general good', but did not realize that Cunningham was in fact ill at the time. Auchinleck told Churchill that indeed he could make any statement that he saw fit about Cunningham, but it would not have been correct to say '...proposed dispositions were not in accord with the principle of relentless offensive'. Auchinleck was clear to Churchill when he said that there was nothing wrong with the planning, but he doubted that Cunningham's state of mind would have allowed him to carry out the operation with 'the resolution that was essential'.[44] Auchinleck was nothing but loyal to his commanders and refused to let them be treated harshly if he felt it unfair.

There were other indications that maybe Auchinleck should take direct command of the Eighth Army, as can be seen from an extract from a field censorship summary. A 'senior officer' was quoted as saying: 'Things have been fairly unsettled here but I hope the worse is now over and that the "Auk" will be able to hit the Hun after all. He is such a grand man – I wish to meet him some time.' Another report said of him:

> General Auchinleck is now in charge of the Eighth Army. He will be capable of dealing with the threat better than anybody else out here. He is a fine chap and seems well respected by the troops. He is showing a good example by roughing it too in the desert; he sleeps at night in the open without a camp bed.[45]

This had echoes of his command in Cairo when he tried to extol to his staff the virtues of roughing it with the men and sleeping in the desert. His staff didn't think much of the idea and eventually Auchinleck gave up, but now the sense of urgency had enabled him to realize his ideas of shared hardship as war had come to Egypt and the comfortable life enjoyed by many had come to an end, at least in the immediate future.

There were still rumblings, though, connected to the dismissal of Cunningham and his delicate health. It was reported that Cunningham continued with his lack of co-operation regarding his dismissal, while it was noted that at least six senior officers had considered that Cunningham was unfit to command during November 1941.[46] It seemed that Auchinleck was beginning to get to the end of his tether with Cunningham and his shenanigans as he remarked to General Smith that Cunningham, as an army commander, could not be treated as a junior subaltern and told not to do it again as he remarked 'The issues are too great!' Auchinleck went further and said that Cunningham would have to 'lump it' until an announcement could be made that would not harm the Allies' cause.[47] Auchinleck was trying to prevent the Germans from finding out about Cunningham, but his hand was finally forced when the Australian press discovered Cunningham's dismissal. Churchill wrote: 'It will be necessary for me to make a statement on this point [Cunningham], and generally on the battle in Libya on Wednesday at noon.'[48] It should be noted that Australia provided very fine troops who stood shoulder-to-shoulder with their allies, but at times the Australian press and the Australian government seemed determined to undermine the work of their servicemen and no doubt vexed commanders such as Auchinleck who were trying to destroy the German ability to dominate and destroy the civilized world.

By December 1941 there was still a fear among the British planners that the Germans might be able to advance through Turkey and the Caucasus; something that the new CIGS General Sir Alan Brooke addressed when he wrote to Auchinleck. Brooke did not like there being two commands that bisected this area: the Middle East command which fell to Auchinleck and the India command. In Brooke's view this meant that the force that would have to oppose any such German advance would be under divided control. The answer according to Brooke, who had studied the problem, was that Auchinleck's command should extend and include Iraq and western Persia and asked for Auchinleck's views on the matter.[49] The next day Auchinleck expressed his fears of the war spreading to Anatolia, Syria and Iraq in the New Year.[50]

Clearly there was a great fear of a Soviet defeat during the winter of 1941–42 but the situation grew worse as Japan attacked US shipping at

Pearl Harbor on 7 December 1941. This changed the war and allowed the question of Cunningham's dismissal to be quietly buried in that news. It was, in 1941, one good day to bury bad news, even though the news was terrible. In the same communication to Auchinleck, Churchill agreed with Brooke's ideas of 10 December and proposed that Auchinleck's command should reach to cover both Iraq and Persia, which gave a local unity in the event of Turkey and the Caucasus being threatened. This change was to happen as soon as it was convenient to Auchinleck and Wavell, who had the India command and was to look east owing to the Japanese threat.[51]

Ritchie arrived at Eighth Army HQ on 26 November where it was clear that the German tanks had met their match against the 4th Indian Division at Sidi Omar. Even so, the Germans had successfully entered Bardia to the north and had also captured the HQ of the 5th New Zealand Infantry Brigade. It was at this time that Rommel intervened and ordered his forces to concentrate on the encirclement of Tobruk. During this reorganization the 15th and 21st arrived at the New Zealand position at Sidi Rezegh, but the New Zealand Division was minus its 5th Brigade. The odds were too much for the New Zealanders who were driven away with more casualties. However, the enemy was not getting away lightly and was beginning to suffer tank losses which could not be replaced as no tanks, Italian or German, had been received from across the Mediterranean since CRUSADER began. The enemy was wholly reliant on workshop-repaired tanks. British bombers were covering the battle area as well as hitting the enemy-held ports behind the front line; British air supremacy was complete. Finally, the siege around Tobruk was lifted by XIII Corps on 29 November 1941. General Godwin-Austen, commander of XIII Corps, signalled 'Tobruk relieved and so am I.' Auchinleck forwarded this as a greeting to Churchill the next day as it was the prime minister's 67th birthday.[52]

Once Ritchie was in post he began to discuss tactics and objectives with Auchinleck and was clearly more dynamic than his predecessor Cunningham had been, but then he was yet to undergo the challenges of high command. Ritchie suggested to Auchinleck that Benghasi [*sic*, Benghazi] port on the Libyan coast was key to enemy power and that Tobruk was secondary to the enemy, therefore it might be worth trying to capture Benghazi.[53] Such an attitude must have seemed like music to the ears of Auchinleck; a commander with ideas and aggression looking to attack the enemy with a purpose. Ritchie maintained this aggressive stance as in a further communication with Auchinleck on 22 December he told the latter that he considered that day was to be crucial as the Germans had to be destroyed or the Allies were to witness another German escape into Tripolitania. Ritchie admitted that he had a problem keeping in contact with his forward troops as they advanced against the enemy.[54] Maintaining contact with other units was always going to be a problem in the desert at this time, especially with fast-moving units advancing into a featureless terrain in a time before drones, GPS or satellite surveillance; aerial observation was the best that they might have had and that was clearly limited as well.

On Christmas Eve 1941, Auchinleck reported to Churchill that the 1st Royal Dragoons had occupied Benghazi from that morning,[55] such good news for the weary yet resilient Churchill and some light after the darkness of 1941. At around the same time Ritchie wrote to Auchinleck wondering if there was a change in the tide, having heard that Hitler had taken direct command of the German army.[56] Events were certainly changing as the Red Army was beginning to take the war to the Germans, events in Africa were not too bad for the Allies, the USA was in the war and the fact that Hitler was overseeing the German army was also good news as it meant that professional and sound decisions would become overturned by Hitler; he was not a professional soldier, but his word was law.

There was more news as Leo Amery wrote to Auchinleck expressing that a 'great battle in Cyrenaica had been won'. Amery considered that the aim of the ongoing offensive should be the Atlantic coast via Tripoli and Bizerta, unless on reaching Bizerta the offensive should change direction, go to the Mediterranean and invade Sicily. Amery also expressed a fear of having to give up troops for operations in Burma or Malaya.[57] As Greenwood wrote, it could be said that CRUSADER was over by the end of 1941. The enemy losses were estimated as being 33,000 killed, wounded or captured. They had also lost about 300 tanks. The Eighth Army losses were about 18,000 killed, wounded or captured and more or less the same tank losses. Playfair considered that by the end of November 1941, after a fortnight of heavy fighting, even though CRUSADER was far from over, an important stage had been reached: the British were able to bring up fresh troops and the enemy could not. This shows that Auchinleck was correct in his approach of keeping up pressure on the enemy. This had been a risky strategy, but had clearly paid off.[58]

A post-mortem of the operation found that many things had not worked as well as might have been expected. A major concern was that Rommel had managed to get away with much of his force and was soon able to launch a determined counter-attack. British equipment was also found to be wanting as much of it was tested on the flats of Salisbury Plain in a gentle Wiltshire climate but could not function well in the more demanding conditions of the desert. The Crusader tank relied on a pair of water pumps for its cooling system, but these could not take the heat and sand of the desert and the majority of the pumps began to leak after only a few hours' use. By the time XIII Corps reached Benghazi almost 200 tanks were in workshops being repaired. Godwin-Austen signalled to GHQ requesting that 400 water pumps be flown immediately from the UK, only to learn from the War Office that there were none available.

Greenwood also discussed the difference between German and British guns. The British relied on the 2-pounder gun mounted on all their tanks and also used as the standard anti-tank gun. This weapon, albeit well-designed and extremely reliable, was too small to be effective over 500 yards. Colonel Norman Berry, DDME at Eighth Army HQ, examined a captured German anti-tank gun and discovered it to be a British 3in AA gun fitted to a Soviet gun carriage. This was equipment sent from the UK to the Soviet Union under the Lend-Lease programme, captured by the Germans, repaired and sent to Rommel as part of his reinforcements. According to Greenwood these were examples – and there were others – of the inadequate equipment which underlined British complacency under Chamberlain until the end of the 'Phoney War', but he warned that Auchinleck's problems were only just beginning.[59]

*Chapter Eight*

# Rommel Counter-Attacks and the Consequences

There was much going on after the success of CRUSADER and most of it was going onto Auchinleck's plate. On Christmas Day 1941, he agreed to the extension of his command to encompass Persia and the German threats to the Caucasus Mountains. He also agreed with the concept of strong armoured forces being made available for use in Syria, Iraq and Persia. He admitted that when he was C-in-C India he would not have agreed, but service in the Middle East and North Africa had shifted his perspective of problems and objectives. Auchinleck also said that aid to the Soviet Union via Iraq, the Persia Wheeler Mission and the evacuation of the Poles from the Soviet Union would all have to be taken over by Middle East command.[1] There were many things going on there, but what was most interesting was the evacuation of Poles from the Soviet Union where most had been in Soviet captivity since late 1939 following the Soviet invasion and annexation of eastern Poland whence hundreds of thousands of Poles were deported to face humiliation, starvation, being used as slave labour and murder. It should be remembered that the Soviet Union aided Germany as an ally between 1939 and 1941 and had conducted vicious repression in eastern Poland and the Baltic republics. This involved the massacre of tens of thousands of Polish officers during April 1940 in the Smolensk region: the infamous Katyn massacre. General Władysław Anders, who was to lead the Poles out from Soviet captivity into Iran and to form what was to become the 2nd Polish Corps, or more popularly 'Anders Army', also suffered hideously from Soviet ill-treatment and this coloured his view and that of his men of anything regarding the Soviet Union; they remained resolutely hostile towards that country and communism in general.

There were other things happening in the world as the war expanded across the globe, and as previously thought there was a request for equipment to be sent to the Far East following Japanese attacks on British possessions there. Churchill wrote to Auchinleck asking for materials for the Far East including at least 100 American tanks as well as four squadrons of Hurricanes as modern fighters were needed to counter Japanese aircraft operating from aircraft carriers.[2] Then Rommel struck back, as was recorded in a letter from Brigadier Scott-Cockburn DSO to the commander of XIII Corps. It ran thus:

> The enemy attacked from the west with his tanks and from the north and north-west with three columns. We were able to hold off the enemy attacks for four hours, but shortage of ammunition and battle and mechanical casualties obliged us to take up a position further east. I should say that amn [ammunition] and petrol vehicles which usually accompany units had to move off owing to the attacks by enemy columns from the north and the north-east. A conservative estimate of enemy tanks destroyed is 30. He had, we thought, about the same number in action at last light. One we captured intact, a Mark IV the day before, was a new vehicle with 400 kilo [kilometres] on the clock. This may indicate recent reinforcements of tanks. I hope what we have done in is a big percentage of their effectives. I cannot report personnel casualties yet but will send them over the air. Heyworth was wounded yesterday and also his 2nd in command, Joy; neither seriously but both have been evacuated. We've been bothered a lot by Stukas.[3]

Even though Rommel was counter-attacking and making the British hurt, an old African hand, Field Marshal Smuts, found a silver lining as he wrote to Auchinleck: 'I am rather pleased to find Rommel making a stand at Agedabia. It would obviously suit us better to dispose of him there than to pursue the westwards fighting rearguard actions. I hope that it will be possible to cut off his further retreat.' In crayon Auchinleck wrote a reply: 'Thank you for your telegram G 10752. I too am glad of chance to smash Rommel at Agedabia and we have done all we can to this end.' This was dated 30 December 1941.[4]

Ritchie also wrote to Auchinleck regarding an armoured engagement south of Agedabia on 27 December 1941:

> I received your message on this subject last night and am not surprised at the uneasiness that our sitrep [situation report] caused you. I am sorry that this happened but as a result of my enquiries yesterday and reports received at 13 Corps I feel much less unhappy about what happened that day; in fact on balance I feel that we inflicted greater casualties on the enemy though he was in possession of the battlefield, and this is the most unsatisfactory feature. In connection with this I attach at Appendix 'A' a report by Scott-Cockburn on what happened. He claims that 30 enemy tanks were knocked out, but after careful cross-examining by Godwin-Austen I think that we can safely say that 22 were destroyed – definitely destroyed and unserviceable – while another 22 were hard hit and some of them may not be fit for operations again. I must admit to having some misgivings myself about our tactics and general employment of our armed forces and I have discussed this at considerable length with Strafer and with Martell. The facts are that:- We are outgunned in tanks and until this is righted which may not be until we get a 6-pdr, our tactics must be modified accordingly. The British Cruiser tanks are not robust enough in my opinion to withstand the rigours of campaigning in this type of country. The M.3 American tank is on the right lines. One might describe it as an 'owner-driver' type of tank and it is mechanically miles ahead of ours. But as a fighting machine it is not, and certainly not up to the Germans. It is, in fact, a light tank and nothing more. There is no doubt that in this campaign the gun is everything and the tank in my opinion, should be built around the gun, and not the reverse. I know you will be seeing 'Q' Martell and Strafer Gott shortly and will get their views on the matter.[5]

Ritchie's points are valid as the main thing was that the tank was a gun being moved across the battlefield and not an armed vehicle. The war in North Africa was about vehicles and movement. A mobile gun such as a tank was essential in order to advance, but it had to be a large-calibre gun to take on the enemy, especially the Germans with their large tanks. It would take time for the Allies to learn this. The sense of the war in the deserts of North Africa can be learned by the contemporary reader via searches on the internet. Captured German film illustrates the large number of vehicles immediately available to Rommel and the type of modern weaponry, especially artillery, deployed by both the Germans and the Italians.[6]

In the New Year Ritchie received a reply from Auchinleck. He agreed with Ritchie about the question of tanks, but considered that the Allied superiority in numbers would redress the balance. We have already seen that the Germans were struggling to receive new equipment as the British were able to destroy and disrupt Axis convoys at sea as well as bomb German-held ports in North Africa from the air. The British had other methods of supply and Auchinleck's idea of his L of C beginning in India rather than being the end of it was paying off, even if the Japanese were beginning to advance in South-East Asia; Hong Kong had already fallen to the Japanese on 25 December 1941. Auchinleck discussed the tanks available to Ritchie and himself in the deserts of North Africa and conceded that the cruiser tank was too complicated for the Near and Middle East while the American M3 was mechanically sound but as fighting machines were not as good as cruisers or German medium tanks. Auchinleck noted that somehow they had to 'muddle through' with what they had available to defeat the Germans. He also added the following note about leadership:

> If we are to add to our inferiority in material an apparent inferiority in leadership, then we shall be in a bad way and not deserve to win. Mind you, I do not say our leadership and tactics are inferior. I am not in a position to pass any judgement, still less a hasty judgement on anybody. All the same, I have a most uncomfortable feeling that the Germans outwit and outmanoeuvre us as well as outshooting us, and I must know as soon as possible if this is so. If it is so, then we must find new leaders at once. No personal considerations or the possession of such qualities as courage or popularity must be allowed to stand in the way. Commanders who consistently have their brigades shot away from under them, even against a numerically inferior enemy, are expensive luxuries, much too expensive in present circumstances.

Auchinleck concluded by considering that there was a need to discover what had happened to the 22nd Armoured Brigade and its failing the week before which had failed to hold the enemy, let alone defeat it.[7] The Germans may have had the best equipment in the early stages of the fighting in North Africa, including the dreaded 88mm flak gun which could be used as either an AAA piece (its original function), but owing to the ability of the gun to be depressed low enough, also served as a fearsome anti-tank gun which packed a greater punch than anything the British had in this field and was far more adaptable. It is incredible to realize that the 88mm AAA gun being used as an anti-tank gun was first noted by the War Office during the Spanish Civil War (1936–39).[8]

Despite having some of the best equipment, the inability of the Germans to receive regular supplies for various reasons meant that they were unable to replace wrecked and damaged equipment as well as receive adequate numbers of men to carry on the fight. The evidence was obvious, while footage of the Eighth Army in North Africa is testimony to the contemporary reader of the scale of destruction of enemy resources in North Africa by British armed forces.[9] The British did indeed 'muddle through' but even so, it still had a lot to do with superior planning in the end, while the Germans, lacking adequate resources, were also outmanoeuvred and finally holed up on the Tunisian coast and forced to surrender.

The matter of the tanks caused conversation as Smuts also agreed that the British tanks were inferior to those of the enemy and that there was a need to 'make strong representations' to the War Office.[10] General Brooke as CIGS also agreed that British tanks were inferior, both in terms of firepower and mechanical reliability when compared with the German Mark III and Mark IV tanks. The most immediate change according to Brooke was an alteration to the 2-pounder main gun of British tanks and to give the guns a higher charge and ballistic cap to try to make it more effective in terms of destruction and suggested that the Crusader tanks should be refitted with a 6-pounder gun as the main weapon. Brooke also wanted remedies found for the defects in all British tanks and have them applied to those in the field and those being produced at that time.[11]

Auchinleck replied to Brooke on 7 January 1942, advising him that Rommel still had plenty of fight in him and pointed to the attack on

Scott-Cockburn's 22nd Armoured Brigade on 28 December 1941 and 30 December 1941. During the attack of 30 December, the brigade lost forty-six tanks out of fifty-six. Many of these had been left on the battlefield from where the enemy could take them and repair them or whatever they wished. Auchinleck's complaint was that the enemy had inferior numbers and the terrain was against them, but they still defeated the 22nd Armoured Brigade and regarding that Auchinleck was quite blunt: it was a weakness in British armoured commanders. Auchinleck was certain that Rommel would begin a counteroffensive from Agedabia. It was also noted that the British had 1,223 tanks while the Germans on 18 November 1941 had only 439.[12]

The next day, 8 January 1942, Ritchie confirmed Auchinleck's fears as he made contact and told him that captured documents suggested that the enemy was withdrawing to the line of El Agheila-Marada. Ritchie observed that this meant the British and their allies would have to move 60 miles further over difficult terrain before engaging the enemy.[13] Churchill was not slow to ask searching questions, as in his message to Auchinleck on 11 January 1942. Clearly Churchill had received information as he wrote to Auchinleck:

> I fear this means that 7.5 enemy divisions have got away round the corner and will be retreating directly along their communications. I have noticed 9 M/V (merchant vessel) ships of 10,000 tons are reported to have reached Tripoli safely. It was understood that you believed that your advance down Trig El Abd would certainly cut off Rommel's Italian infantry but now it appears they are out of the net. How does this all affect ACROBAT? I am sure that you and your armies did all in human power, but we must face facts as they are which greatly influence both GYMNAST and SUPER-GYMNAST.[14]

The operations mentioned by Churchill were all operations against French North Africa: ACROBAT was a proposed attack on Tripoli, while GYMNAST and SUPER-GYMNAST eventually evolved into TORCH which was indeed the American and British amphibious landings into French North Africa. At the time of Churchill's writing, operations against French North Africa were points of discussions and meetings with the British General Staff and operational commanders such as Auchinleck. Clearly Churchill was nervous about the successful German withdrawal and threatened counter-attack and how they might affect future operations.

Ritchie was to deliver more bad news for Auchinleck as he admitted that Rommel had outwitted the British during his retreat and was forming a 'box' made up of the Mersa Brega marshes, the Wadi El Faregh and the El Chebrit marshes.[15] This made a formidable position given that a wadi is a dried-up water course and often steeply banked. Auchinleck made a reply to Churchill's message of 11 January. In his reply he said that only low numbers of Italian and German infantry had escaped and that the alleged escaped divisions were incomplete. Auchinleck also disputed the number of ships that had got into Tripoli as he claimed that only six vessels of 7,200 tons had got into harbour. Auchinleck continued to have faith in ACROBAT, if only to force the Germans to fight on two fronts: Libya and the Russian Front. Auchinleck also informed Churchill that

> I promise you will NOT repeat NOT be led into any rash adventure NOR repeat NOR will General Ritchie but in view of the heartening news from the Russian front, I feel that we should do all we can to maintain the pressure in Libya. We have full and interesting records of daily conversation between our prisoners General Ravenstein and Schmidt. Making all allowances for mental depression natural in prisoners-of-war there is no doubt that German morale is beginning to feel the strain not only in Libya but in Germany. They speak freely also of huge losses in the recent fighting, mismanagement and disorganisation and above all the dissatisfaction with Rommel's leadership. I am convinced that the enemy is hard pressed more than we dared to think perhaps.[16]

This must have been a fillip for Churchill as at times it seemed that Rommel was beyond all reproach by both the Axis and Allied forces who both seemed to admire him, but this revealed that he was only human and had human failings as we all do.

Auchinleck sent a further message to Churchill on the same day as the previous missive and confessed that he had underrated the Italian armour and had discounted the entire Italian Ariete Armoured Division and he had been wrong to do so. The Italian armed forces had fought well against the British; however, Auchinleck, fair-minded as he was, still could not countenance that perhaps the Italians may have been good troops as he suggests that German troops had 'stiffened' the Italians, especially the armoured units. Auchinleck discussed the period of 24 to 26 November 1941 when British tank strength was less than that of the enemy in the battle zone and that Cunningham had told Auchinleck if the British had carried on fighting as they had been, they would have lost all of their tanks. He also told Churchill:

> If I am correct in my views, and if it is a fact that we may have to fight the Germans in Anatolia, Syria, Iraq and Persia next summer with the same equipment as we have had in the Libyan campaign, then it is obvious that we must improve our leadership and tactics generally so far as the handling of armoured forces is concerned.

Auchinleck also added that from information gleaned from the captured German generals Ravenstein and Schmidt, it was obvious that Tripoli needed taking.[17] Auchinleck's message must have given Churchill a lot to think about and perhaps understand how Auchinleck thought and the nature of the problems that beset him in this alien desert warfare as they tried to nurse inadequate armour across the terrain as well as push the enemy back and hopefully induce him to surrender.

By mid-January 1942 Auchinleck was considering the next steps in the desert campaign. In a message to Ritchie, he said that he wasn't too bothered about the Poles; he was referring to the Carpathian Brigade under the command of General Stanisław Kopański. This brigade had been formed in Syria from Polish soldiers who had escaped from internment camps in Hungary and Romania and had made it to Allied-controlled territory. After the fall of France, the Carpathian Brigade left French-controlled Syria to avoid internment by the French collaboratist regime, the Vichy regime, and moved to British-controlled Palestine where it joined the British army. From just under 4,000 men and officers, the brigade grew to roughly 5,000 men. In August 1941 the Poles were moved from Palestine to the besieged town of Tobruk where the brigade took part in the final four months of the siege. The siege was lifted in December 1941 and the brigade joined British forces in pursuing Axis forces who were withdrawing from the area around Tobruk as well as fighting in the Battle of Gazala, west of Tobruk, which took place between 26 May and 21 June 1942.

However, in January 1942 Auchinleck was considering what he wanted to do with the Polish forces under his command: the Carpathian Brigade. He told Ritchie that he considered the Poles to be unimportant to him and that he wanted to them to be sent to Syria as soon as he could get them there, but not so that it left Ritchie in an embarrassing situation; in other words, if Ritchie could not spare them, they were to remain in North Africa. Auchinleck thought that the Carpathian Brigade might be relieved by South African troops who were due to go to Cyrenaica, so he suggested that perhaps the 2nd South African Brigade should relieve the Carpathian Brigade. This is interesting as according to Polish historiography of the Second World War it seems that the British were very lucky to have the Poles on their side, but in reality the Poles were unimportant with their penny-pocket outfits and this episode with Auchinleck rather underlines this; just another small foreign contingent once the larger view is taken. In any event it was withdrawn to Palestine in March 1942 and became absorbed by the Polish forces led by General Anders which had been evacuated from the Soviet Union and was re-formed into the 3rd Carpathian Rifle Division. The brigade officially ceased to exist on 3 May 1942. This is not to dismiss the work of the Carpathian Brigade who on 9 December 1941 seized the strategically-important Medauar Hill and town of Acroma and broke through to the Eighth Army. The various actions of the Poles across Europe and North Africa were important but never unique. They were too small in number to be overwhelmingly important, despite some of the propaganda in the early days of the war and before American and Soviet successes could be enjoyed.

Auchinleck also had to deal with local issues and personalities, as various exchanges illustrate. The Second World War produced two citizen armies: the British and the American armies. These armies were

Subedar Ganpat Patel receiving the Military Cross from General Sir Claude Auchinleck, 1944. (*Courtesy of the National Army Museum, London*)

Field Marshal Sir Claude Auchinleck inspecting members of the Women's Auxiliary Corps (India), 1947. (*Courtesy of NAM*)

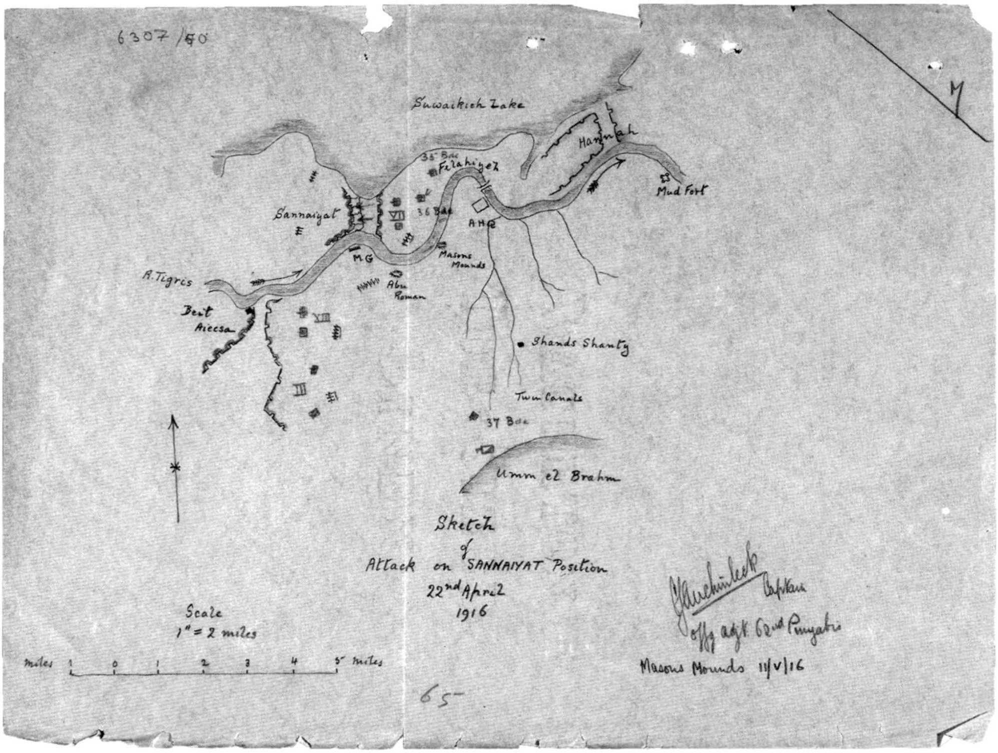


Sketch of attack on Sannaiyat position, Mesopotamia, 22 April 1916. (*Courtesy of NAM*)

Operation CRUSADER, November 1941. (*Courtesy of NAM*)

The visit of Field Marshal Sir Claude Auchinleck to South India, March 1946. (*Courtesy of NAM*)

Pakistan independence day at Razmah, Waziristan, 15 August 1947. (*Courtesy of NAM*)

Mahratta soldiers of an Indian anti-aircraft battery giving a demonstration, November 1944. (*Courtesy of NAM*)

Field Marshal Auchinleck, C-in-C of the Indian Army, with Naga troops in ceremonial dress, 1946. (*Courtesy of NAM*)

Defensive position of 'C' Company 3rd Battalion, 9th Jay Regiment, Waziristan, 1923. (*Courtesy of NAM*)

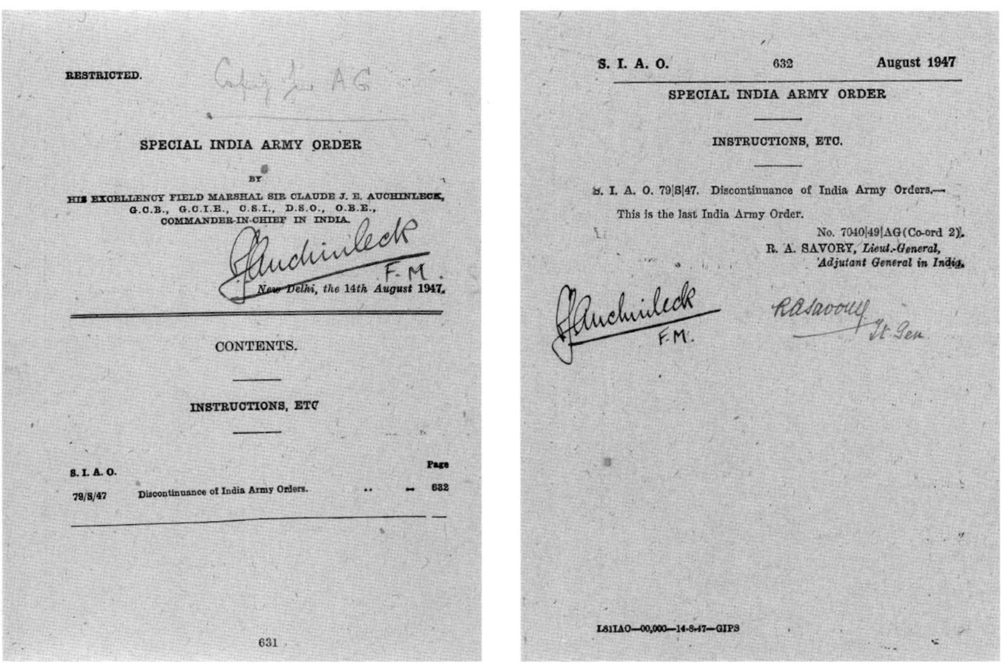

RESTRICTED.

SPECIAL INDIA ARMY ORDER

BY

HIS EXCELLENCY FIELD MARSHAL SIR CLAUDE J. E. AUCHINLECK, G.C.B., G.C.I.E., C.S.I., D.S.O., O.B.E., COMMANDER-IN-CHIEF IN INDIA.

New Delhi, the 14th August 1947.

CONTENTS.

INSTRUCTIONS, ETC

| S. I. A. O. | | Page |
|---|---|---|
| 79/S/47 | Discontinuance of India Army Orders. .. .. | 632 |

631

S. I. A. O. 632 August 1947

SPECIAL INDIA ARMY ORDER

INSTRUCTIONS, ETC.

S. I. A. O. 79/S/47. Discontinuance of India Army Orders.—

This is the last India Army Order.

No. 7040/49/AG (Co-ord 2).

R. A. SAVORY, *Lieut.-General*,

*Adjutant General in India.*

LSIIAO—00,000—14-8-47—GIPS

Copy of the last India Army Order, printed in New Delhi on 14 August 1947. (*Courtesy of NAM*)

A Gurkha soldier demonstrating how to use a kukri fighting knife, November 1944. (*Courtesy of NAM*)

Indian troops gathered around a carrier, 1947. (*Courtesy of NAM*)

Japanese propaganda leaflet distributed by the Indian Independence League, 1944. (*Courtesy of NAM*)

Men of the 2nd Battalion, Highland Light Infantry, in action near Nahakki, 1935. (*Courtesy of NAM*)

Vickers light tank, Mohmand, India, 1935. (*Courtesy of NAM*)

FIELD MARSHAL SIR CLAUDE J. E. AUCHINLECK
GCB, GCIE, CSI, DSO, OBE, ADC.
C-in-C India 27 Jan. 41 to 10 Aug. 41 and 21 June 43 to 14 Aug. 47
Supreme Commander Pakistan and India 15 Aug. 47 to 30 Nov. 47.
1st. Punjab Regiment 1904.- .......

( 19 )

Field Marshal Sir Claude Auchinleck in full dress uniform, 1947. (*Courtesy of NAM*) the product of conscription in which men and women from all walks of life became members of the armed forces at a time of facing a common enemy: the Axis armies. There was only one aim of these armies and that was the destruction of their enemy and the ending of the war and then after this returning to their previous lives. They were not professional soldiers, sailors or air personnel but were just serving to win a war against a common tyranny, not to further a political cause save perhaps that of democracy. This was the very reason why Auchinleck remarked in a message to General Brooke that the RAC (Royal Armoured Corps) had to learn to associate with other branches of the armed forces and not try to be a 'Corps d'elite with separatist tendencies'.[18]

Auchinleck was railing against the attitude of some of the professional corps who considered that they were above those who were serving only for the duration of the war. There was also the question of removing senior officers who were beyond their 'sell-by dates'. Brooke wrote to Auchinleck and discussed the problem and cited the case of 'Jumbo' Wilson, properly known as General Henry Maitland Wilson, who he considered to be too old to be on active service, but he was only three years older than Auchinleck, as were other officers who had already been retired from active service by Brooke and were protesting about the situation.[19] The question of elderly officers trying to hang on to positions and trying to be of some use to the war effort is described by Evelyn Waugh in his Second World War trilogy *Sword of Honour* as men set out to be included in the war despite their age and lack of suitability for military service – including Waugh himself – and how they fared. It should be noted that General Wilson continued in his career and was finally promoted to field marshal.

Churchill was more disturbed by events as he had heard from the naval liaison officer to the Eighth Army who spoke of evacuations from Benghazi and Derna. Churchill was quite surprised that such a situation had arisen and was disturbed by what he had heard. He asked Auchinleck if he had a really heavy defeat in the Antelat area and was it a case that the British tanks had been unable to cope with the 'resuscitated' German tanks. To Churchill it was a serious crisis and an unexpected one at that; he was querying further why it had all happened so quickly. Churchill wanted to know whether the 4th Indian Division could not hold out at Benghazi as the Germans (Churchill, as ever, wrote 'the Huns') had at Halfaya. The proposed evacuations caused Churchill to fear the confirmation of the failure of CRUSADER and 'the ruin of ACROBAT'.[20] This was characteristic of Churchill as he wanted to know everything; indeed, he had a point as he needed to know what was going on in the war, but at times it seemed that Churchill might have wanted to have been a bit more hands-on given half a chance, even fighting on the front line. He was an impulsive and romantic man and needed restraining at times so that commanders could do their work properly and win the war. Auchinleck since Narvik had learned that ministers, especially Churchill, were quite willing to send inadequate forces into battle, but Auchinleck was not willing to do any such thing in North Africa.[21] This, of course, was to eventually set him on a collision course with Churchill.

Auchinleck wrote to Lieutenant General Sir Arthur Smith in response to Churchill's letter. Smith was the general officer commanding the London military district and so would have had the ear of Churchill. Auchinleck explained the situation to Smith:

> The Poles are at and around Mechili while the 150th Infantry Brigade should move fast today [25 January 1942] to a point south of Tengeder to block any attempt on the part of the enemy to send fast-moving columns by that route against our L of C. The crux of the whole matter is the condition of the 1st Armoured Division, which G-A [Godwin-Austen] told Neil [Ritchie] can no longer be counted on as a fighting force. Its losses are said to be 40 guns and I suppose about 100 or more tanks, and there is much doubt as to whether it was able to inflict any appreciable loss on the enemy. G-A is apparently very pessimistic about it and says that it cannot possibly be counted on to cover the flank of the 4th Indian Division if the latter remains at Bengasi [Benghazi]. However, Neil told G-A that he was to issue orders to do this and to remain at Charruba and to take the offensive against the enemy at once. These orders were issued yesterday afternoon. The Poles and the 150th Infantry Brigade are being told to be as aggressive as possible with mixed columns and I hope that Tuker will be able to worry the enemy – Tuker seems aggressive enough with the 'right idea'.

Auchinleck also observed that the RAF had been 'blowing the enemy to bits' along the Msus-Antelat road and that the 'blood is up amongst the fighters'.[22]

Field Marshal Smuts, in a letter to General Theron, the South African commander of artillery of the 1st South African Division in North Africa, gives vent to his concerns regarding the situation in Cyrenaica and expresses his shock but is seeking clarification of the situation there as well as reassurance that things are not as bad as he thinks they might be. At a time of the Japanese appearing to be running rampant in the Far East, Smuts was looking for something to inspire confidence in the Allied war effort and at that time North Africa seemed to be the most obvious place. Smuts asked if there were any attempts being made to cut Rommel off both from retreat and from further advance.[23] This was a desperate time and the Allies were yet to achieve a major victory to which they could point and celebrate, so it was not surprising that Churchill and Smuts were getting worried. Auchinleck's next letter to Churchill certainly would not have helped the mood, as he told his prime minister that

> I am reluctantly compelled to the conclusion that to meet German armoured forces with any reasonable hope of decisive success our armoured forces as at present equipped, organised and led must have at least two to one superiority. Even then they must rely for success on working in the very closest cooperation with infantry and artillery which perhaps for their weakness in anti-tank guns are fully competent to take on their German opposite numbers.

Auchinleck also warned Churchill that the Royal Armoured Corps was losing confidence in their equipment, but everything was being done to rectify this.[24] This was not the most welcoming of letters for Churchill to receive, but it was the truth. German armour was superior but in time became limited as the Axis forces were unable to resupply the Afrika Korps or the Italians easily once the Royal Navy began to boss the Mediterranean Sea. However, this was to take time and the Americans were yet to supply the mass-produced equipment manufactured in the USA. It was only early 1942 and victory was on its way, but the political leaders had to keep faith with their commanders and not panic.

Churchill, however, did keep faith with Auchinleck at this time as is witnessed in a letter from General 'Pug' Ismay who was Churchill's military advisor. Ismay, writing from the British prime minister's official country residence Chequers, told Auchinleck that Churchill had complete faith in him and said 'there is no shadow of a doubt' of this and in addition added the following compliment and praise: 'You have done magnificently old friend, and I am proud of you.'[25] These are fine words of support from a somewhat frustrated and thwarted Churchill who had little patience with many things including waiting for operations to be concluded successfully and victory secured. Therefore Auchinleck's professional caution no doubt irked him.

Auchinleck wasn't the only professional soldier who frustrated Churchill as Brooke also stuck to facts rather than fancies as he wrote to Auchinleck on 6 February 1942 following Rommel's counter-attack. Brooke said that if he looked at Rommel's work from a detached point of view, he could not help but feel that over optimistic-intelligence reports were largely the reason for the British woes. He asked whether Auchinleck and he had both doubted the reports and had considered that they were too optimistic, which had led to the enemy being constantly underestimated regarding its powers of recuperation, resistance or evasion. Brooke, throughout his message, was critical of Shearer, the compiler of the reports and his DMI (Director of Military Intelligence), and questioned whether he should be retained in this post. Brooke was of the opinion that Shearer had also failed Wavell by sending him inaccurate intelligence reports which underestimated the enemy and seemed to be a feature of his work.

After this Brooke discussed tactics to be used in North Africa. Drawing on Auchinleck's experience of fighting on the North-West Frontier in India which used small supply columns and that everything was small-scale compared with fighting on the European mainland, it was decided that the smaller supply pattern might be beneficial in North Africa. In a recent large-scale exercise, it had been learned that commanders were unable to carry out attacks even of a single division as they were more used to operating on the smaller scale of a brigade group. Brooke took Auchinleck's idea that they should work at such a level and approved his proposed reorganizations, but they were already talking about reforming organization for the future at corps level and that corps commanders must be able to control everything by wireless including the close co-operation of infantry, artillery and tanks in armoured divisions which had become the norm in the UK for the previous eighteen months. There was good news as Brooke confirmed that the 2-pounder anti-tank gun was to be replaced by the 6-pounder.[26] The replacement of the lighter anti-tank gun with one with a larger payload was no doubt welcome, but it was still not the 88mm shell which the Germans were using to deadly effect.

Even though both Auchinleck and Brooke often had to deliver Churchill news that he did not want to hear; Auchinleck also had good news as can be seen in a message to Field Marshal Smuts during the same week that Auchinleck and Brooke were exchanging ideas. Auchinleck told Smuts that the recent fighting had cost Rommel about two-thirds of his original army of 100,000 men, while the British had lost fewer than 20,000 men. This he considered to be an achievement which 'must have upset Axis plans'. Auchinleck considered that the Axis attacks on the Soviet Union had been weakened and that the threat to Egypt from the West was indefinitely postponed. Of the present campaign in the desert, Auchinleck's attitude was that it was bound to ebb and flow but felt that even if the fighting at that time was not necessarily going the way of the Allies, he was convinced that the British would defeat the enemy in North Africa.[27]

In further discussions of tactics, Auchinleck approved the use of mobile units roaming the desert, especially those hitting enemy landing grounds at Derna and Martuba.[28] The vast wastes of the deserts allowed for some unorthodox forms of warfare at which the British excelled but the Germans or the Italians never seemed to take to. Various motorized units were formed that specialized in long-range reconnaissance as well as hit-and-run raids against enemy targets. Notable among these groups were the Long-Range Desert Group and the Special Air Service or SAS which is still operating in the British army today; probably not many people know of its original use in the deserts during the Second World War. Auchinleck liked this form of warfare and spoke of it approvingly. General Arthur Smith, when discussing 'Jock columns' which were basically 'hit and runs' against enemy targets, also called for looser supervision of small units as they set out into the desert seeking their targets and might be out of range of Allied units for days, if not weeks. It is also interesting that in early December 1941 Auchinleck had anticipated a counter-attack by Rommel using the last of his armoured reserves.[29] Jock columns had been the brainchild of Lieutenant Colonel John Charles 'Jock' Campbell.

Auchinleck confided to Ritchie that there were signs that Rommel was seriously underestimating the British strength and capacity to resist further attacks by him. According to Auchinleck, this was fairly typical of Rommel. Not surprisingly, Auchinleck realized that this should be used against Rommel. As Auchinleck remarked to Ritchie:

> If we are to take advantage of the enemy's apparent underestimation of our strength, and his possible consequent decision to attack us with inadequate forces, we must achieve surprise. Surprise can only be achieved first by hiding from him our strength in tanks, and secondly by stationing them where they can be used to best effect, which implies keeping them concentrated. To give of their best, our tanks must have the maximum support of our artillery and infantry firmly established in positions from which the enemy cannot shift without risking heavy casualties, which he cannot if our information is correct. We must not be led away by feints and movements designed to mislead us, at which the enemy is very good. If we are to avoid this, we must have continuous and intensive ground and air reconnaissance of the most offensive kind. Above all we must try to keep track of his main tank concentrations.[30]

The war in the desert was very much a question of trying to deceive the enemy in an apparently featureless environment and being reliant on good reconnaissance and patrolling – in other words, good intelligence – and this was very important to Auchinleck, as the following discussion between Brooke and Auchinleck reveals.

Auchinleck, returning to the earlier discussion about the intelligence work of John Shearer, told Brooke that he did not agree with Brooke's conclusions. Auchinleck agreed that Shearer's early reports were perhaps 'too rosy' but put this down to inexperience of reporting from the battlefront and claiming that too many enemy tanks had been destroyed and so on; however, recent reports were much more reliable. Auchinleck wrote of Shearer: 'He is certainly optimistic rather than pessimistic but a really pessimistic DMI would not be welcome to me I'm afraid.' Auchinleck conceded that Shearer made mistakes, but fewer than other intelligence officers.[31]

Even so, the question of Shearer's competence or otherwise would not go away. Neil Ritchie wrote to Auchinleck and told him that there was a general loss of confidence in the intelligence work of Shearer. General Ritchie could not really account for this loss of confidence, but said that many people felt Shearer tried to make his information fit any situation rather than accepting that perhaps he was sometimes wrong.[32] Just over a week later Auchinleck agreed that Shearer had to go; not because of his alleged overoptimistic views that Auchinleck considered not to be true but an invention, but because of the general loss of confidence in him which was largely owing to Shearer's personality. Auchinleck does not enlarge on that view at the time, except to add that the question of trust in Shearer's reports had grown worse to 'a serious extent'.[33]

Finally the full story of John Shearer was revealed by Auchinleck in the first week of March 1942. Auchinleck told Brooke that Shearer was being returned to the UK. The loss of confidence in him had continued, especially among certain commanders in the Eighth Army. Shearer's problems seemed to have been those of mental health or wellbeing and his inability to admit that he could be wrong on occasion. Auchinleck admitted that this was a bad fault in an intelligence officer and was also creating a lack of confidence in the general staff as a whole. He reflected that without doubt Shearer had many enemies with plenty of people being jealous of him and that he was a victim of intrigue. Auchinleck continued along the lines that Shearer was not excessively optimistic but suffered 'just the above faults'. In defence of Shearer, Auchinleck wrote:

> You will realise that we have here literally masses of captured documents, which allow us to check our deductions and conclusions. We have just had conclusive evidence that we over-estimated the enemy strength at Agheila before we counter-attacked in January last. We are not yet sure as to the extent of our overestimation but there is no doubt that we did. However, this does not alter the

> fact that he [Shearer] must go, despite his undoubted ability and organising powers.

One can sense the sympathy that Auchinleck undoubtedly had for Shearer, who was in turn frustrated that he knew he was right and captured enemy documents were beginning to point to this, but as he had lost the confidence of commanders and was beginning to endanger the credibility of the local general staff, Auchinleck reluctantly had to let him go. The latter's reluctance is seen in the last sentence of the matter when he informs Brooke that Shearer was 'too valuable to be idle' and needed re-employment.[34]

This episode concerning Shearer, the intelligence officer, reveals Auchinleck's professionalism and his humanity; qualities he had in abundance. As Warner notes, Auchinleck felt that Brooke was wrong in his opinions of Shearer, but knew that confidence in the accuracy of intelligence would not return until Shearer was replaced. On 23 February 1942, Auchinleck agreed to the appointment of F.W. de Guingand who was a lieutenant colonel working in the planning department of GHQ Cairo. De Guingand was told to report to Auchinleck, and in his own words the interview went thus:

> Auchinleck looked up from his desk. 'Freddie, I want you to take over DMI.' This was a shattering thing for a lieutenant-colonel with no previous intelligence experience to be told. When I recovered my breath I replied: 'But I have never done anything of the sort before sir.' 'Excellent,' said the Auk. 'That's why I've chosen you, you'll do it all right. I want you to take over at once.'[35]

Auchinleck was later criticized over some of his appointments, but it seems that the appointment of de Guingand was a good choice. However, the appointment of General Corbett, who at the time was a corps commander in Iraq, did raise some eyebrows as he had little experience of desert warfare. Nevertheless, Churchill took time out from the litany of reversals that marked the beginning of 1942 and sent Auchinleck a telegram dated 12 February 1942 which read: 'Have been thinking much about you and your affairs with complete confidence you will come out on top.'[36] Clearly, even in his darkest times, Churchill had faith in Auchinleck. It was just as with his other commanders; Churchill had little patience with them if they could not deliver an offensive quickly enough as they weighed up the pros and cons. Churchill, at times, rather like the character Brigadier Ben Ritchie-Hook in Waugh's trilogy *Sword of Honour*, just wanted to 'biff' the enemy at every opportunity, regardless of the consequences.

Auchinleck not only had to deal with Rommel but also the press and the usual armchair generals who seem to come to the fore at times of a country's military setbacks. An example that had to be dealt with was who, if anybody, was to blame for the perception that the British advance on Tripoli had come to a halt owing to Rommel's counter-attack. Auchinleck was sent part of a signal sent to the Secretary-of-State for Air from the AOC-in-C referring to a speech about air estimates. The senior airman in the North African campaign urged the Secretary of State to issue a

> sharp rebuke to newspaper leader writers and ill-informed contributors to correspondence columns who attribute our reverse in the Western Desert and our failure to reach Tripoli already, to lack of air support and failure to exploit our air superiority to the best advantage of the Army's operations. I am most concerned lest this ignorant and ill-informed press campaign should, if not stopped, have a serious effect on the morale of the RAF crews in the desert at the present critical time. The least harm it may do if not stopped is to engender ill-feeling between the two services which would be deplorable. Auchinleck agrees with me on this.[37]

Auchinleck certainly did agree with his RAF counterpart and wrote in support to the Secretary of State for Air. Auchinleck said that the reverses in the desert had had nothing to do with lack of aerial support but was the result of trying to bluff the enemy with weaker forces in the forward area while trying to bring in reserves from Benghazi to bring stronger forces forward. As he observed, the enemy called the British bluff, got the upper hand and was able to control the desert. Auchinleck attributed Rommel's success to having a superior strength in tanks which resulted in heavy British losses and making it impossible for them to remain in

Benghazi or anywhere else in the Cyrenaican bulge owing to the certainty of communications being cut. This was the reason why the British fell back to Gazala to stabilize their positions as this was the most westerly line on which a stand could be made without a grave risk of being easily outflanked or cut off from the base in Tobruk. Auchinleck asserted that the RAF had been magnificent in supporting the army which had nothing but praise for them and concluded his message with this sentence: 'I view with greatest anxiety any attempt to revive the controversy between the Army and the Air Force which had been successfully buried at any rate in the Middle East. Revival must cause bad feeling between the services and might have disastrous results.'[38] It is probable that he was referring to the summer of 1940 and the fall of France as many troops struggling back to the beaches at Dunkirk were critical of the perceived lack of air cover at that time. The reality was that the RAF had been recalled to the UK ready to defend the British Isles against German invasion.

While these various sideshows were being played out, Auchinleck still had to win the war in North Africa and figure out how best to organize it. There had been a call for him to attend a conference in London to discuss the progress of the campaign in the Western Desert, but Auchinleck declined to attend as he was reorganizing the Middle East command and suggested that perhaps Brooke should come out to the Middle East to either Cairo or Baghdad, but he did offer to send either Wavell or Peirse to the conference.[39] Churchill was not happy with Auchinleck's refusal to attend. In a message he told him that both the Chiefs of Staff and the Defence Committee were anxious about progress in the Middle East – by which he meant the lack of progress as he viewed it – and therefore regretted that Auchinleck was not available to attend.

Churchill's fear was that the enemy might be able to outpace Auchinleck, causing him to fear for the safety of Malta which was under siege from the sea and the air, while he also noted that Auchinleck's losses were less than those of the enemy which continued to fight. Churchill hated Auchinleck's caution and made some withering if unfair observations. The British prime minister made the point that the 7th Armoured Division had been withdrawn to the Nile delta to rest, even though its losses had been far less than those of the 15th and 21st German Army divisions who had struck back at British forces 'with so much vigour'. Churchill also lamented that a strong German counteroffensive was expected in the Soviet Union and that he found it intolerable that Auchinleck had 655,000 men who had come from Malta who were not fighting but were waiting to do so in July. Churchill suggested that a limited offensive to Derna would be of some use as it would force the enemy to use up his resources. He considered that if British armour was defeated at Derna, then it could be withdrawn to a defensive zone and if the British won, the people at home in the UK would not understand why the advantage was not pressed home.

Churchill did have some praise for Auchinleck, including supporting him in sacking General Cunningham and General Godwin-Austen, and said:

> I have done everything in my power to give you continuous support at heavy cost to the whole war. It would give me the greatest pain to feel that mutual understanding had ceased. In order to avoid this, I have asked Sir Stafford Cripps to stop for a day in Cairo about 19th or 20th on his way to India and put before you the view of the War Cabinet.

Churchill told Auchinleck that Cripps would be accompanied by General Nye who was travelling separately but was in full possession of the opinions of the Chiefs of Staff and that it was impossible for General Brooke to come.[40]

It seems that Churchill was missing the point regarding Auchinleck's tactics as the latter had already said that he was not going to engage the enemy in smaller operations, was preparing for a larger new offensive and that he needed to remain in situ to ensure everything was taking shape as he was planning. Churchill, the COS and the Defence Committee may have had an overview of what was happening in the desert, but could not see the day-to-day minutiae as Auchinleck could. The idea of sending Cripps out to see Auchinleck was risible as he knew nothing of military matters and was a lovely old champagne socialist with the sense of reality of a 4-year-old child. It was perhaps good that he was accompanied by General Nye, but it seemed that nobody understood what Auchinleck was planning.

Auchinleck, in a dispatch to Smuts, observed that training and modernity were key to success and that he could not say how long the war would last.[41] Cripps also made his views known to Churchill and wrote:

> …danger that Auchinleck is apprehensive that an attack might develop in Syria or the north via Caucasus or Turkey or upon Cyprus, while the operation was on in the Western Desert in which event it would seem necessary to withdraw a considerable proportion of the air forces from the Western Desert and surrender air superiority. This would mean abandoning the battle with extremely serious results. In my view this is a risk which most unfortunately must be taken unless we are to abandon all hope of an offensive till the autumn.[42]

It's debatable whether Cripps really understood what he had put his name to, as Auchinleck writes his own thoughts in a memorandum during March 1942 and it is quite bellicose.

Auchinleck's priority was to secure Cyrenaica, and to achieve that he recognized that as much as possible of the enemy's armour must be destroyed. Auchinleck made thorough preparations as he realized that to take and hold Cyrenaica, the British needed to be able to maintain sufficient forces in the El Agheila region in order to hold it against a heavy enemy attack and that the sooner the offensive was launched the better. In Auchinleck's opinion there was a need for a 50 per cent numerical superiority of tanks over the Germans and equality with the Italians to give the offensive a reasonable chance. He was determined to make a bold statement by capturing and holding Cyrenaica rather than undertaking a limited operation to secure the landing grounds in Derna-Martuba that was likely to need the same number of tanks but with a far lesser reward.[43] Auchinleck was not cautious as such but careful and could see the bigger picture. He was ambitious enough to aggressively attack the larger target rather than play it safe and capture a small target which required the same commitment as a larger objective but with smaller gains.

What Auchinleck had concluded after the winter fighting of 1941–42 was that for further operations in 1942 two important changes had to be made in the organization of the army in North Africa. He, like the enemy, had seen that British armour, artillery and infantry had been unsuccessful in coordinating their operations on the battlefield. Therefore Auchinleck decided that the three arms of the army should be directed to work 'more closely at all times and in all places'. He thought that the British type of armoured division would be better balanced if there was less armour and more infantry, like a German Panzer division. In future, an armoured division was to consist of one armoured brigade group and one motor brigade group. The armoured brigade group was to contain three tank regiments, one motor battalion and a regiment of field and anti-tank guns, while the motor brigade group would have three motor battalions and a similar artillery regiment. Both would have the necessary service units and light AAA. The other decision was about the infantry brigade. Auchinleck considered that a permanent grouping between the various arms would make for better co-operation between them. Thereafter, an infantry division would consist of three infantry brigade groups, each containing three battalions, a regiment of field and anti-tank guns and a proportion of light AAA, engineers and other service personnel. These changes led to other alterations in some regiments. A regiment of horse or field artillery was now to contain three batteries each of eight 25-pounders and a battery of sixteen anti-tank guns replacing existing anti-tank regiments. A motor battalion was to consist of three motor companies and one anti-tank battery of sixteen guns. An infantry battalion was to consist of a headquarters company, three rifle companies and a support company of a mortar platoon, a carrier company (mounted on Bren carriers) and an anti-tank platoon of eight guns. The intention was to give the artillery the new 6-pounder anti-tank guns and the infantry and motor battalions the 2-pounder.

New armour was also received by both sides during the previous winter. The Allies received the Crusader Mark II which had slightly thicker armour than its predecessor the Mark I, but was no more mechanically reliable in desert conditions. The British had also begun to receive their first American medium tanks, the M3 or General Grant. The Grant's main gun was a 75mm gun firing either a high-explosive shell or a 14lb uncapped armoured-piercing shot. This should be contrasted with the Stuart tank's 37mm gun which was provided with capped ammunition that had greater strength in piercing enemy armour as the shot did not break up on impact. Nevertheless, the Grant was welcomed in the Middle East as 'a resounding event...for it provided the means of killing German tanks and anti-tank crews at ranges hitherto undreamed of. And this can be done from behind the heavy armour of a reasonably fast and very reliable tank.' Playfair noted that in the turret was a high-velocity 37mm gun similar to that of the Stuart. The Grant would have been better if it had its 75mm gun mounted in the turret instead of a sponson at one side and if the latest armour-piercing ammunition had been available for it.

All the changes in armour had caused further changes through the British armoured regiments, including those of the type of ammunition to be used. One can begin to understand why Auchinleck was cautious as when he began his next offensive as he had to ensure that adequate supply positions were in place before beginning a new campaign as well as taking into account what the Germans may be doing. It was known that the Germans had received a new model of tank: the Pzkw III called the 'III Special', armed with a long 5cm gun similar to the highly successful PAK 38 anti-tank gun. The extra length of the barrel gave greater muzzle velocity and penetration than the short 5cm gun with which the bulk of the Pzkw IIIs were still armed. Furthermore, the Germans had also received large reinforcements since January 1942.[44]

In a message to Ritchie, Auchinleck agreed that the Germans were more aggressive in their approach towards deployment and would push on into the middle of their army, while the British tended to look at their flanks and over their shoulders too much. Auchinleck was also alive to the situation in the Soviet Union which was beginning to release Poles from captivity and raise a Polish army on Soviet soil. The problem was that the freed Poles hated the Soviets for their inhumanity endured by millions of Poles since 1939 and wanted to leave the Soviet Union for the West and fight alongside the Allied armies and not with the Red Army. As a consequence, Stalin began to provide rations for many of the truculent Poles and wanted them to leave the Soviet Union. Auchinleck was willing to accept Polish troops. He had some already under his command – the Carpathian Brigade – but as all of the British commanders found they were odd, Auchinleck wrote:

> They are a queer crowd with no thought of anything but their own convenience and gain. However, I am very glad to have the Poles, if we can get the equipment for them. We hope to keep about 40,000, which will be a great reinforcement in these hard times.[45]

The Poles, like all the minor Allies from the French upwards, were notoriously difficult to deal with and for little gain, but Auchinleck's major bugbear was his own Prime Minister Winston Churchill, as he had to listen to him and then make his case. The Poles could be ignored until they were wanted.

In a private letter to Auchinleck, General Brooke wrote: 'We have got the PM [Churchill] to accept your dates and arguments but not in a pleasant manner. He is accepting the delays under protest and with little grace! It is a pity that you could not come home as I believe it might have assisted matters.'[46] One can see the problems faced by Auchinleck. He had difficulty in convincing his prime minister of the need to wait, but luckily his colleagues in the general staff had his back and supported him. Churchill may have thought that he knew much about military strategy, but he was not a dictator and so bowed before the collective skills and experience of his general staff and gave in, even if he was somewhat ungracious in this. However, this incident was one of many in which Churchill and his senior officers clashed over operations and the future of the war. It is also interesting to note that Auchinleck explaining his ideas in person to Churchill might have been more beneficial than Brooke explaining them to Churchill. Perhaps Churchill felt that Auchinleck was snubbing him. A letter from General 'Pug' Ismay to Auchinleck sheds more light on the situation as he wrote and told Auchinleck that Churchill was furious with him (Auchinleck). Ismay urged Auchinleck to return to the UK, to see Churchill and to put things right and argue his case for delay in the Western Desert. Even so, Ismay did conclude his letter with an acknowledgement that Churchill 'thought the world' of Auchinleck.[47]

However, the war in North Africa was part of a larger story; one that Auchinleck was aware of and could comment on. Brooke expressed to Auchinleck that he feared Cyprus and Turkey might well fall if naval and air cover were removed from the Eastern Mediterranean for commitments elsewhere in the war.[48] Auchinleck was also concerned about how the war was panning out, with the Germans and Japanese seemingly being able to push forward and advance at will and stretching the Allies almost beyond endurance. In reply to Brooke's message, Auchinleck also confessed his own misgivings about the current situation and wrote the following:

> I also am not too easy, and we have a problem under active examination this moment. Will send full reply earliest possible. I know how you realise how desperately short we are of infantry at present and urgent need of keeping something in GHQ reserve if only two bde [brigade] gps [groups] at present. Have considered weakening TENTH ARMY but am NOT at all happy about possible results on internal security (in) that area witness recent need for troops for Tehran. So far we have considered likely we shall get adequate warning.[49]

This missive from Auchinleck illustrated perfectly just how stretched the Allies were by 1942, but the Germans and the Japanese were also beginning to overreach themselves as they advanced into the Soviet Union and towards India respectively.

British commanders began to consider what they might do for the coming summer and as Auchinleck signalled to the Air Ministry in London, India could not be lost to the Japanese. He would rather forgo the idea of an offensive in Libya that summer and run a risk on the Northern Front (Iraq and Iran) and still hope to maintain the current Allied position in the Middle East as well as retain oil supplies in Iraq and Persia. He was even willing to risk holding the Germans in Libya using a reduced force which he claimed would not endanger Egypt.[50] Auchinleck, as the author of the supply line running east to west, knew exactly just how valuable India was and that a Japanese conquest of the subcontinent could well put the British out of the war and allow for a Japanese-German victory as without doubt the Soviet Union would have collapsed. Retreating behind the Urals would not have been an option for the Soviets if the Germans and Japanese already had captured territory to the south and east of the Urals. The traditional Russian withdrawal route would have already been cut off.

There were other problems concerning one of the British allies, the Soviet Union. The double-dealing of the Soviet government was legendary with east-central Europe suffering the most, especially Poland, but in 1942, Soviet chicanery in Iran was concerning the British Foreign Office (FO) as was reported from the Iranian capital Tehran. The line being suggested by British diplomats in Teheran regarding Soviet activities was as follows:

> The policy we should adopt regarding Soviet infiltration into Central and Southern Persia needs, I agree, careful consideration. The establishment of various Consular posts in the area has extended the influence of the Soviet government. Furthermore, we know that Lease/Lend trucks are to be taken over by Russian drivers at Bushire and they are proceeding there for that purpose. Already the Russians have taken delivery of trucks at Andimesh; at Basra they have aircraft and at various places en route they have established meteorological stations. They may make other requests. I am alive to the dangers to our position here inherent in the fact of Russian penetration, but since the Russians are our Allies we should, particularly at this critical stage, give them every possible assistance against a common enemy. Since the supply route to the Gulf is a main line for them, we should adopt a realistic attitude and concede to them the right to use it in the way that appears to them to be the most efficient. It is true that to adopt such an attitude may possibly endanger our future status in this country but as our main object is to beat Germany before all else, we must run the risk involved. The general world situation after the war will largely determine our position in Persia, and I therefore think that our attitude to the Russians now should not be obstinate, or influenced by pre-war apprehensions, but should be reasonable whilst being firm, as over the railways issue, and against illegal activities, as over Azerbaijan. I believe our object should be to establish friendly local relations, with the consistent object of eradicating Russian suspicion, which past policy may possibly have encouraged, and more than anything else to ensure that there can be no grounds for allegations that our assistance to Russia is not all that it possibly could be.[51]

This was a sound approach towards a temporary policy and bearing in mind the Soviet influence in Iran. The Soviet infiltration of Iran was part of a Russian policy that had its roots in pre-revolutionary Russia as part of a Tsarist foreign policy to sow the seeds of intrigue and doubt in countries such as Afghanistan and Iran against the British in India. It was all part of the so-called 'great game' as the British and Russians vied for influence in the area and led to several wars in Afghanistan as the two imperial powers clashed over territories in neighbouring India but with the British fighting Afghans rather than Russians. Auchinleck, as an old 'India hand', would have been well aware of the situation.

Auchinleck's concerns about India are revealed in a message to Brooke as they discussed the possibility of a British offensive in Libya in the face of a possible Japanese invasion of India and the consequences this might have for operations in North Africa. Auchinleck wrote to Brooke with his fears:

> Our line runs through the Indian Ocean from South Africa to Suez and from India to Basra and Suez – with the Japanese at Colombo and Bombay I wonder how long we should be able to supply ourselves and how long it would be before our oil supplies from the Persian Gulf are cut off? I quite realise the value of the Middle East as a base for a future offensive to reopen the Mediterranean and to carry the war against Germany into Europe. We put this project clearly to the Chiefs of Staff some months ago – before Japan had gained her very startling successes against us on the sea, on the land and in the air. The situation has completely changed.

It would seem that Auchinleck, as with most European and American service chiefs, had underestimated the Japanese and as he observed, India was vital to the existence of the British Empire and if the Japanese captured it, the chances of its recovery were very slim. Therefore if he had to choose between losing India or the Middle East, Auchinleck stated clearly that he would rather lose the Middle East as he maintained his stance that India could be held without the Middle East. He urged Brooke not to be mistaken in his approach to further operations as he wrote the following:

> Do not mistake me. I am not advocating a withdrawal from the Middle East. Far from it, and I see no immediate reason for such a drastic step, even if you do decide to weaken us to strengthen India. Even if we had to leave Egypt after having thoroughly blocked the canal, we might well hold on to Iraq and the oil supplies until the tide turned.

Here it should be seen that Auchinleck is not being defeatist as he clearly believes in an eventual victory for the British, but is somewhat thrown by Japanese successes and therefore realizes the need to adapt to the situation as it unfolded before him. He concluded his message to Brooke with these words:

> As to our projected offensive in Libya, I fully realise its desirability from the political and strategical point of view, but it must be admitted that the material value to be had from it so far as it may affect the course of the war is small at present. Had Japan not entered the war, its effect might have been much greater, and, ultimately, possibly decisive.

Once more he called for the need for tank and air superiority.[52]

Brooke sent Auchinleck his reply as he saw the progress of the war. He did not think that Japan would directly attack or invade either Australia or India as the Japanese rapid advance into the South Pacific islands had considerably stretched their resources. The Japanese were now holding a line reaching from Burma through the Andaman Islands into today's Indonesia to New Guinea, and anything further threatened to tax Japanese strength. Brooke had more concerns with China and the Soviet Union than he did with Japan. He was concerned with events in India as there was a fear of mutiny among local native troops, concerns about 'fifth columnists' and the worry about Japanese propaganda in India. He certainly feared a Soviet collapse and worried about the Soviet ability to defend itself and its oilfields on the northern front. Overall though, Brooke remained optimistic as he said that the Polish General Władysław Anders, who had been in Soviet captivity between 1939 and 1941, was pessimistic about the Soviet chances of defending themselves against a coming German attack. Brooke considered that Anders was exaggerating the numbers that the Germans might field as he considered they did not have the forces for an attack such as that predicted by Anders. Brooke wrote that if the Russian Front did collapse, the British already had sufficient troops to defend the Levant-Trans-Caspian Front and there would be no need to take them from Indian defences.[53]

Then it was time to return to Rommel. The Allies knew from a captured Order of the Day issued to Italian forces on 26 May 1942 that the enemy was about to go onto the offensive.[54] This was probably why Churchill considered that Auchinleck should have anticipated this move.[55] No matter what, Rommel's initial attack was launched by the Italian XXI Corps against the 1st South African Division around Gazala. It was a feint, and a clever one too. Rommel had authorized the use of special vehicles, fitted at the back with old aircraft engines and propellers, to circle around the desert creating clouds of sand and dust to give the impression of columns of tanks advancing; it was most effective. Rommel's main attack began at first light on 27 May in the southern sector south-east of Bir Hacheim. He used both his Panzer divisions plus the 90th Light Battle Group. Initially it seemed that the Germans were once more going to sweep all before them. Then the British counteroffensive was launched by 28 May as mentioned in a letter from Amery to Auchinleck.[56]

On 1 June Auchinleck had very good news to report to Churchill regarding the fighting in Libya. He wrote:

> The skill, determination and pertinacity shown by General Ritchie and his Corps Commanders, Lieutenant-Generals Norrie and Gott, throughout this difficult and strenuous week of hard and continuous fighting have been of the highest order. You may also like to mention, if security reasons do NOT (repeat NOT) forbid, excellent performance of Grant tanks with which its users are well pleased and also six-pounder anti-tank gun which had done great execution [*sic*]. The story of General Messervy's capture, deception of the enemy and escape, and resumption of command of 7th Armoured Division all within a few hours is a good one.[57]

Messervy's escapade was a remarkable one as elements from the 15th Panzer Division had overrun the HQ of the British 7th Armoured

Division and General Messervy was captured. He was only 48 years of age but was already grey. Just before he had been taken prisoner he had managed to tear off his badges of rank and red tabs of a staff officer and bury them in the sand with his red hat which would have also betrayed his seniority in rank. He then pretended to be an officer's batman. A German officer even remarked that Messervy was a bit too old for active service, with which he wholeheartedly agreed, complaining that although he was a reservist, he should never have been called up at his age. The Germans were deceived and lacked the necessary men to guard their prisoners adequately, which meant that Messervy was able to make good his escape during the night.[58]

Smuts signalled Auchinleck, expressing his pleasure at how the battle was going. The veteran South African considered it now appeared that there was an opportunity to cut off Rommel's retreat and so finish off the work that the British had begun in Libya.[59] There was further good news to be had as Auchinleck told Smuts that the Eighth Army was doing all it could to achieve victory. He also considered that the enemy armoured units were fighting hard and that there was parity in tank strengths but hoped that British tank numbers were on the rise.[60] The Germans having parity in armoured strength was a danger as German tanks were superior to those of the British. The Allies were quite dependent on large numbers of inferior tanks against the better German tanks which always took longer to produce and replace, while the use of American mass-production techniques ensured a large number of tanks being available to replace those lost by the Allies in battle. The Germans did not have this luxury, but the battle was totally destructive of tank crews from both sides and exploitative to boot. There was even a message from King George VI on 2 June. The British monarch saluted Auchinleck and General Ritchie for their work as well as all ranks of the three branches of the armed services and remarked approvingly on the skilled land-air co-operation.[61]

However, by the next day it seemed that operations were going wrong. Auchinleck signalled to Ritchie on 3 June with the news that the offensive was not going well. He reported that the 150th Brigade had been destroyed and that the enemy was consolidating itself on a broad and deep wedge in the middle of the Eighth Army position which obviously was very dangerous for the British. Auchinleck considered that

> if the enemy is allowed to consolidate himself in his present position in the Sidra-Harmat-Mteifel area our Gazala position including Bir Hacheim will become untenable eventually even if he does not renew his offensive. That situated as he is, he is rapidly able to regain the initiative which you have wrested from him in the last week's fighting. This cannot be allowed to happen. I repeat that in my opinion you must strike hard and at once if you are to avoid a stalemate, that is unless the enemy is foolish enough to fling himself against your armour. I wish he would, but I don't think that you can count on this at present.[62]

Auchinleck now had to retrieve the initiative before it was too late. Churchill and Auchinleck began to mull over the situation in North Africa with Churchill trying to fight the war from London; nevertheless he endorsed Auchinleck's decisions and signalled '…decision to fight it out to the end most cordially endorsed. We shall sustain you whatever the result. Retreat would be fatal. This is a business not only of armour but of will power.'[63] Churchill may well have been right about willpower, but also the Germans were finding it hard to get reinforcements and new supplies of equipment, so it was a case of the British not panicking and waiting for the Germans to run out of steam. Rommel, on the other hand, knew that he needed to panic the British into making errors of which he could take advantage and perhaps reach the Suez Canal.

Auchinleck explained the situation to Smuts, writing the following:

> …a strong counterattack was put in against the enemy centre on 5–6 June and had initial success but was counterattacked in its turn by a strong enemy force and driven back with heavy losses. Hacheim had in my opinion largely fulfilled its purpose and I think that Ritchie was right to evacuate it when he did although it may have released some though not many enemy troops to move against us in the North. Chief enemy attacks against Hacheim seem to have been by bombing and shell fire. Free French losses were not heavy apparently and they are now reorganising. After discussion with Theron who now fully understands am communicating your message to the Free French through General Catroux and not to General Koenig as

> former commands all Free French forces. Have just got back from 8th Army HQ. Situation is serious but by no means irretrievable and I am confident that Ritchie will retrieve it. Enemy is not, repeat, not in an enviable position and is being attacked and harassed on all sides. There is no doubt that superior anti-tank gun gives him very great advantage which he is wholly exploiting to the full and our tank losses are serious enough although every effort is being made to recover damaged tanks and replace losses.[64]

Auchinleck had orders already in the pipeline as he outlined to Churchill who he informed of his orders to Ritchie. General Ritchie was ordered by Auchinleck to deny the enemy the Acroma-El Adem-El Gubi line and furthermore not to allow Tobruk to become besieged. Ritchie was ordered to attack the enemy whenever the occasion offered.[65] Basically Ritchie was to assault the enemy at every opportunity and the question of Tobruk began to loom large.

Auchinleck, writing to Smuts, said that he had no intention of giving up Tobruk and hoped that it was only temporarily isolated. He remained convinced that Ritchie would defend the port city and the 'strong' Salum Hamra Maddalena position which had been prepared long before in anticipation of such a problem as the besieging of Tobruk.[66] However, doubt was being sown concerning whether Tobruk could hold out, as the Middle East Defence Committee on 21 June noted that even though Tobruk was still fighting, it was doomed to fall. The reason given for the possibility of Tobruk falling was that the enemy was stronger in everything essential for battle in open country and was well provided with vehicles.[67]

Churchill was a recipient of this report. The fact that the enemy had adequate vehicles was essential as troops had to be ferried around the desert because marching in such conditions was more or less ruled out. In his history of the Second World War, Churchill claimed that he was not in possession of all the facts regarding the situation at Tobruk and later realized that some of Auchinleck's orders to Ritchie regarding the defence of the city were ambiguous and that if he had seen the orders in full, he would have been dissatisfied.[68]

However, in Warner's work we learn that Tobruk was not quite the fortress that people assumed and still assume that it was. For example, the perimeter was too large to defend properly. The need for adequate water meant that the perimeter was too long for comfort, militarily speaking. The strongest point was the south-west corner which had been built up during the Italian occupation and included concrete blockhouses, minefields and anti-tank ditches. Rommel had attacked here unsuccessfully several times. The weakest part was the south-eastern corner. Its weaknesses were a mixture: much of its material had been taken to strengthen the Gazala line, and partly because that corner was dominated by two hills that could be used by an attacking force.

On 20 June 1942 the Germans attacked the south-eastern corner, preceded and accompanied by concentrated bombardment from the air and by artillery. The defences of this corner had been neglected latterly as there was an impression that further attacks against them were unlikely while the troops inside the defences were no longer the hardened 'diggers' of the 9th Australian Division who had withstood the previous siege. However, the worst thing was that Ritchie made no serious attempt to counter the German attack on Tobruk and this appalled Auchinleck further.[69]

Within days, Tobruk fell. Auchinleck was devastated and he wrote to Brooke as follows:

> The unfavourable course of the recent battle in Cyrenaica culminating in the disastrous fall of Tobruk impels me to ask you seriously to consider the advisability of retaining me in my command. No doubt you are already considering this and quite rightly, but I want you to know that I also realise the probable effects of the month's fighting. Personally, I feel fit to carry on and reasonably confident of being able to turn the tables on the enemy in time. All the same there is no doubt that in a situation like the present, fresh blood and new ideas at the top may make all the difference between success and stalemate. I acted on this idea myself last summer when I replaced Beresford-Peirse and Creagh by new men. After steeping oneself for months in the same subject all day and every day one is apt to get into a groove and to lose originality. For this theatre originality is

> essential and a change is quite desirable on this account alone apart from all consideration such as the loss of influence due to lack of success, absence of luck and all things which affect the morale of an army. It occurred to me that you might want to use Alexander who is due here in a day or two. Personally, I do NOT think that Wilson could do it now, but he might. I have thought over this a lot and I feel I must tell you what I think.[70]

Auchinleck was not only being humble in this message as well as observing his work over the previous few months in which he admitted that he sacked men who had failed to come up to scratch, but he also offered good reasons as to why he should be retained as he saw that the battle was not over and considered there was a chance of defeating the enemy. Even so, he was still cautious of the enemy as a few days later he messaged Brooke saying that in the Western Desert the enemy had more tanks as well as considering that if there was a chance of the Germans occupying Egypt, then perhaps they might divert troops from the Russian Front to ensure this happening.[71] However, there was at least one ordinary soul who supported Auchinleck and Ritchie against Churchill and the British government as an old Indian army hand, Colonel Rodney Foster, who in 1942 was serving in the Home Guard on the Kent coast, confided in his diary that he considered Churchill to be quite craven when things went wrong and would normally scoot overseas to see President Roosevelt. In the case of Libya, Foster predicted that Ritchie and Auchinleck would be sacrificed, while the government would weaken another front in order to defend Egypt.[72] In 1950, Churchill, in penning his account of the Second World War, wrote of Auchinleck and Ritchie that the personal association between the two generals did not allow Ritchie much room for independent thought which is essential for commanding a battle. It was the lack of clear thought and ill-defined responsibility between Auchinleck and Ritchie that led to the fall of Tobruk. Yet as Connell observes, in military matters Churchill's views should not be taken as gospel.[73]

This episode illustrates the problem that Auchinleck suffered once post-war memoirs and histories began to be published and of course people such as Churchill and Montgomery were highly visible and people considered that their pronouncements were infallible. Even so, Playfair reminds us that it was clear from February 1942 that there was never going to be a second siege of Tobruk, which led to the town not being properly prepared for another siege or even a determined assault. Playfair also observes that neither Auchinleck nor Ritchie understood the full extent of the Eighth Army's defeat after it had withdrawn from the Gazala positions. If they had done so, they would not have attempted to carry out three simultaneous policies: to continue the battle in the Tobruk area, to organize the defence of the Egyptian frontier, and to prepare a counteroffensive.[74] When Tobruk did surrender in June 1942, what devastated Auchinleck were the large number of troops captured – 30,000 in number – as well as a large amount of equipment including fuel, and the speed at which resistance collapsed.

Auchinleck's logic was quite astute as he knew that he could defeat the Germans and the Italians in the desert. The Germans were not natural desert fighters but had adapted well to the conditions and had learned the tactics necessary to be successful in the desert; however, Auchinleck was also aware that it was difficult for them to receive equipment, supplies and men to further their campaign. Auchinleck had adequate experience of desert warfare; indeed, it was more or less the only form of warfare that he had ever experienced save for the Norwegian campaign and then the Norwegian high Arctic was more like a snowy desert. This experience meant that he understood about supply problems over long empty miles of terrain, but his fear that Hitler might send troops from the Russian Front to North Africa is interesting and perhaps novel.

Germany had only become involved in North Africa to save its ally Italy from being driven into the sea. If there were no Axis force in Africa it was possible that the Allies might launch an invasion of Italy via Sicily from Africa, which indeed did happen in 1943. Therefore the Germans had to act, but the fighting in North Africa was mainly a sideshow for them. Yet a chance of capturing Egypt and the Suez Canal was something that perhaps Hitler could not pass up, but he did as he was totally obsessed with the destruction of the Soviet Union. Even so, Roger Parkinson rather dramatically wrote that only the Eighth Army could stop the Axis advance into Egypt and 'avert the world-wide catastrophe'. The Eighth Army was in full retreat and in total chaos 'thoroughly mixed up and disorganised. I did not see a formal fighting unit, infantry, armour or artillery.' According to Parkinson, everything depended on one man – Auchinleck – who left on 25 June 1942 to fly for the front and assume personal command of the Eighth Army.[75] Playfair notes that Auchinleck taking over Ritchie's command was more or less radical as the former had been quite correct in his relationship with Ritchie and the observation of the chain of command which sometimes meant that a superior officer might well allow a junior officer to have his head, even if events were not going well. Rommel had no such scruples and totally dominated Axis proceedings in North Africa.[76]

On taking command of the Eighth Army, Auchinleck changed its policy. He felt that they lacked the armour and artillery to hold on to Matruh and Sidi Hamza. He also considered that the enemy had superior numbers of armour which might well pierce the centre of the British positions or crush the southern flank; if either happened it would have meant defeat for the British. Auchinleck was determined to avoid this and keep open the Eighth Army's freedom of movement and could not afford for it to be pinned down at Matruh. At 0415 on 26 June 1942, Auchinleck issued new orders, of which he had given the gist to corps commanders shortly before midnight. In the new orders, Auchinleck decided not to fight a decisive action at Matruh or Sidi Hamza. Instead the action was to take place between Matruh and the El Alamein gap. In Auchinleck's words the aim was

> to keep all troops fluid and mobile, and strike at [the] enemy from all sides. Armour not to be committed unless very favourable opportunity presents itself. At all costs and even if ground has to be given up I intend to keep 8th Army in being and to give no hostage to fortune in shape of immobile troops holding localities which can easily be isolated.

This was quite revolutionary for the time and entirely unpractised. Previously British tactical withdrawal policy insisted that anything like a running fight should be avoided. Suddenly the Eighth Army was in the oddest position: its commander had been replaced, it was retreating before an aggressive enemy, it had barely prepared itself for one kind of battle when it was suddenly ordered to fight another, and in the midst of all this was also told to change its organization and tactics. Before anything could be reorganized, the enemy attacked.[77]

At the beginning of July 1942, Auchinleck was ready to go once more. He wrote to Smuts:

> On the eve of what may prove to be the turning point in our campaign of the Western Desert I wish to tell you how proud I am to be in direct command of 1st South African Division in my capacity as Commander Eighth Army. This magnificent Division is holding an important sector of the El Alamein front and I am certain that it will throw back the enemy however often he may come on. I know that I can implicitly rely on Major General Dan Pienaar and on every man under his command to fight to the last of the courage, tenacity and sagacity which are the characteristics of the South African soldier of whom you are a shining example.[78]

Something not really mentioned are the distances involved at El Alamein. Bungay reports that the front at El Alamein was twice as far from Tripoli as Moscow was from the German-Polish border and there were no trains. Everything had to be moved by lorry which had to travel over a space that was just vast and empty like an ocean.[79] This is not to mention the heat and lack of water that both the Allied and Axis forces had to endure in North Africa. During the winter of 1941–42 Auchinleck had realized that the further the British advanced into Cyrenaica, the more difficult the supply problem became.[80]

Clearly Auchinleck had got over his setbacks, but there was a reason why which becomes obvious later on 3 July in a message from Churchill. It is interesting to note that in 1939 during his leave in the UK when he had attended the course in Aldershot, Auchinleck had taken part in a paper exercise concerned with the defence of Egypt in which close attention was paid to the potential offered by the location of El Alamein. Auchinleck remembered this 'war game' which was now coming to life. It was quoted as being

> the only so-called position that one could hold without going much further back, and it had several advantages: it had its flank on the

> Qattara Depression which prevented a wide outflanking movement on the left, and of course the right flank was on the sea. It had certain defensive qualities – slight rises which were not usual in the desert.[81]

This lesson was one that was to eventually win the war on the Western Front.

Leo Amery at the India Office sent his support to Auchinleck, saying that he totally trusted the latter with his offensive and was quite ready to hear that Rommel had been fought to a standstill and was being pushed back as far and as fast as supplies could make possible. Even so, Amery did consider that Auchinleck might be forced to fight in Egypt before finally coming out on top. This was Amery musing to his friend but laying out what might actually happen, yet the final thought was that the British would prevail and vanquish the enemy.[82]

On 3 July 1942 Churchill messaged Auchinleck and referred to 'our special information' which was in regard to information received about enemy moves in the near future. This 'special information' was probably ULTRA, the result of being able to read German communications once Allied code-breakers had been able to crack the German security codes. This information was used carefully so as not to alert the Germans to the fact that the Allies had cracked their codes. What had been learned in relation to operations in Libya was that the enemy, after making a feint at the British southern flank, would then attack the centre of the main position where 18 Brigade was positioned before turning north and cutting off El Alamein. Churchill remarked that this was what the enemy appeared to be trying to do and asked if Auchinleck was getting 'these priceless messages (which have never erred) in good time. Every telegram ought to be in your hands without a moment's delay.'

Churchill continued with his questions, asking how the 8th Armoured Division was 'getting on' and when it could partly or wholly become operational. He also enquired about the 9th Australian Division and had they got all their artillery. Churchill was almost hinting that there might be a disaster, as he asked how Auchinleck considered German armour might manage in operating along the canals and irrigation ditches of the Nile Delta. However, it should be seen that this was not a big fear of Churchill's as he was not pressing for immediate action on this question.

Point four of this message from Churchill is very interesting as it is very clear that the British were reading German messages as the Germans were asking (who is not clear, but it certainly wasn't the British!) if inundations had been made in the Nile area; that is, defence through using flooding. Churchill said that this had been planned for the past two years with Wavell, with the assumption that it had been carried out.

As Churchill remarked, Egypt was to be defended as 'drastically as if it were Kent or Sussex without regard to any other consideration than the destruction of the enemy'. Clearly Egypt was not going to be given up lightly, but as we have already seen, Auchinleck, even though he considered Egypt important, did not consider its defence to be vital, but the Germans were obviously concerned about what they might meet if they were able to invade Egypt. The final point of Churchill's missive was one of huge support for Auchinleck and his leadership of the fighting in Libya as there had been an overwhelming vote of confidence in the government and Auchinleck's army given in the House of Commons.[83] Warner points out that this vote of confidence emboldened Churchill as he still needed a military victory; one that Auchinleck was stubbornly refusing to give him and, despite telegrams suggesting Churchill's support for Auchinleck, he was actually beginning to lose confidence in him.

On 12 July 1942 Auchinleck received an ultimatum from Churchill: both defeat and destroy Rommel or there would be no strengthening of the Middle East's northern front which was endangered by the German advance into the Soviet Union. On 13 July, Rommel suffered heavily in an unsuccessful counter-attack near El Alamein and by 17 July, he told the Italian high command 'Any more blows like today and I do not anticipate being able to hold the situation.' Neither Churchill nor Brooke could see that the war in the desert was being won by Auchinleck, so when on 27 July 1942 Auchinleck put the Eighth Army onto the defensive, Churchill had had enough and deemed the news to be 'very depressing'. He also did something else. As Auchinleck had steadfastly refused to go back to the UK for meetings and conferences on the situation in North Africa, Churchill decided that he and Brooke should go out to Cairo to meet and discuss the situation with Auchinleck.[84] What seemed to have passed Churchill by was that Auchinleck had stopped Rommel's advance into Egypt. This was the First Battle of El Alamein; the one that, as we shall see, Montgomery tried to ignore. This was because he was a better politician and communicator than Auchinleck.

As the fighting around El Alamein got going, Churchill had received a reply to his telegram of 3 July 1942 via General Corbett, who answered for Auchinleck to avoid delay. He answered point by point. Every 'special message' went directly to the Eighth Army and was received there as early as at GHQ. It was confirmed that these messages were of great value, but the timings were not always useful as some arrived in time to be of use operationally and others not so. Auchinleck suggested that perhaps timings should be checked from the UK. Point two concerning the 8th Armoured Division was answered in full. It was revealed that two squadrons of Valentine tanks had already gone forward to reinforce the Eighth Army and these tanks were manned by personnel from 1 Army Tank Brigade. Personnel from the 8th Armoured Division were to start landing on 4 July 1942 and that, depending on the physical condition of these men, it might be possible to move forward one armoured brigade group in its entirety by the middle of July. However, it was still not possible to predict the readiness of a second brigade owing to the necessity of receiving replacement tanks which had already been sent to the Eighth Army as well as artillery support.

Regarding the 9th Australian Division, less one brigade group, it had already arrived in the Alexandria defence area from which one battle group had been sent that day to join the Eighth Army. The dispatched battle group consisted of twenty-four 25-pounder field guns with proportionate anti-tank and infantry support. The remaining Australian brigade group was to complete its arrival in the Alexandria area on 4 July 1942. Steps had already been taken to put the entire division on a mobile basis. The divisional artillery consisted of seventy-two 25-pounder field guns and fifty-five anti-tank guns of which fifteen were 6-pounders. Point three related to preparations for the defence of Egypt. Churchill was informed that tank movements among waterways and irrigation channels were very much restricted both for the Allied and enemy tanks. What is interesting is that large numbers of tank-hunting Commandos had been formed from schools and depots for operations in the enclosed delta area.

Regarding inundations in the Alexandria area as queried in point four, Churchill was told that complete inundations were impossible as it would rule out use of the aerodrome; however, the remaining inundations were being carried out. In the Cairo area, a partial inundation was being carried out, with the completion of the scheme being dependent on negotiations with the Egyptian government. It was also revealed that places in the west branch of the Nile that were normally fordable in many places during the summer were having their water levels increased to try to prevent the enemy crossing easily. In total, arrangements had been made to defend the Nile delta area with 'every available man and all resources'.[85]

Auchinleck's work and steadfast faith in his men and planning proved to be fruitful as was witnessed in a message from Smuts to Auchinleck in which it is revealed that the enemy had been stopped at El Alamein and that Smuts was very proud of the role that South Africa had played owing to the presence of the 1st South African Division and the South African Air Force (SAAF). There was bad news as Tobruk had fallen, but as Smuts wrote: 'We [South Africa] shall continue to give fullest support until not only Tobruk is avenged but Africa is cleared of the enemy.'[86] The question of the fall of Tobruk was one that was to rankle for some while and began when the Vice Chief of the General Staff (VCIGS) asked General Corbett, one of Auchinleck's staff officers, to report independently to the War Cabinet on events surrounding the enemy capture of Tobruk. Whitehall was concerned that Tobruk fell after a relatively short resistance with many prisoners being taken and a substantial amount of material being captured by the enemy. The VCIGS commented that it '...seems from this distance quite inexplicable'. Enemy reports point towards the commanding general having surrendered and that Axis propaganda was making the most of this, causing the VCIGS to comment that 'It is evident that the greatest capital can be made by the enemy from this whole incident which had caused considerable criticism in this country of the fighting spirit of our Commanders.' Then Corbett was ordered to find out and report on what had happened and 'in particular on the conduct of the General in command'.[87] This unprofessional approach to Corbett angered Auchinleck who was not slow in expressing his ire to the Chief of the Imperial General Staff, General Brooke.

Auchinleck wrote to Brooke and was clearly outraged by the War Cabinet ordering Corbett to report independently on the said operation which, as Auchinleck pointed out, had been conducted under his command.

Auchinleck demanded an early explanation of the request made to Corbett which he considered to be extraordinary. He did not deny the Cabinet the right to send out a Committee of Enquiry to North Africa, but he wrote '…to depute a staff officer of mine without my sanction is not tolerable to me and I am sure was NOT intended.' Auchinleck reminded Brooke that he needed to be kept in the loop especially for important decisions and was not to be passed by. He also confirmed what Corbett had already told the VCIGS: that he had already established an enquiry into the fall of Tobruk which was to be conducted by General Wilson who Auchinleck considered to be a 'very competent judge'. Apart from that, Auchinleck did not propose to take any other action.[88]

Almost a week later Brooke replied to Auchinleck and confirmed that the Cabinet had decided to have an enquiry into events at Tobruk; not an independent one, but one carried out by one of Auchinleck's staff officers. Brooke claimed that the intention of the enquiry under Corbett had been to not burden Auchinleck with details of a post-mortem at a time when he had other anxieties and responsibilities to take care of. Brooke supported the appointment of Wilson to undertake Auchinleck's enquiry, apologized for the misunderstanding and stated that the Cabinet enquiry had been set up with the best of intentions.[89] The relative tardiness in answering Auchinleck's complaint is suspicious and one is inclined to believe that Brooke's letter was eventually cobbled together by an anonymous civil servant trying to face the Cabinet and the Imperial General Staff.

On the same day Auchinleck was complaining to Churchill about the poor state of equipment being received in North Africa which had been shipped from the UK. The state of the Valentine tanks supplied to British forces was exercising Auchinleck. The problem lay with the fact that the tanks could only arrive in North Africa after a long journey which involved being moved by road, rail and sea under various climates and as Auchinleck wrote '…tanks cannot be battleworthy after such a voyage without considerable attention'. To go into details, Auchinleck told Churchill that once the tanks were landed and the first 67 were inspected, it was discovered that there were 500 faults requiring workshop attention varying from 140 to 200 hours' work per tank. Even so, this was an improvement on previous deliveries but still below the standard expected. All of the tanks' main guns needed checking and Auchinleck remarked that this should have been done in the UK and he criticized further: 'Approx 160 items of tank fittings were deficient of which 120 such as towing shackles, armament components, periscope components, power traverse control boxes. Some of these items may have been pilfered in transit.' He added that there was no evidence of bad stowage or serious damage in transit.[90] It would seem that all the problems regarding the sending of equipment such as tanks stemmed from the UK and a lack of attention to detail as well as the possibility of theft before the tanks were loaded onto ships being a problem. It beggars belief that civilian contractors would steal from equipment necessary for fighting the war, but human nature is what it is.

Smuts continued to support Auchinleck and his operations in North Africa and wrote:

> Looking at actions last and this week it appears that [the] enemy is trying to repeat his successful Gazala tactics, attacking two places well apart to secure points for further advance and confuse us as to where to reinforce most strongly. While holding Northern attack we have lost Qarat el Himeimat in the extreme South. This taken in conjunction with the strong position [the] enemy is creating locally in locality 877275 seems to indicate his intention to create another Bir Hakeim situation and move to Southern flank. This should be prevented before it is too late.[91]

Auchinleck replied to Smuts, thanked him for his advice, confided how he was fighting the present campaign and said:

> We are fighting this battle on quite different lines to Gazala and for the last ten days [the] enemy had been conforming to our moves and not we to his. Himeimat means nothing to me at present. There is NO Bir Hacheim here. El Alamein is a BASTION on which our flanks rest. I am NOT saying we have won [the] battle but [the] enemy is NOT making us dance to HIS TUNE.

In pencil Auchinleck added a postscript: 'Have just heard that our mobile troops have reoccupied Himeimat from which the enemy withdrew.'[92]

Clearly the operation was going well in addition to proving the fluidity of the campaigning being experienced in North Africa. Auchinleck found time to discuss the war with Brooke and agreed that the Northern Front did look 'ridiculously heavy', but Persia and Iraq still concerned Auchinleck who saw it as part of the line to supply Egypt from India. He also thought that 'Straffer' Gott might take command of the Eighth Army. Since the German invasion of the Soviet Union during the previous summer, Stalin had badgered Churchill about a 'Second Front' to try to divert German forces in the Soviet Union if they were forced to fight a war on two fronts with the British and Americans attacking in the west. Auchinleck's comment on a Second Front was

> We feel that you have already a 'second front' of no mean importance here! As to it being necessary to establish a 'second front' in Europe, Northern Africa and the whole of the Mediterranean basin is, I suggest, really 'Europe' for strategic purposes, and is inseparable from it. Would it not be a good thing to try to make the public understand this? I still hold very strongly that the way to beat the enemy is from the South, through Italy into Austria and thence into Southern Germany. I feel convinced that an attempt to battle a way into Germany from Northern France through the strongest part of his defensive line into the stronghold of Prussianism is likely to land you in a way of position which may last as long as the last one did![93]

Auchinleck may have had a point in 1942, but what he considered then as potential folly became the main thrust of the Allied offensive in the West in 1944. Even his concept of a southern route became a reality. It was also the slow bogged-down affair that lasted from July 1943 until the end of the Second World War and never broke free of Italy until the unconditional surrender of Germany during May 1945.

On 27 July 1942 Churchill signalled Auchinleck and said he was convinced that the latter had the better of Rommel in the air, communications and above all had more reinforcements, which Churchill remarked were luckily sent in time. He also remarked that General Brooke was coming out to North Africa shortly bringing plans and orders, etc.[94] This proved to be true, as on 8 August 1942 Auchinleck received a letter from Churchill relieving him of his command.[95] Auchinleck had been sacked. Parkinson noted that Churchill's gross undervaluation of Auchinleck's work during July 1942 is symbolized by the fact that he never named the 'First Battle of El Alamein' with any name at all.[96] It was a major victory but an anonymous one and would have remained so if it had not been for the likes of Dorman-Smith/O'Gowan who was determined that Montgomery would not be able to claim that it was only his generalship that had led to victory in North Africa. Parkinson also noted that Churchill failed to understand that Auchinleck had been in the midst of battle rather than sitting in Cairo.[97]

The problem for Auchinleck was that he had not appreciated the political problems that Churchill was having with the Soviet dictator Stalin, with whom he was to meet for a second conference once Churchill left the Middle East. Stalin demanded a Second Front, and that was why Churchill was badgering Auchinleck. As Warner points out, what was necessary was a date suggesting that an offensive against Rommel was imminent, even if this was not true. It would seem that Churchill was embarrassed by recent events in North Africa, especially the recent panic in Egypt, and so needed something to encourage Stalin to continue the Soviet resistance against the invading Germans. So Auchinleck's mention of 15 September as the earliest possible date for an offensive did not endear him to his prime minister. Warner also notes the irony that the Second Battle of El Alamein, or the Battle of El Alamein as so many refer to Montgomery's well-known victory, was five weeks after Auchinleck's proposed offensive. However, Montgomery knew how to handle Churchill,[98] and of course timing was everything. Even so, Auchinleck had not known that he was about to be replaced, but he perhaps should have been more astute. Back in January 1942, after the loss of Benghazi, Brooke had written his private view in his diary that he felt that Auchinleck was not the man for the Middle East, while Churchill later wanted to dismiss Auchinleck for 'insubordination' after refusing to return to London during the summer of 1942.[99] Auchinleck may have been a good soldier, but he was not so brilliant at politics and stroking the ego of Churchill, who didn't like facts or reality when it suited him not to.

*Chapter Nine*

# Back to India

In his letter to Auchinleck relieving him of his command in the Middle East, Churchill explained his reasoning. He referred to the time when Auchinleck had offered his resignation in June, just after the fall of Tobruk, and explained that at the time the government was not willing to take up the offer as it was experiencing a crisis and a major resignation on the operational front would not have helped. Churchill admitted that Auchinleck had 'stemmed the adverse tide and at the present time the front is stabilised'. However, in Churchill's opinion it was time for change and the War Cabinet agreed with him, so it was proposed that Iraq and Persia should be detached from the Middle East theatre of operations. General Alexander was to be appointed to the command of the Middle East and General Montgomery was to command the Eighth Army. In return, Auchinleck was offered the command of Iraq and Persia including the Tenth Army with headquarters in either Basra or Baghdad. Churchill admitted:

> It is true that this sphere is to-day smaller than the Middle East, but it may in a few months become the scene of decisive operations and reinforcements to the Tenth Army are already on the way. In this theatre, of which you have special experience, you will preserve your associations with India.[1]

Churchill was making the most of an unpleasant situation and a probably unpopular move. Auchinleck certainly had his supporters and those were from varied backgrounds. Part of Churchill's thinking was his belief that the failures in the Middle East, as he perceived them, might not have occurred if Auchinleck 'had not been distracted by the divergent considerations of a too widely extended front'.[2] Churchill might be forgiven for his considerations, but it seemed that Auchinleck was the only senior commander who could see how his command was joined up with the L of C coming from India through the Middle East to the front in North Africa. Of course Auchinleck had not failed, and had indeed prepared the way for final victory in North Africa. In 1964 O'Gowan wrote that Churchill had come to Cairo in August 1942 looking for a crisis but did not find one, which denied him the opportunity to exert his 'decisive control over events' in Egypt. What Churchill found himself faced with was complete control and calm once he arrived in the Egyptian capital and indeed, he was not needed. As a result, he could hardly sack Auchinleck for saving the situation in Egypt and so he split the Middle East command, thereby reducing Auchinleck's authority if he accepted the Persia-Iraq command. Auchinleck, at the time, considered that the defence of Iraq and its oilfields at Abadan was vital but lacked the resources to do much about the situation there.[3] He clearly understood the situation.

General Tom Corbett wrote to Auchinleck on 14 August 1942 expressing his support and praise for his work, writing: 'Your achievement in stopping the rot in a beaten army, in restoring its morale so speedily, in wresting the initiative from a triumphant enemy, and inflicting on him crippling losses, will one day be recognised. I shall make it my business to see that it is.'[4] Another letter of support came from the Polish C-in-C Middle East General Zając, who wrote to Auchinleck on 19 August 1942 expressing deep regret that Auchinleck was going. Zając spoke not only of Auchinleck's military skills and prowess as a commander, but also of his human side as he wrote that

> Whilst at the post of the Commander of all Allied Forces in the Middle East you have shown profound understanding for the Polish troops as well as a great heart to me and also to my subordinate commanding officers and men. Allow me, Sir, to take this opportunity to assure you that I have always shared the admiration for your courageous decision to voluntarily withdraw to El Alamein line. This daring decision, in my opinion, not only enabled us to check Rommel's offensive but also dismissed [the] menacing danger to the Nile Valley. May I express once more my sincere regret to see you leaving us, and allow me Sir, to assure you that Polish troops

> will always remember the period during which they had the honour to be led by such an experienced Commander, Soldier and Friend.[5]

This was quite a tribute from Zając as the Poles were not always the easiest of the Allies, but the respect is obviously genuine otherwise why would Zając have written the letter? Nevertheless, Auchinleck was disappointed that he was not being kept on in the Middle East, as he confided to the Viceroy of India, Lord Linlithgow. Auchinleck wrote that he had been sent to India 'on leave' and that there was to be no publicity about how he was moving away from the Middle East. Without doubt he was feeling very bitter, as he told Linlithgow that he had plans to defeat Rommel and considered that Alexander would not find it easy to beat the enemy. It is very clear that Auchinleck was greatly disappointed with the outcome of events in North Africa during the summer of 1942.[6]

As autumn 1942 progressed, it was quite clear that there was ample support for Auchinleck and that some questioned his dismissal. Leo Amery wrote to Auchinleck on 2 September 1942 and gave his opinion of the situation and some sage advice, writing the following:

> I need not tell you how deeply distressed I was to hear of your supersession. I am in no position to judge the merits of that decision in the particular circumstances of the moment: all I would say to you is don't for one minute look upon your star as set. Take your present spell of rest wholeheartedly as rest and recuperation for the next chapter, which may very well be as important as any in your life. I know, from my talks with them, that both the Prime Minister and Brooke are really well disposed towards you and in no sense regard you as out of the picture for the rest of the war. So be of good heart, keep fit, and above all don't lose confidence in yourself or your power to do big things.[7]

Connell observed that at the time of Auchinleck going to the Middle East, it had been clearly understood that once he had completed his task there, he would be returned to India in order to carry on his work in that sphere. Therefore in June 1943 when Wavell was offered and accepted the post of viceroy, Amery made representations in the strongest terms on behalf of

Auchinleck, saying that he would be the ideal successor as C-in-C India. Amery considered that there should be only one candidate for the post and that was indeed Auchinleck. This recommendation was grudgingly accepted by Churchill. The problem was one of not understanding, as Churchill considered that Auchinleck was an old-fashioned, orthodox soldier who could not understand modernity while he, Churchill, was the total opposite and was dynamic with many constructive projects in mind. Connell wrote that it was the other way round: Churchill was set in his ways and it was Auchinleck who could take the long view. Even so, there was nothing to shake Churchill from his view and furthermore, even if Auchinleck had been able to return to India as C-in-C, it was unlikely that he would have been able to have had operational control over any attack on the Japanese in South-East Asia.[8] However, Amery was not to know that Auchinleck was perhaps about to embark on the most important task of his life as he was soon to oversee the dismantling of the British armed forces in India and divide the Indian armed forces between India and the newly-formed Pakistan during 1947 against a backdrop of extreme violence and upheaval owing to inter-communal violence between Muslims and Hindus once the British government had granted independence to India.

Auchinleck was also to get support from the great Australian commander from the First World War, Field Marshal Lord Birdwood, who noted that Auchinleck was the first Allied commander to thwart Rommel.[9] However, the tide was beginning to turn in Auchinleck's favour by November 1942 following the success of the Second Battle of El Alamein with which Montgomery was given full credit for the victory while more or less ignoring Auchinleck's success earlier that year. Amery was swift to observe that if it had not been for Auchinleck's work during the summer, perhaps the autumn victory might not have been possible, as he wrote:

> I know what you must be feeling just now. You always have the satisfaction of knowing that the victory of today was only made possible – and indeed the whole Middle East saved – by your getting back to Alamein and holding the position there by your personal intervention. There would have been no champagne today if you

> hadn't put the cork in the bottle in July. So, possess your soul in patience.[10]

Churchill made a speech about Montgomery's victory, but failed to mention that the plan followed by Monty was virtually Auchinleck's. This omission angered many officers who had served under the latter.[11] This argument of Montgomery versus Auchinleck was to be reignited during the 1950s when Montgomery published his memoirs. That will be considered later in this work.

However, in 1942 Auchinleck also began to receive more praise and support from within the exiled Polish camp as can be seen in a letter from Victor Cazalet, a lieutenant colonel of the British army, liaison officer to the exiled Polish wartime leader General Sikorski and a Conservative MP. Cazalet wrote to Auchinleck during November 1942 expressing his understanding and feelings after the Second Battle of El Alamein:

> I do not know anything beyond what I have seen in the papers about recent changes, but I do want to send you this line to say how much I and many others have been thinking of you recently. In the House [of Commons] last Thursday I ventured to remind Members how much we owed to you and all I can say is that my few remarks met with very warm approval from everybody present. I know when the battle began, Sikorski said that his first thoughts were of you. We shall always remember the charming way in which you received us in Cairo and hope very much that our paths will meet again.[12]

Both Sikorski and Cazalet were fated to die within a year, killed in an air crash just off Gibraltar on 4 July 1943.

Auchinleck also received a letter from Sikorski's enemy, General Władysław Anders, who was largely responsible for the release of thousands of Poles from Soviet captivity and the establishment of a large Polish force which left the Soviet Union and was later to serve as the Second Polish Corps in Italy. This force is often known as the 'Anders Army', such was the charisma of General Anders who wrote to Auchinleck:

> It is a pleasure to receive your letter; I return often to the brief period of our meetings. Soldiers appreciate each other quickly; and consequently, it came as no surprise to me when – during the period of the worst crisis – you succeeded thanks to your great energy and military authority, in stopping Rommel at the very gates of Cairo and Alexandria. I have the greatest admiration of that achievement, and I have no doubt that military history will make it clear the importance of stopping the Germans in that particular operation. I am certain that the present improved situation would be far different had that event turned out otherwise, and we might never have heard of this great advance through North Africa. We know what it means to undertake stopping a victorious enemy with an Army shaken by reverses. Those without precise knowledge of such things little appreciate the call for difficult decisions, and the expenditure of energy demanded of the Commander. I, myself and all of us here will be happy if it so happens that we find ourselves upon [*sic*] your command when we face our enemy again. Personally, it would be a great pleasure either to see you here as my guest or to take the field with you. We are now quickly completing our preparations. But we have one great trouble: that is, the attitude of the Soviet Government in refusing to allow all our people – soldiers, wives and children remaining in Russia – to leave Soviet territory. If this attitude does not quickly change, they will, I fear, be lost. Morale and discipline here is good, and as to Germany, the men are anxious to start a settlement of accounts for what that nation has done to Poland.[13]

Anders was both a very frustrated man and a very brave man. He had received harsh treatment as a prisoner of the Soviets. Initially he had been treated as a prisoner of war by the Soviet authorities following the short Polish-Soviet War of 1939 in which Anders was captured as he had been withdrawing eastwards following the earlier German invasion of Poland. Following the German invasion of their former ally, the Soviet Union, during June 1941, Anders was suddenly released and charged with forming a Polish army on Soviet territory. He did this, as well as ensuring that thousands of Polish women and children were able to leave the Soviet Union, having been deported into the Soviet interior during the autumn of 1939. During 1942 Anders was able to leave with his men for Iran but even so, hundreds of thousands of Poles were left stranded in the Soviet Union once Stalin forbade any further evacuations of Poles from Soviet territory. From exile Anders raised the question of Soviet behaviour and how the Soviet Union annexed large areas of east-central Europe, including Poland, while claiming that these territories were being liberated. Anders never returned to Poland and died in London in 1970.

By the summer of 1943 Auchinleck was back where he belonged – in India – when he was reappointed as Commander-in-Chief, India. This new appointment delighted many who also supported Auchinleck over his dismissal from his Middle East command. General Arthur Smith wrote to Auchinleck during June 1943 expressing his pleasure at the latter's appointment, but considered that Auchinleck might have been disappointed that Burma had not been included as part of his remit. Smith returned to the subject of El Alamein and said that justice had not been done for Auchinleck for his work at the First Battle of El Alamein and he considered that Auchinleck was responsible for the saving of Egypt from a German invasion and a possible conquest as far as the Suez Canal. Smith based this view on what others who had served under Auchinleck had said of those days in 1942.[14] Lord Linlithgow wanted to go further back and discuss the situation in Iraq during 1941, which had been headed off by some British resilience and grit. Linlithgow wrote:

> I have a strong wish that our joint endeavour in meeting the danger in Iraq in 1941 should be fully recorded in some document of a permanent character. I cannot feel confident, remembering the confusion of those times, that the story is adequately presented in any war diary. Moreover, I am only too well aware of the enormous mass of material that awaits those unfortunates who will be charged with the duty of writing the Indian part of the history of this war. Half the fun, you'll recall, was the stubborn failure of the Foreign Office to comprehend the nature of the emergency and to provide adequate support in coping with it. But I can hardly expect that that aspect can be brought out, except perhaps obliquely! That it was

> an emergency, I have no doubt, and I think there is a pretty good reason to regard the happenings of those anxious days as one of the turning-points of the war.[15]

Linlithgow's assessment of the FO is slightly unfair because, at least in the privacy of his diary, Sir Alexander Cadogan, the Permanent Under-Secretary of State for Foreign Affairs, was taken up with the question of Iraqi aggression against the RAF outpost at Habbaniya. Indeed, Cadogan recorded that he had authorized the commander at Habbaniya to inform the hostile Iraqis that if the air base was attacked, Baghdad would be bombed in retaliation. The period that encompassed the Iraqi crisis, May 1941, was one of a number of crises ranging from the battle for Crete, concerns about Djibouti, intelligence reports suggesting that the Germans were on the verge of invading the Soviet Union (which was delayed by six weeks owing to the German forces being diverted to Yugoslavia to put down a revolt there), the hunting and sinking of the German battleship *Bismarck*, and finally the arrival of Hitler's deranged deputy Rudolf Hess, who had flown in secret from Germany to the UK to try to seek peace between the two countries.[16] It was a busy month, and Iraq came somewhere after Crete which fell to the Germans and drove the Allies out of Europe for a couple of years while the questions of what to do with Hess and the intelligence reports which pointed towards a German invasion of the Soviet Union vexed the British authorities including the FO. The arrival of Hess and the threatened invasion of the Soviet Union were without doubt linked.

Even though Auchinleck was made C-in-C India in 1943, he had actually been in India since 21 August 1942, but after finishing his dispatches before the end of the year, he was left a full general aged 58 on full salary but unemployed. At this time the Allies were waging war in Europe, Africa and South-East Asia. Auchinleck was outside of these things and quite naturally frustrated even if there is no record suggesting this, but it would have been outside his nature and sense of duty to be doing nothing while the rest of his compatriots were fighting. Even worse, Auchinleck and his wife did not even have their own home in India, but they had good friends who tried to entertain them and put them up. Eventually it dawned on Churchill that Auchinleck was still of value to him and the war, but was still making bad decisions regarding how he could be usefully employed.

At the Casablanca Conference (January 1943) it was decided that General Eisenhower should be Supreme Commander of all the Allied forces in North Africa with Alexander as his deputy. Wilson, who had taken the Iraq-Persia command after Auchinleck's refusal to do so, was to become C-in-C Middle East and for some reason Churchill thought that Auchinleck might this time take the Iraq-Persia command. Once in Cairo, Churchill contacted his Deputy Prime Minister Clement Attlee, leader of the Labour Party, and suggested that perhaps Auchinleck should be offered the post but Attlee cast doubt as to whether Auchinleck would accept the position having refused it once before, and informed Churchill that if he did refuse the command, then the only course to be followed was to retire him.[17] The British diplomat and writer Harold Nicolson was privy to a conversation with Churchill during November 1942 at the time of the British triumph at El Alamein and was able to record the conversation in his private diary. Churchill referred to this third battle as 'the battle for Egypt', but he also spoke about his dismissal of Auchinleck. He admitted that it was a terrible thing to do and said how Auchinleck had taken the news: 'It was a terrible thing to have to do. He took it like a gentleman. But it was a terrible thing. It is difficult to remove a bad General at the height of a campaign: it is atrocious to remove a good General.' Churchill admitted that he wanted General Gott as commander of the Eighth Army, but in the space between deciding and then going swimming, Gott had been killed when the aircraft in which he was travelling was shot down over the Western Desert. Churchill appointed Montgomery in Gott's place.[18]

In 1963 Auchinleck spoke to O'Gowan about why he refused to take the Iraq-Persia command. He wrote as follows:

> As to the Iraq-Persia command, I honestly believed it was militarily unsound in the conditions existing and I refused it for this reason. Moreover, I felt that I could not do myself justice at an essential command properly if I appeared as a commander discredited in the field. It would not have been fair on the troops. I felt this very strongly at the time. It was not pique – also I think that I was pretty

> tired though I would have thrown that all off in a month or so I think. Churchill's visit tired me much more than Rommel ever did.[19]

This statement is very much Auchinleck, who always wanted the best for his men and army and was loyal to them, even to the point of being unemployed for a while. He was also not a fool and knew that this really was a demotion, even if it was denied by those trying to undermine him. Furthermore, Churchill was tiresome to most of his generals; it was only a few mavericks like Montgomery who seemed to 'get' the British prime minister.

It would seem that Montgomery managed to whisper some poison into Churchill's ear as Churchill had decided that he should employ Auchinleck once more as early as November 1942 and had sent for Montgomery. Churchill desired to see Montgomery as he understood that there had been some confusion and difficulties between the two generals. In early February 1943 Churchill returned from the Casablanca Conference via Montgomery's HQ in Tripoli and it appears from a note sent to the CIGS that Churchill had, following talks with Montgomery, altered his opinion of Auchinleck. This note, dated 8 February 1943, read: 'I want to have another talk with you sometime this week with regard to General Auchinleck, in view of the very strong line taken by General Montgomery upon his work.' It seems that Montgomery's views of Auchinleck carried the day and nothing else was heard of the latter being offered the Iraq-Persia command.[20] It might have been face-saving for Churchill to receive Montgomery's briefing against Auchinleck. This may have decided Churchill against offering Auchinleck the Iraq-Persia command, not having to suffer the humiliation of his declining the post once more and avoiding the question of having to retire a very able general at the very height of the war. It was now a question of finding a suitable post for Auchinleck.

The problem was that Churchill had been sufficiently poisoned by Montgomery for him to decide that Auchinleck was no longer suitable for a field command. This became obvious as the Casablanca Conference had discussed a possible joint service operation against Burma to be launched later in 1943. On 17 February 1943, Field Marshal Wavell signalled to the Chiefs of Staff in London suggesting that Auchinleck should be army commander for the proposed campaign. Once more, Churchill conferred with Montgomery and then claimed that both he and the CIGS had lost confidence in Auchinleck as a field commander. Churchill conceded that Auchinleck's abilities and knowledge of India made him quite suitable for a governorship. It would seem that Churchill was willing to do anything other than give Auchinleck another military appointment and tried all forms of musical chairs to prevent him returning to a military post. This included trying to juggle all forms of governorships, but eventually it began to dawn on Churchill that the right place for Auchinleck was C-in-C India with the appointment being announced on 18 June 1943. On 20 June he travelled to New Delhi to take up his post: Auchinleck was assuming control of all armed forces in India which in the conditions of war meant that he was in command of more than 2 million service personnel. The next day Auchinleck was 59 years old.

Once in post, Auchinleck set about reorganizing the structure of military command in India and altered it from four commands – Northern Command at Rawalpindi, Eastern Command at Barrackpore, Central Command at Agra and Southern Command at Bangalore – to three commands: North-Western Army, Eastern Army and Southern Army. He retained all the senior staff and commanders. However, when Auchinleck assumed command of India, the Japanese army was at the India-Burma frontier and threatening to invade India, but he was denied a role for the conduct of operations against the Japanese as the British War Cabinet decided to set up a separate command for this; the South-East Asia Command which was tasked with waging war against the Japanese. Nevertheless, he was able to get a measure of involvement via the unlikely discipline of long-range penetration warfare with groups operating deep behind Japanese lines.

These groups known as Chindits were commanded by an eccentric officer, Brigadier Orde Wingate, who just prior to the return of Auchinleck to India had led a successful expedition into Japanese-occupied Burma. Wingate was an extremely unpopular officer with immense ambitions and a huge ego, but a successful campaign which liberated Italian-occupied Ethiopia and restored its ruler, Haile Selassie, to his throne, had made Wingate's name along with his reputation for unorthodoxy. Wavell saw the value of Wingate and had him sent to India. A subsequent interview in New Delhi in which Wingate explained his thinking and his way of waging war as well as those on world strategy made Wingate a sensation overnight.

Wingate's first venture into Burma was known as the First Chindit Expedition and he sent the dispatches of this directly to the Secretary of State for India who passed them directly to Churchill, so Auchinleck and the India command were bypassed. Churchill was very excited to receive these papers and, considering that he could see a way forward in defeating the Japanese, railed against the perception that British commanders were competing with one another for materials and funds and so demanded that Wingate should command the army in Burma. Having the ear of Churchill, Wingate was able to convince the prime minister that the Japanese could be driven from Burma if he was given the best officers, the best NCOs and indeed, the best men, the best equipment, best aircraft and best gliders. Greenwood even claims he demanded the 'best castrated mules'; all to be used as Long-Range Penetration Groups behind Japanese lines. Wingate, after consulting with Churchill, returned to India with the rank of major general and the authority to contact Churchill directly, at any time, if he felt it necessary to do so. One message to the Chiefs of Staff from Wingate which of course reached Churchill was wretched and misleading. It read as follows:

> [General Auchinleck] finds himself unable to recommend the formation and training of more than the existing L.R.P.G.s. The grounds on which he bases this opinion are that the creation of any more L.R.P.G.s will denude the Army in India of essential forces. There are in India today, and have been for a considerable time, something in the neighbourhood of a million men under arms.[21]

This provided extra ammunition for Churchill to use against Auchinleck.

Auchinleck was made responsible for finding the necessary officers and men for Wingate, as well as providing the organization, training facilities and equipment demanded. As Greenwood remarks, Auchinleck found Wingate to be someone with whom it was hard to have any form of relationship owing to the latter's quite odd behaviour which often drove many people to distraction. Auchinleck genuinely wished to help Wingate in his endeavours and arranged to meet him at his jungle training camp in the Central Provinces. Auchinleck kept the appointment but Wingate was missing; however, it was soon learned from an embarrassed staff officer that he was in his tent and was not to be disturbed. Greenwood was sent to Wingate's tent to see what was happening and found him sitting bare-chested in a deckchair, reading a large bible while eating a raw onion. Auchinleck remarked that Wingate was a 'scatterbrain allowed power without any responsibility'.[22]

There were other events happening in the world that were to impinge on India and on Auchinleck. Churchill and Roosevelt had met in Quebec and made further decisions about the future conduct of the war, which included appointing Lord Louis Mountbatten as Supreme Commander of a new command established to wage war against the Japanese in Burma and South-East Asia as a whole. The American General Joseph 'Vinegar Joe' Stilwell was to be Mountbatten's deputy. Stilwell's nickname reveals his caustic nature; furthermore he did not trust many people and certainly not the British. Mountbatten, a British aristocrat and cousin of King George VI, no doubt was a shock to him.[23] The appointment of Mountbatten, which Churchill had convinced Roosevelt to accept, was a brave decision as Mountbatten at age 43 was a captain and had commanded nothing other than destroyers. However, Mountbatten was not only a cousin of the king but also believed in himself and had endless energy and self-confidence. He had often been told that the best time to take over a post was when things were at their worst and this was one of those times, with the Japanese poised to invade India.[24]

Mountbatten arrived in New Delhi on 6 October 1943 wearing the uniform of an acting admiral of the Royal Navy, all 'dazzling in white and gold'. Auchinleck, with a retinue of distinguished persons, met him and took Mountbatten to stay at the commander-in-chief's house until Wavell was installed as viceroy on 12 October. Montgomery had warned Mountbatten that Auchinleck was odd, someone who suffered from an inferiority complex and who went onto the offensive very quickly. It seems that Montgomery was certainly poisonous as far as Auchinleck was concerned; he had a bee in his bonnet about his fellow officer. However, Greenwood considers that Auchinleck was not charmed by Mountbatten either and claims that he viewed the latter's arrival with misgivings.

Mountbatten's chief of staff, Lieutenant General Sir Henry Pownall, wrote in his diary:

> It doesn't sound as if Mountbatten had got on too well with the Auk. The former effervescent and dynamic, the latter very mulish at times and, like a mule, without warning and over very minor matters. I wouldn't say his nose is out of joint, but he cannot exactly relish a Supreme Commander coming to sit down in what is so very much his parish.[25]

Indeed, the modest Auchinleck was put out by the flamboyant Mountbatten while rumours began to circulate that Auchinleck's marriage was in trouble as Jessie was seen with another man on frequent occasions while Auchinleck was increasingly alone, even undertaking engagements on his own. White-Spunner notes that Mountbatten needed to foster a good relationship with Auchinleck, his C-in-C, and that this relationship was not going to be easy. For one thing, Auchinleck was a great friend of the Viceroy General Wavell, who was also part of that small club of the C-in-C Middle East sacked by Churchill. Auchinleck knew that his post as C-in-C India was a consolation post and that it was to lose its operational responsibility for South-East Asia. This was to pass to the South-East Asia Command (SEAC) which was commanded, of course, by Mountbatten. Auchinleck, in effect, had been demoted. Mountbatten was dubbed 'pretty Dickie' by Auchinleck, while his staff laughed at what they considered to be the ineffectiveness of the SEAC. As India approached independence and Partition, Auchinleck and Mountbatten had to get on together.[26]

It was during this time that Auchinleck began one of his crusades. In a way it was yet another battle with Montgomery's undue influence when connected to Auchinleck and his career. In March 1944 Auchinleck received a reply to a letter that he had written to Brooke congratulating him on being promoted to field marshal, the highest rank in the British army, while asking him also to support his campaign to reverse the decision that only those who had fought under Montgomery should be entitled to the '8' emblem on the ribbon of the Africa Star. Brooke informed Auchinleck that the Honours Committee had refused his request. Auchinleck considered it unfair that those men who had saved Egypt in the First Battle of El Alamein or those who had fought in the Eighth Army since its establishment should be denied this recognition. The Honours Committee claimed that if this distinction was made in Auchinleck's favour, then a whole can of worms could be opened with other units making similar claims to other awards and they felt unable to deal with this.[27] However, whenever it came to a situation between Montgomery and Auchinleck, it seems it was always the latter that lost out.

There were other ways in which Auchinleck lost out to Montgomery as it was quite clear that Monty was the blue-eyed boy as far as Churchill was concerned and this was no more obvious than at the time of the Normandy landings in June 1944. Montgomery was C-in-C, 21st Army Group and by the end of the summer of 1944 Churchill had ensured that Montgomery had been promoted to the highest rank of the British army, that of field marshal. This was to ignore two things. Normandy was a very untidy campaign with the 21st Army Group making a lot of mistakes and it took the 1st Polish Armoured Division to pull the 21st Army Group's irons out of the fire with their valiant stand on Hill 262 or the Mont Ormel ridge which the Poles referred to as the *Maczuga* ('mace'). The 1st Polish Armoured Division wrecked the German withdrawal from Normandy. The other thing that Churchill had overlooked at the time of Montgomery's promotion was that General Alexander was C-in-C of the Allied armies in Italy and was senior to Montgomery in both service and active command. This led to much criticism, forcing Churchill to tell Alexander during September 1944 that he was preparing to promote him to the rank of field marshal with the promotion being backdated to the fall of Rome on 4 June 1944, which then preserved Alexander's seniority to that of Montgomery. Then as Greenwood observes in December 1944, General Wilson was also promoted to the rank of field marshal, the fourth such promotion made during 1944, and Auchinleck had been superseded for the third time.[28] The Home Guard veteran Colonel Foster made a comment on this odd arrangement in his diary, remarking: 'Alexander has been made a Field Marshal, with seniority over Montgomery; a strange method of promotion.'[29]

Greenwood, as Auchinleck's ADC, was witness to the comings and goings of visitors to Auchinleck and so was able to furnish history with a colourful picture of 'Vinegar Joe' Stilwell who visited for the first time 'armed to the hilt and his Philippino [*sic*] ADC, Major Young, arrived with a Sten gun across his shoulder.' No doubt Stilwell thought that he was entering 'enemy territory'. Stilwell was not only Mountbatten's deputy but was also the Commanding General of the United States Army Forces in China, Burma and India. Throughout lunch with Auchinleck, Stilwell continued to smoke a cigar as well as shouting orders to Young who was seated some yards away at the end of the table. Greenwood, however, recalled that in spite of the obvious differences between the two men, they did get along together. When Stilwell was finally recalled to the USA for a supposed lack of diplomacy when he argued with the Chinese leader Chiang Kai-shek, he wrote a personal letter to Auchinleck in which he thanked him for his friendship and hoped that he would visit him in his home in California.[30] Auchinleck had a knack for getting on with most people, so perhaps the problem with Montgomery lay with Monty and not with Auchinleck.

However, as 1944 turned into 1945 and the war in Europe seemed pretty much won, the war in the Pacific and South-East Asia continued. It was clear that the Japanese would be defeated, but the question was just how long this might take and at what cost to the Allies. The cost of defeating the Japanese was uppermost in some minds as morale was low in the Fourteenth Army fighting its way across Burma. These troops considered that they were the forgotten army and that every other front was better armed, better regarded at home and basically having a better time than they were. Furthermore, they considered that their wives and girlfriends were seeing soldiers from other countries, notably the USA, while the erratic supply of mail caused problems for those who had been in Burma for up to four years but had had no home leave. The British response was to erroneously blame the India command for inefficiency. Therefore the British government decided that all soldiers who had been overseas for more than three years and eight months should be repatriated to the UK. This, of course, would have weakened the forces in the Far East. Auchinleck in a letter to Wavell during December 1944 pointed to the folly of the proposed Whitehall plan. He must either be allowed to retain men longer than three years and eight months or operations against the Japanese would take longer and the war would be prolonged. Whitehall could not have it both ways, observed Auchinleck.[31]

Even if troops could be released from Europe, once Germany had been defeated, just how safe was the world? Nazism might well have been close to collapse, but Stalinism was beginning to sweep across east-central Europe as the Red Army advanced, installing Soviet-friendly regimes in its wake. For Auchinleck the most immediate concern was for the war in Asia and how it might turn out for the British and the Indians at a time of local discontent with British rule and the demand for Home Rule growing further.

For Auchinleck, 1945 started on a positive note as he was knighted in the 1945 New Year's Honours List, receiving the Knight Grand Cross of the Order of the Bath (GCB). In later life, Auchinleck only used this title as a suffix, ignoring all his other titles; therefore Field Marshal (as he became) Sir Claude Auchinleck, GCB. However, 1945 was also the beginning of a more difficult phase for him once the Japanese threat receded and the Japanese were finally defeated in August 1945. There were consequences for India once peace was restored in Asia as there had been an element of Indians who had sided with the Japanese during the war and now these men were to face up to their actions which some regarded as treasonable while others saw them as liberators. Auchinleck offered wise counsel during this period.

Early in 1945 a reorganization committee (India) was established to study the post-war composition of the British army with the assumption that India was to receive a measure of self-government, which meant that this study would encompass the Indian army. A major area of concern was the future of the Gurkhas who had served the British faithfully for well over a century by 1945. The viceroy was in London during March 1945 having consultations with the British government about India and its future. Auchinleck wrote to him, giving his comments and advice. It seemed unlikely that all the Gurkha outfits would be needed by the Indian army in the future; however, what was very important was just how the British government were going to employ the Gurkhas post-war. If the British government wanted to retain these men post-war, there was an added problem with the Nepalese religious authorities: would they allow their soldiers to serve overseas in peacetime? There was also the question of what to do about Gurkha officers who remained with the post-war Gurkha units serving in the Indian army. It was expected that the Indians would use their own officers, while the Nepalese would be resentful unless alternative training and employment could be found for Nepalese officers serving in the Indian army.

After being summoned to London to support his recommendations for post-war India, Auchinleck left Delhi on 28 April 1945. The European war was nearly at an end and on the day that Auchinleck travelled from India, the former Italian dictator Benito Mussolini was executed by his own countrymen. Auchinleck arrived in the UK shortly before the German surrender to Montgomery on Lüneburg Heath, Germany. He spent much of his time in London attending conferences at the India Office and at the War Office. However, during his time in London he failed to notice the gap between himself and his wife and the closeness of Jessie and Sir Richard Peirse. A private investiture was arranged at Buckingham Palace so that Auchinleck could receive his GCB from King George VI and Auchinleck went alone. However, Jessie did return in time to accompany Auchinleck to lunch at Chequers where Churchill entertained them on 20 May 1945. Auchinleck was spared any questions as the British prime minister was obsessed with the coming General Election.

All the same, Auchinleck spoke about the war in South-East Asia and spoke well of General William Slim, commander of the Fourteenth Army which had just recaptured the Burmese capital of Rangoon. Slim was considered the victor in Burma. Auchinleck considered that Slim was the best general of the Indian army and expressed the desire that in time, Slim might succeed him as commander-in-chief in India. However, change was in the wind as Auchinleck had received a letter from Slim on 17 May reporting that Oliver Leese proposed to relieve Slim of the Fourteenth Army so that mopping-up operations could continue in Burma and then garrison the country with a new army, the Twelfth Army. Slim was to hand over to General Philip Christison who would then prepare the Fourteenth Army for the invasion of Malaysia. Slim concluded his letter by stating that he did not wish to serve under a general who did not value him and have confidence in him. He then informed Auchinleck that he wished to retire.

Auchinleck, as the most senior officer in the Indian army, immediately went to see the CIGS and learn more of the situation regarding General Slim. On 22 May 1945 he lunched with Brooke, with Slim being the main subject of conversation. Auchinleck was soon to discover from Brooke that the situation was largely the fault of Mountbatten, who lacked leadership qualities. Brooke later recorded in his diary that 'Seldom has a supreme commander been more deficient of the main attributes of a Supreme Commander than Dickie Mountbatten.' On 22 May the Secretary of State for War, Sir Henry Page Croft, gave a lunch at his home for Auchinleck with Brooke present. Once more, the main subject of conversation was Slim and the question of Leese v. Slim. Once more it was concluded that Mountbatten and his poor leadership qualities were to blame. Greenwood certainly discusses the tensions felt at the beginning of May 1945 when it was first mooted that Slim should be removed and a defence of Slim was first mounted. May 1945 was a bad month for Auchinleck, not only because of the chaos surrounding the future of Slim but also because his marriage fell apart. On 26 May he returned to India but Jessie stayed in the UK with Sir Richard Peirse and Auchinleck was never to see her again.

Once back in India the question of Slim rose again. Auchinleck held a dinner at his home two weeks after his return and invited Mountbatten, while Leese was a house guest of Auchinleck and was present at the meal. On 27 June 1945 Auchinleck received a letter from Mountbatten marked on the envelope as being 'Top Secret – Strictly Personal and Private'. In it Mountbatten was by then trying to rid himself of blame for the situation that had arisen regarding Slim. Now, after learning of opposition from Brooke to the dismissal of Slim, he was trying to distance himself from the entire affair and was proposing removing Leese and promoting Slim. Auchinleck agreed with this approach, but refused to allow his name to be circulated as he did not want the impression given that he had been interfering with appointments made in the South-East Asia Command (SEAC). By 1 July 1945 Mountbatten was forced to sack Leese and elevate Slim.

As had been predicted, Mountbatten was a dead loss but was a royal and so people had to put up with his defects, even in time of war. It was not the last mistake that Mountbatten was to make during his time in Asia and one that was going to have a profound effect on millions of people and history. Therefore we can move on to the next stage of Auchinleck's active life as a military officer as he perhaps had much on which to reflect following the collapse of his marriage as well as having Dickie Mountbatten to contend with at a time that should have been seen as delicate as India moved towards independence.

The war in South-East Asia ended very suddenly owing to the use of nuclear weapons by the Americans. Many people had considered that the war against the Japanese had a few more years to run as there was still a lot of territory to re-conquer from them, and even more sea space. The Japanese fought fanatically, and it was clear that to take Japan itself would require a great deal of effort and would see hundreds of thousands of people dead. However, during the summer of 1945 the Americans had been finalizing tests of a nuclear or atomic bomb as it was then called. On 6 August 1945 an atomic bomb was dropped over Hiroshima and 80,000 people were killed instantly. Three days later, a further device was dropped over another Japanese city, Nagasaki. The impact of a second nuclear attack with a horrendous casualty rate compelled the Japanese people to accept unconditional surrender, but only the Japanese emperor was able to order his people to accept defeat, which he did in a broadcast to the nation. The war was over at last.

However, the Second World War was to have far-reaching repercussions. Even before the war was over, in the General Election of July 1945 there had been a huge shock when Churchill and his party were ousted from power as the Socialist-minded Labour Party won a landslide victory of 390 seats over the Conservative Party's meagre 195. This meant that the Labour Party was able to begin a radical programme of social reform without any hindrance owing to its vast majority. The ruling Labour Party also decided that India should be given dominion status, the same as Canada, New Zealand and Australia. However, nationalist Indian leaders such as Nehru and Jinnah considered that complete independence could not be too far away. Auchinleck also realized that radical reform was needed for the Indian army. A most obvious necessary reform was that of command as in 1945 the most senior-ranking Indian officer was a brigadier.

By the autumn of 1945 Auchinleck and his friend Field Marshal Brooke, who was now Lord Alanbrooke but still CIGS, were able to take advantage of the more liberal regime. Alanbrooke was able to travel to India, something that Churchill may well have forbidden; also the censures of international warfare had dictated the moves of various senior political and military figures. However, the new British Prime Minister Clement Attlee was happy enough for Alanbrooke to visit India. There were serious matters to be discussed and settled: the future of India and how the British were to withdraw from what had been the jewel in the imperial crown, which would prove to be no light undertaking.

A major problem with the British exit was how to deal with Indian troops who had served in the Indian army against the Japanese but had had the misfortune to be captured by their foe. During their time spent in Japanese captivity a large number of Indian troops had turned against the British and enlisted in the Indian National Army (INA). Many Indians, but not all, considered these men to be heroes as they were considered to be fighting for Indian independence, while the ruling British authorities, post-war, took quite a different view. It was something that Auchinleck had to deal with, but as an old India hand he was better than some gadfly like Mountbatten. A further aspect of Auchinleck being a safe pair of hands regarding the termination of British rule in India was the legacy of the Indian Rebellion of 1857–58, known in India and Pakistan as a War of Independence but more commonly known in the UK as the 'Indian Mutiny'. Neither side covered themselves in glory by the time the British restored order. Auchinleck's father had been witness to the fighting during the Indian Mutiny and without doubt would have witnessed the horrors carried out both by British troops and Indian troops loyal to the British and those Indian troops or sepoys that had revolted against British rule. The massacre of British women and children by sepoys was uppermost in the collective British mind. Mountbatten, as we shall see, lacked sensitivity and understanding while also lacking the common sense and intelligence to deal with the complexities that were India by 1945. Sugata Bose, a descendant of Subhas Chandra Bose, notes that the 1857 revolt inspired the INA.[32]

The problems of the INA began just before the Japanese surrendered as there is a record of talks beginning in July 1945, but the bulk of the problems carried on after the Japanese surrender. The leader of the INA was a Bengali civil servant called Subhas Chandra Bose who had been educated at Cambridge but had over time become a violent and dictatorial nationalist.[33] This might have been the British view but for the brutal actions of INA members against those who refused to join them while in Japanese captivity. After the war had ended the INA were returned to India, were segregated and graded into categories based on the gravity or otherwise of the crimes committed during their periods as prisoners of the Japanese. It was decided that only the ringleaders and those charged with atrocities would face courts-martial. Immediately the All-India Congress Committee, which after 1947 became the government of India, protested that the INA was only fighting for the freedom of their country and so demanded the immediate release of the INA defendants.[34]

However, it is worth taking a swift look at the INA. Some 60,000 Indians were captured at Singapore in February 1942. Many of these men had been separated from their original units, or their officers and NCOs had been killed. This meant that many of the men entering Japanese captivity were leaderless and bewildered. Despite their predicament, many Indian soldiers endured everything that Japanese captivity held and many died rather than betray their comrades. However, 25,000 were deceived into joining the so-called Co-Prosperity for South-East Asia Sphere from which they believed that with co-operation from the Japanese, India might achieve independence. Bose was not the first choice of leader as a Sikh officer, Mohan Singh, was the first leader but once he realized that the Japanese were not going to aid India, he resigned. In October 1943, under Japanese control, Bose set up the Provisional Government of Free India, aka Azad Hind, in Tokyo, taking the main portfolios of Head of State, Commander-in-Chief and Foreign Minister. He appointed a Cabinet, declared war on the UK and the USA and sent ambassadors to Germany, Italy and those countries under Axis control. The Japanese would not permit more than 16,000 men in the INA; the rest were returned as prisoners. A further 4,000 had resigned with Mohan Singh but fresh volunteers were found among those Indians living in Malaya and Singapore. Eventually 15,000 were formed into a single division and sent to Burma and Assam but were under-armed. The Japanese only allowed them rifles to fight with and so they were wasted. Their record was not good: no battles won, 750 men killed (only 3 of whom were officers), 5,000 deserted, 1,500 died of disease and the remainder were captured.

The Japanese objective was to maximize propaganda out of the INA who were depicted as an oppressed people striving to free themselves and their compatriots from imperial British bondage; the fact that their existence was virtually unknown in India was unhelpful. Bose was killed in an air crash in Taiwan on 18 August 1945 en route for Tokyo just after the Japanese surrender. It looked as if the INA's day was over but Nehru, as Indian independence was being argued over, took up their cause and they became a bargaining chip. Indian leaders who would soon be in power in independent India considered that the INA were trying to achieve independence for India and therefore should not be tried by either the British or a future Indian administration. Warner argued that if Bose had lived, this position would not have been possible. Indeed, not all Indians agreed with the position regarding the INA, while Auchinleck considered that the entire affair was Indian and that trials of the INA should be for the Indians and not the British.[35] The numbers involved regarding the INA vary as at Singapore the Japanese claimed nearly 50,000 Indians went over to them; the British claim 40,000.[36] Whatever the figures of 2011 read, it is certainly a lot more than was being debated in previous decades.

A conversation that took place at a small party on 15 November 1945 at the Chelmsford Club in Delhi underlined the problem facing the British as they attempted to try to convict members of the INA. It seemed that pro-independence lawyer Bhulabhai Desai was doing much of the talking, with the main subject being the INA and the forthcoming trials. An opinion was expressed that it was a great pity the trials had stirred up hatred and discontent throughout India, but Bhulabhai Desai parried this opinion with his own view that the real bitterness had begun on 21 October when Captain Nag and other defendants had been cross-examined. Desai observed that if any of the INA were executed by the British, it would create martyrs and probably lead to an armed revolution. He was asked about Indians who had remained loyal to the British and the king-emperor and had seen their own colleagues, during their periods of Japanese captivity, tortured by members of the INA for refusing to join them. Now these eyewitnesses wanted to see the INA prosecuted for their crimes. However, Desai dismissed these claims and accounts as being little more than from Indians tutored to make such allegations and demands.[37] If the British were astute they could avoid much of the fall-out from what was essentially an Indian problem as India was rapidly moving towards independence and the British would, in the long run, have no say in Indian matters. What the British wanted was a clean exit from India, so getting too mired in the question of the INA would have not been beneficial to this aim. An old India hand like Auchinleck would have been very well aware of this and so able to deal with what could have become an extremely sticky situation instead of one of relative harmony that allowed the British to leave India in 1947 with their dignity more or less intact.

The INA did indeed attract sympathy as it was reported that Major Charles M. Cockin said to Colonel K.S. Himatsinhji, who was on the general staff in New Delhi, that it was morally wrong for the British to judge them.[38] It was reported that there was sympathy in the Indian army for the INA, even if they doubted the motivations of INA members, considering them to be somewhat muddled and a mixture of wanting a better India or, more realistically, an independent India as well as saving their own lives.[39] A similar situation was experienced by Poles held captive as slave labour by the Soviets between 1939 and 1941 who without doubt reluctantly joined the Soviet-backed Polish army raised after 1941 on Soviet soil. These Poles, having failed to join the Western-backed Polish army also raised on Soviet soil, the so-called 'Anders Army', had to make do and fight alongside the Red Army but in the Soviet-dominated Berling's Army (named for General Zygmunt Berling) which was communist in name but not in nature with its members merely wanting to live and not die in the wastes of some wretched mine in the Soviet interior. It was a matter of life or death for both the Indians and Poles, while the question of consequences would have been a matter for the future, assuming they ever lived to tell their tale, especially those Poles fighting on the Russian Front. Of the Indian case, Connell notes that in the case of the surrender of Singapore in February 1942, 85,000 men surrendered to the Japanese army. Of the 85,000 captives, 60,000 were Indians of all ranks. Of this 60,000, 25,000 men joined the INA.[40]

On 12 February 1946 Auchinleck wrote his report on the question of the INA. It was very insightful. He suggested that every Indian worth his name was a 'nationalist' but that did not make him 'anti-British'; however, as far as Indian independence went there were no 'pro-British Indians'. Auchinleck considered the three worst of the INA offenders or defendants, depending on one's view, were Colonel Prem Sahgal, Colonel Gurbaksh Singh Dhillon and Major General Shah Nawaz Khan, all of whom had been captured by the Japanese in Malaya, Singapore and Burma and later fought alongside the Japanese in Imphal and Burma. Auchinleck reckoned that they had committed the worst crimes that a soldier could commit.[41] This overall, once the entirety of the INA trials were considered, comprised torture, murder or abetment to murder. The three senior officers were the only ones in the INA trials who were charged with 'waging war against the King-Emperor' as the 1911 Indian Army Act did not provide a separate charge for treason. Auchinleck questioned why these three senior officers had been treated so leniently, as he noted that they had only suffered being cashiered or transported and to where: the very remote Andaman Islands in the Bay of Bengal. He also noted that 20,000 men and officers had joined the INA.[42] Clearly he had both questions and concerns as it was quite clear that the British would be unable to try all 20,000 INA members even if they had the ability to do so at a time when even British officers, as we have already seen, questioned the moral right of the British to try INA members, especially as the British were about to leave India.

Auchinleck received a letter from Colonel K.S. Himatsinhji of the 7th Rajput Regiment. Himatsinhji wanted to discuss the situation in India which was simmering with resentment. This was not only against British rule, even though the British were close to leaving; there were also other political frustrations linked to fears for the future and where India was actually going in the near future. Himatsinhji wrote:

> Never before has the entire country been in such a hostile mood against the British Government as it is today. This is due to political frustration, and several other factors of which your Excellency is well aware. The demobilised ex-servicemen who remain unemployed, the released political detainees and INA personnel will make the

> situation worse. Whatever the motives of the INA, it has made a phenomenal impression upon the masses. It is believed by a vast majority of Indians that this was an army of liberation and would bring freedom to our country. It is the only issue upon which there is agreement between Congress and the Muslim League. The INA has aroused the imagination of all shades of opinion in the country: the Indian army (in spite what unit commanders may say!), students, merchants, the labour and Government servants alike. Certain 'prophets' in the IA [Indian Army] used to predict that when ex-INA personnel returned to their villages, the ex-prisoners of war would 'lynch and flay them alive'. Nothing of this sort ever happened. As a matter of fact, the ex-INA personnel have been well received by their villages. Morally this may not be justified. But the fact is that these men are the 'pets' of the country today. The following problems will stare the Government in the face in the near future:- Food crisis: Resultant deaths and consequent national agitation against the Government. The impending Parliamentary statement concerning the constitutional reforms to be given to India, which will be issued shortly and which is bound to have a mixed reception and generate further agitation against the government. Agitation for Pakistan. I therefore submit that as the government are likely to be confronted with certain major crises soon, it would be expedient to precipitate crises on matters other than those mentioned in para such as the INA. If any punishment is awarded to INA personnel, it would be denounced by all political parties. In view of the general policy of the government, it is unlikely that any accused in the INA trials will be awarded capital punishment. As a national government is bound to come into being in the near future, it is a foregone conclusion that they will release all INA personnel serving various terms of imprisonment. Knowing therefore that the sentences will be remitted within a few months, I suggest it would be a feather in the cap of the present government if it released all INA prisoners.[43]

Clearly Colonel Himatsinhji was considering the future of his country and made a lot of sense in his letter to Auchinleck. He was correct in that the INA basically united Indians against the British and he identified an issue that was beginning to make itself felt and would be a devastating legacy of post-empire India: the call for a separate homeland for Muslims, which was of course Pakistan or, as it was in 1947, a divided Pakistan; East Pakistan and West Pakistan with East Pakistan becoming Bangladesh after 1971. The division of India in 1947, known as Partition, brought about some of the worst examples of intercommunal violence seen in India and hundreds of thousands of people were killed as members of the differing religious communities found in India turned on one another with the main strife between Hindus and Muslims. It was for people like Auchinleck to consider advice given by those with valuable insight into problems that might blight independent India and then pass on his thoughts on to the British government as it prepared to grant independence to India and allow the British to leave. Auchinleck was certainly an influential figure and best prepared to peacefully lead the British army out of the country.

However, it was never that easy to try to whitewash the sins of the INA. While it was true that perhaps they were fighting for Indian independence – which is debatable as it was unlikely that the Japanese saw it that way – genuine crimes were also committed. These could not go unpunished, but the question was who should try to punish: the British or the Indians. Field Marshal Wavell, in his capacity as viceroy of India, wrote to Auchinleck to discuss the seven-year jail sentence that Captain Burhanuddin (2nd Baluch Regiment) had received. As Wavell pointed out, it was deserved as one Teja Singh had been placed on a table with his wrists bound to a rope 8ft from the ground and then the table was removed, leaving the hapless Teja Singh suspended; then he was beaten by 120 men under the orders of Burhanuddin until he lost consciousness and subsequently died.[44] This was straightforward torture and murder and no excuse can be accepted for this.

However, by May 1946 it was obvious that the INA were going to get their way as Nehru wrote to Auchinleck expressing his delight at the withdrawal of all the trials of INA personnel, saying that 'I am sure this decision will be widely welcomed and will help in producing an atmosphere which we all desire.' Nehru also claimed that while the regular Indian army was largely ignored, the INA was lionized. He was not certain why that should be, but made the observation that while

Indians were proud of the courage and capacity of the Indian army, it was often looked down on as an agent of a foreign power (Britain), yet Nehru was convinced that the motivation of the INA was patriotic and a desire for Indian freedom.[45] It could be that the lower ranks of the INA may have considered they were fighting for Indian freedom, but it still does not explain the brutality against those who did not wish to join them and the motivation of some of the senior officers can only be speculated upon.

In June 1946 Auchinleck reached the pinnacle of his military career when he was promoted to the highest rank of the British army: that of field marshal. Leo Amery was quick to send in his congratulations to Auchinleck and said that he had done better for India and the Empire than if he had marched from El Alamein to the Alps.[46] Amery was making an obvious reference to Auchinleck's victory at the First Battle of El Alamein which prepared the ground for Montgomery's seminal victory there at the second battle but never acknowledged Auchinleck's preparatory work. Of course Auchinleck was always happiest and most at ease while in India and it is there his legacy is best remembered as he was able – using his experience, understanding and tact in dealing with leading Indian personalities as well as the genuine affection that Indian troops had for him – to allow the British armed forces to withdraw from India with their dignity intact.

The British press was full of accolades for the newly-minted field marshal. *The Times* commented:

> His [Auchinleck's] period of command in the field was one in which the British forces were still inadequately equipped but the forces under his command nevertheless managed to snatch victory at Sidi Rezegh, and though defeated in the next campaign, succeeded in barring the road to Egypt against all expectation.[47]

Douglas Kay, writing in the *Daily Mail*, gives quite a testimony to Auchinleck:

> In that sense 'the Auk' is an unlucky soldier. Who now remembers, save those who wear their African ribbon without an '8', that it was he who formed the 8th Army and trained it for desert warfare?

> Who, except a few surviving 'Desert Rats', recalls those tense and triumphant days of November and December 1941 when he and they cleared Cyrenaica within a month, sent Rommel scuttling back beyond Benghazi with fewer than 50 tanks and put out of action 22,000 Germans and 39,000 Italians – a bigger bag than at El Alamein? The defeat of the next summer is remembered, for defeat rankles. Again, few know how close we came to victory. Many forgot that it was 'the Auk' who took command in person in the critical 48 hours early in July when the stopper was driven into the Alamein bottleneck and the Axis dream of victory in Africa was ended for ever.

Kay observed that Auchinleck was sacked before sufficient arms were made available for his forces in North Africa. Kay continued in his appraisal of Auchinleck by quoting Lieutenant General Sir Giffard Martel's work *Our Armed Forces* which read: 'Before he left the Middle East, General Auchinleck had planned a counter-offensive which was to be launched as soon as he had the necessary reinforcements in troops and equipment. There was no great difference between his plans and those finally adopted by the new commanders.'[48] Clearly there were some who still remembered Auchinleck's skilled tactics in North Africa and knew what his successors in that theatre owed him, but all too soon events in India involving the INA were upon him as the nation drew ever nearer towards independence.

On 17 June 1946 Auchinleck received a letter from the private secretary to the viceroy which discussed the matter of the Royal Indian Navy (RIN) courts-martial. These were the results of mutinies on various RIN ships and shore establishments which in many cases had amounted to little more than refusals to work, raising the Indian tricolour or shouting pro-Indian and anti-British slogans. However, the matter of HMIS *Kathiawar*, a minesweeper, there were four cases of mutiny which Auchinleck's correspondent considered to be 'mutiny on the high seas' and 'too serious an offence to be dealt with other than severely'. The worry was that if very serious cases of mutiny were not punished adequately, it might be a problem in the future.[49]

Auchinleck may have suspected that this was correct, but it was not to be a British problem in the future of India; furthermore, there was limited support for the discontent within the RIN. No doubt Auchinleck may have considered the Invergordon Mutiny of 15–16 September 1931 – which was more of an industrial action – when around 1,000 sailors in the British Atlantic Fleet mutinied over a cut in wages with some pro-communist underlining. Some of the ringleaders were imprisoned, while about 200 were dismissed from the Royal Navy. No doubt Auchinleck considered these events while trying to deal with what some considered to be traitors, while others considered them to be heroes. It should also be noted that there had been mutinies among the British army owing to the slow pace of demobilization.[50] Alex von Tunzelmann notes that in 1946 India was 'a mess' with many British civil and military officers waiting to go home.[51] There was no reason for the British to continue in India and those from the citizens' army, which was what the conscripted Second World War British armed forces became, just wanted to go home. A new socialist government had been elected and the UK was changing; also after years of separation, serving and fighting a terrible war, it was not surprising this was what many Brits wanted to do. The British withdrawal was swift: in 1947 there were only 11,400 British troops in India and by April 1948, the figure was just 4,000.[52]

Auchinleck, as he was tasked with leading the British army out of India, always had an eye to the future as can be seen in two documents, which in many ways seemed centuries apart in their discussion. The first is a statement of the geo-political situation in India once the British left and reads thus:

> With the coming of atomic warfare there is increased necessity for space, which will allow for the proper dispersion of base installations. It is not possible to estimate whether Russia would actually establish bases in India, but with her taste for world power politics, it is considered likely that Russia would take advantage of an unprecedented opportunity to establish herself in a position from where she could threaten the whole fabric of the British Commonwealth. History had shown that nature abhors a vacuum and if the British step out, we can expect the Russians to step in.[53]

Without doubt this was true as the Soviet Union was seeking to continue gaining war booty after annexing East-Central Europe between 1944 and 1945. The Soviets were looking for further trophies and taking India from the British would have been a major feather in the Soviet cap, especially as India had been the jewel in the imperial British crown. The use of the word 'Commonwealth' rather than 'Empire' is also interesting and was part of the British strategy for leaving India. They wanted to leave a 'decent record' on their departure from India and hoped that their influence would overall be seen as positive. This had largely worked in today's India but less so in modern Pakistan where other influences are at play, but Soviet influence never really manifested in what had been British India.

Then in total contrast, Auchinleck, instead of discussing atomic warfare, made the following statement: 'I think we want a new hand-to-hand weapon (on the lines of the kukri) to replace the bayonet, which must follow the rifle into the museum.'[54] If he was considering the terrifying yet overlong sword bayonet used with great vigour in North Africa, he had a point. In close combat such as urban fighting or jungle fighting, such a bayonet fixed on a rifle was too long and too unwieldy, coupled with a bolt-action rifle which had also had its day as automatic and semi-automatic rifles had made their presence felt on the battlefields since at least the First World War. Bayonets became shorter and were certainly instrumental in open warfare thirty-six years later in the Falklands War of 1982.

By October 1946 some of the leading mutineers had been convicted and sentenced and it had not gone all the way that some Indian nationalists might have wanted. However, those who had been sentenced to imprisonment had not been convicted of political crimes but of genuinely serious criminal acts such as murder and torture. Suba Shingara Singh of the 5/14 Punjab Regiment was charged with waging war against the king-emperor, but his crimes also included three counts of murder and two of bodily harm. For this he received fourteen years of rigorous imprisonment (RI) or, in the British vernacular, 'hard labour'. Jem Fateh Khan of the same regiment received the same sentence. Captain Burhanuddin, 2nd Baluch Regiment, for waging war against the king-emperor as well as committing 'grievous harm' received seven years' RI. The trials took place between August 1945 and March 1946 with sentences commencing from the date of the end of the trial. Under normal circumstances, it was related, these sentences would all have been reviewed in January 1947.[55]

What should be considered is that in normal circumstances, the two murderers would have been hanged, including Europeans who had committed such heinous crimes. There was no excuse, but everyday norms were being subverted to try to avoid a difficult passage out of India for the British. The horrendous crimes of these men had been made public knowledge with trials at the Red Fort, but little would move the British to seek the death penalty for murderers as in a few years it would not be their problem once India became independent. There was no advantage in stirring up an already furious hornets' nest of Indian discontent with the British. Nehru, writing to Baldev Singh Ji on Christmas Day 1946, wrote of his concerns about INA men still in jail which was fuelling the growing agitation in Punjab.[56] This was the problem facing the authorities in India in the period leading to the withdrawal of the British from the subcontinent. No matter what, Indians in jail for some very good reasons which had nothing to do with Indian independence always caused civil strife and widespread rioting against British rule.

Auchinleck was just as concerned about the situation as it deteriorated owing to INA men remaining in jail. As he wrote to Sardar Baldev Singh, even though the continued imprisonment presented a challenge to the authorities, including the interim government, there was little that could be done as the crimes committed were neither conscious nor political but were serious crimes of murder and cruelty. Auchinleck questioned whether these crimes could really be condoned, and he reminded Singh that Indians committed these atrocious acts against their fellow countrymen. He mentioned the two officers who had committed murder and received a relatively light sentence of fourteen years each, while another officer had received only seven years for attempted murder. As Auchinleck wrote, of all the men who had been convicted, not one had been convicted of what anyone could interpret as a political crime 'but of crimes against humanity'. As he outlined to Singh:

> These despicable crimes were carried out against their own former comrades in arms who, through no fault of their own, found

> themselves helpless prisoners of the Japanese, avowed enemies of liberty and civilisation. These men took advantage of their position as collaborators with the Japanese to ill treat and even murder their own unfortunate countrymen.

Auchinleck remarked that one could not remit the sentences of the two murderers and that if one started 'tinkering' with the sentences or releasing men prematurely from jail, such actions would eventually cause problems. His bottom line was that the INA men were not convicted for membership of the INA but for the genuine crimes of murder, mutiny or aiding mutiny.[57]

The question of how to deal with the INA would not go away, as Wavell wrote to Auchinleck in early January 1947 relating a visit he had had from Baldev Singh. He stated:

> Baldev Singh came to see me this morning about the matter of the INA. He said that a resolution is likely to be moved in the Assembly early in February [1947] about the release of the INA men still under sentence, and that will have the support of both the Congress and the Muslim League. He said that further demands were likely to be made for the restoration of payment to the INA men and also for their re-instatement in the Army. A meeting in Calcutta will be held on January 23rd, at which the INA will put forward their demands. Baldev Singh seemed to be inclined to give way over the release of prisoners and of payment of arrears, not because he really thought they were justified himself, but to relieve political pressure. He agreed that re-instatement would be a serious matter but said that it might well be pressed. I warned him most forcibly indeed any concession to the INA, even the release of prisoners, would be fatal for the Indian Army; that it would almost certainly make it impossible for the Commander-in-Chief, or any senior officers of the British Army, to remain responsible for the Indian Army, and I should find it impossible to accept responsibility for the security of India if the confidence of the Army was shaken in this way. I said that it seemed to me to be sheer madness to treat the INA as heroes when most of them were the weakest part of the Army, men who had

> joined our enemies for the most part fear of hardship and danger rather than from patriotism; if those who had stood firm to their oath, who were the greatest part of the captured, were to see the INA treated like this, the effect would be fatal to the Indian Army. Baldev said that he would represent what I had said to the political leaders, but he held out no great hope of being able to convince them. I am sure however that if we stand firm on this, we shall gain our point. I trust therefore that you intend to maintain absolutely that you cannot consent in any circumstance to any further concessions of any kind to the INA. I am sure that all the senior officers of the Army will support you in this matter, and I shall of course do so.[58]

This was the problem for the British as they prepared to leave India: the INA were clearly in breach of criminal law and common human decency, but this failed to impress millions of Indians who appeared to unify around the INA in a common theme of anti-Britishness. This unity transcended all religious commitments, namely Hindu, Muslim or Sikh, the main religions of India, and often descended into intercommunal violence as was the case once the British departed and the new India and Pakistan were born.

As 1947 progressed, Auchinleck was charged to plan and enact the handing over of Indian military resources to the new Indian and Pakistani military authorities prior to the new republics proclaiming their independence. During June 1947, he wrote to General Lord Ismay, who was serving as Lord Mountbatten's chief of staff, expressing his vision of how the division of the Indian armed forces should be carried out:

> I cannot stress too strongly my conviction that the success of any plan for the division of the Indian Armed Forces depends on the willing co-operation of the British officers now serving with them, the greater majority of whom it will be essential to retain during the process of reconstitution. The goodwill of British officers is more likely to be secured if the Partition Committee – on behalf of the future Governments of Hindustan (India) and Pakistan – openly state that the services of British officers are essential to the success of reconstitution, notwithstanding the 'Quit India' cry of the past,

> and request them to remain in positions of command and on the staff during the period of the reconstitution of the Armed Forces. I hope that this may be done, as I am not at all certain in my own mind that the requisite number of British officers will wish to stay on, and I am most strongly opposed to the application of any form of compulsion to them.[59]

The problem was that the question of Indian independence and a British government taking the issue seriously, let alone granting it, had only been a recent thing and had more to do with the effects of the Second World War which had left the UK bankrupt and unable to continue maintaining its empire, especially a seething India which was growing progressively more hostile towards British occupation. Furthermore, a more radical Labour government had been elected in the UK during July 1945 and this government had agreed to Indian independence. The problem was that Mountbatten, the last viceroy of India, had suddenly increased the pace of Indian independence and the British departure from India to a timetable of weeks with 15 August 1947 being slated as Independence Day, while Pakistan proclaimed 14 August 1947 as its own Independence Day.[60] The rushed timetable was not to many people's liking, especially those who understood India, and it probably was the catalyst for the mass killings that soured independence as various religious groups moved to areas of safety for themselves. During these mass movements of people, commonly called Partition, rival religious groups ambushed and massacred their perceived religious foes.

Nevertheless, the British withdrawal from India was happening, as was Indian and Pakistani independence, and the British authorities continued to try to make an orderly withdrawal from the subcontinent. To this end, instructions were issued on how best to re-orientate the Indian army into Indian and Pakistani armed forces as can be seen in a document referred to as 'Terms of Reference of the Armed Forces Reconstitution Committee' dated 5 July 1947, less than two months before the British withdrawal. The basic premise for dividing up the soon-to-be former Indian army was that of religion and so it was decided that

> the next stage would be to comb out the units themselves on the basis of voluntary transfers. All personnel now serving in the Armed Forces would be entitled to elect which Dominion they choose to serve in. To this, however, there would be one exception, that a Muslim from Pakistan now serving in the Armed Forces will not have the option to join the Armed Forces of the Indian Union, and similarly a non-Muslim from the rest of India now serving in the Armed Forces will not have the option to join the Armed Forces of Pakistan. There will, however, be no objection to non-Muslim personnel from Pakistan and Muslim personnel from the rest of India electing to serve in the Armed Forces of the Indian Union and of Pakistan respectively.[61]

It is quite clear that there was very little chance of any religious unity between the two new states and that, even in the collective mind of the British, Muslims were going to Pakistan and Hindus to India. There was to be no meeting of minds in 1947 and the situation was about to get worse, while subsequent wars between India and Pakistan in 1947, 1965 and 1971 illustrate the poor relationship between the two countries. A dispute over Kashmir also serves to aggravate relations between India and Pakistan. However, it was the matter of the INA that still served to queer the pitch of the British withdrawal.

As the deadline for Indian independence approached, there was still correspondence about the INA trials and the verdicts, and it was something into which the British would soon have no input. Auchinleck wrote to the Viscountess of Burma regarding a letter that she had received from a Mrs Kiani dated 8 July 1947, which the viscountess had redirected to Auchinleck. It is clear that the latter had not altered his opinion in connection with the outcome of the INA trials. He wrote:

> My opinion in this matter remains unchanged. It is to the effect that to reinstate the officers and men of the so-called INA in the Indian Army as it exists today would run the gravest risk of disrupting the Army and ruining its reliability and morale, particularly as it is still largely officered, especially in the senior ranks, by British officers. The whole question was reviewed a few months ago by the

> present exclusively Indian Government which made no suggestion whatever that these men should be reinstated in the army as then constituted. They wish to have the twelve convicts of the INA still in prison released but made no other proposals for the condonation or restoration of the INA as a whole. In the circumstances existing today, I feel that all the other circumstances apart, it would be improper and impossible for political reasons alone for the present government to reinstate these men and thus present the Dominion Governments which are so shortly to succeed with an accomplished fact, which they would find difficult, if not impossible to repudiate, however much they might wish to do so. One cannot help feeling some sympathy for these misguided men, but they were lightly punished for the most dreadful crime that a soldier can commit in war and it would be criminal to risk the causing of strife, misery and suffering amongst innocent and loyal men simply to reinstate them. I am sorry for Mrs Kiani, but I suggest that you should tell her that it is now too late to expect this dying Government to take any action in the matter and that she might perhaps appeal to the new Dominion Government or Governments when these take office next month. I must tell you, however, that should my advice be asked by these new Governments regarding the officers and men of the INA, I should say what I have always said on this subject, which is that it would be dangerous to the morale and reliability of the Army or Armies to take them back and I am sure that I am right.[62]

Auchinleck, as a professional soldier, was horrified by the actions of the INA and was genuinely concerned that officers of the INA were going to get away scot-free with their crimes of murder and torture. These convictions had nothing to do with nationalism but were the actions of thugs. However, in the atmosphere of anti-Britishness there was little chance of the ordinary Indian seeing this with so many regarding the INA as heroes and possibly martyrs, the very reason that death sentences were not handed down in the first place. Auchinleck was well aware that the writ of British justice was near its end in India and that within a few weeks the issue of the INA would be a matter for the Indians and they could and would dispose of it as they saw fit. He wished only to advise and try to point out the grievous wrongs that the INA had committed, and that to release them from what seemed to be very lenient sentences would harm the morale of the new armies of India and Pakistan. In this case he was wrong.

Nehru, however, appealed to Mountbatten weeks before independence and made his case about the INA prisoners. He reminded Mountbatten of the legal process to which the INA prisoners had been subjected and that there was much speculation on their futures as there was still a process to be continued because the sentences and judgements were at that time being reviewed by Federal Court judges, probably with a view to releasing the INA prisoners as Independence Day was coming fast. Nehru made his observations clear to Mountbatten:

> As you will no doubt appreciate, an entirely new situation arises because of the political changes that have taken place. Normally speaking it would be entirely inappropriate for any political prisoners or those considered as political prisoners to be kept in prison after the declaration of Indian independence. There would be a wide-spread feeling amongst the people that independence was not real and was only a façade if such prisoners continued to be detained. It seems to me essential therefore that on or before the 15th August INA prisoners should be released. I am quite certain that if this release does not take place, the matter will be raised in the Constitutional Assembly which will be functioning then as a sovereign Legislative Assembly. [Marginalia in pencil – 'not yet political prisoners'.] There is another aspect of this case. It is possible that the Pakistan Government may take some action in this matter and release the prisoners in their charge. Indeed I am told that assurances to this effect have been given. If this happens, as it very probably will, then the retention in prisons at the insistence of the India Government would be very difficult if not impossible and would give rise to tremendous public opinion. In view of this situation I wish to suggest to you that very early steps should be taken to release these prisoners. This can be done quite appropriately and without any reference to the past in view of the new political status of India. If this is not done, a new public demand will arise and

> then we shall have to do it in response to that demand. It is thus far better to keep the initiative with ourselves than be compelled by circumstances to take action.[63]

This was something with which Auchinleck could not agree, and he said so in a letter to the viceroy's private secretary. His attitude was that political change had not yet taken place and that nothing had changed. He did not deny that change was afoot, but nothing was going to happen until 15 August and observed that the INA prisoners were not political prisoners but were indeed 'murderers and brutes'. Obviously he was referring to the fact that many of the INA convicts had been treated leniently, given that some had been convicted of murder and torture. However, Auchinleck conceded that he was willing to

> put into effect without question any recommendations that the Judges' Committee may make, but I cannot agree to take independent action for the summary release of these men on grounds of purely political expediency. There is no logical reason at all that I can see why this should be done and I recommend most strongly that it should not be done. On the 15th August either or both of the Dominion Governments (India and Pakistan) will be at liberty to take any action they like in the matter.[64]

Clearly Auchinleck was determined to continue the British line regarding the INA, one that was very lenient given the severity of the crimes, while his attitude was that once an independent India and Pakistan came into being on 15 August 1947, the matter of the INA would suddenly become an Indian or Pakistani affair and the British were quite happy to leave it at that.

In addition to considering the INA and the future after 15 August 1947, Auchinleck also wrote about the future regarding ongoing military actions, especially on the ever-restless North-West Frontier where rebellious tribes frequently made sallies out from the Afghan frontier area into India. Retaliatory or punitive actions in the frontier were carefully controlled with instructions as laid down in the 'Grey Book'. Auchinleck suggested that the 'Grey Book' was a guide 'to ensure that military action is executed with due regard to the principles in a civilized country'.[65] Given that a supposedly civilized country, Germany, had been found guilty of slaughtering millions of people and pursuing genocidal policies, it was difficult to decide what was meant by a civilized country, but by implication he meant Britain and went further, considering that Pakistan might be less restrained, especially when bombing villages. This was surely a crime in itself. However, Auchinleck declared, regarding the bombing of villages:

> In this event I consider it is important that the position of the British officers and other ranks of the RAF should be made clear. The Pakistan Air Force will be operating under a British Commander and British other ranks will be assisting to service the aircraft. If the methods of the Pakistan Air Force depart from those acceptable to public opinion in the United Kingdom, it may well lead to an outcry in the press of the UK and to questions in Parliament. It would seem prudent to face this very real possibility now, and to inform the Pakistan Government that the loan of British personnel to the Armed Forces of Pakistan is of course on the assumption that safeguards observed in the past to ensure humane standards are also observed in the future.[66]

Auchinleck was right to anticipate bloodshed and a standard that fell far short of what the British might have expected, but the horrors visited on partitioned ex-British India without doubt shocked him. The wholesale massacre of men, women and children by members of opposing religions was horrific. It must have seemed that the massacres of the 1850s that had so haunted Auchinleck's father were happening once more, but this time the British were not involved. A report of the time gives colour to the horrors being visited on India during the weeks immediately after Independence Day, 15 August 1947. Major General J.B. Dalison reported on an attack by Sikhs against Muslims on 24 August 1947:

> …there was then 'pandemonium' at the rear of the train. Meanwhile large numbers of Sikhs stood outside my carriage saying there was no intention of harming the British. Lt. Col.

DRAPER (FARMS) who was in the next compartment says he was told by a NIHANG (armed Sikh warrior) 'We have orders not to harm the British this time.' He speaks Punjabi well. I found that the train had been systematically searched, every MUSSELMAN murdered who had been identified as such and the brake vans were completely looted. No British were touched nor was the luggage which was in the compartments. Some MUSSELMANS who were not readily identifiable were not harmed. For instance, almost immediately after my bearer was killed another servant got through the window of my wife's side of the carriage, exclaiming that he was a HINDU. He, unlike our own bearer, was a doubtful case. The Sikhs poked in their spears and started questioning him but a NIHANG called them off. I feel that in deference to my wife's presence that he did not apply the physical test which, I understand, was elsewhere applied. The Sikhs, though seemingly a rabble, were well organised. For instance their murder and looting was systematic, and parties were specially detailed to cut off those who tried to run for it. Many of the dead were replaced in the train by the Sikhs. Two injured were expected to live. Total casualties are expected to be thirty. I sincerely hope that one of the punishments imposed on the village of MAUR will be a collective fine in which case I should be glad to receive some thousands of rupees in order in some measure to compensate my bearer's family and to enable my wife and myself to replace some of our kit which was looted from the brake van.

Major-General Dalison, Adjutant General AHQ, Pakistan.[67]

This was an obviously horrific incident – similarly carried out many times across India – and this time with an implicit threat towards the British that bore shadows of the Indian Mutiny of ninety years earlier. The physical examination would have been to check if their victim was circumcised and therefore a Muslim; a primitive and somewhat inexact method of checking the identity of one's victims.

Meanwhile, Auchinleck was having his own problems with his position of being Supreme Commander in India and Pakistan once those two countries had achieved independence in mid-August 1947. Mountbatten wrote to Auchinleck and informed him that the Indians resented Auchinleck being Supreme Commander and said:

> I am sorry to say that I have completely failed to convince them – the heated arguments at Tuesday's meeting of the Defence Committee may have been the last straw – and the point has now been reached when I can no longer prevent them from putting up an official proposal to the Joint Defence Council that the Supreme Headquarters should be abolished and replaced by an organisation with a less high-sounding title and headed by a less high-ranking officer. The discussion of a proposal of this kind in the Joint Defence Council would be absolutely deplorable. It is possible that the Pakistan representatives would oppose the proposal out of cussedness, but not, I fear, out of any sincere desire to support you. It is only a short while ago that they were pressing for your removal on the grounds of your alleged anti-Moslem sentiments during the Gurgaon disturbances. But whatever line Pakistan might take, I, myself, would find it a most difficult case to argue.

Then, rather oddly, Mountbatten recommended Auchinleck for a peerage.[68]

Another person agitating for his removal was Montgomery, who was now CIGS, and he wrote to Mountbatten as follows:

> It is my opinion that Auchinleck's usefulness in India is finished. He is sixty-three; he has spent all his life in India under a previous regime; he is too old to re-adjust himself to new ideas which he dislikes in his heart. He is viewed with suspicion by the senior officers of the Indian army. I personally consider that if you want military matters to run smoothly and efficiently you will have to remove Auchinleck.[69]

Montgomery continued to put the boot in whenever he could against Auchinleck, as Zeigler finishes this quote: '…I further consider that if you do *not* do so you will have trouble…. I would tell Auchinleck to retire and recommend him for a GCSI [Knight Grand Commander of the

Order of the Star of India], nothing more.'[70] This was extremely arrogant and rude of Montgomery, as if he had had his way, he would have ignored Auchinleck's long career and considerable achievements during the years he had served as an officer in the Indian army. Yet in so many ways it says more about the inadequacies of Montgomery than his perceived defects in the character of Auchinleck.

Mountbatten was unhappy about how Montgomery suggested that Auchinleck should be disposed of and certainly challenged the attempt to fob him off with a GCSI. He agreed that the Supreme Command of India should close down, but told Montgomery that 'Auchinleck's Indian career had been a singularly long and a fine one, and I have the Prime Minister's permission to ask him if he would wish to have a peerage.' To Attlee, Mountbatten had said it was only a matter of days before the Indian government demanded Auchinleck's recall and told the prime minister that 'I want him to go while he can still go with a reputation as the greatest Commander-in-Chief the Indian Army has had for many years. If he holds on he will lose that reputation.'[71] Timing was all and perhaps Mountbatten was correct; if Auchinleck had tried to resist leaving India, he might have lost the goodwill that he had garnered over his entire military career.

It might have been that Mountbatten was trying to kick the problem of the British Supreme Commander further down the street in his recommending Auchinleck for a peerage. However, this was also to do with trying to remove Auchinleck himself as Attlee had already agreed that Auchinleck should go, while Auchinleck had never liked Mountbatten. Auchinleck was to criticize Mountbatten for his lack of knowledge of India, as well as being surrounded by some 'odd' advisors, but it was not one-way traffic and he was also responsible for some of the horrors that happened in Punjab once India and Pakistan separated from one another. Auchinleck was obsessed with the Indian army as an institution, considering that it had a life and importance above its duty to the people it served. During August 1947, he should have allowed the use of British and Gurkha troops to protect those who were massacred. White-Spunner considered all of this and argued that the British should have been used to protect those migrating and religious minorities, but were reluctant to suppress 'internal unrest' despite that being its job. The main problem – one dating back to the Indian Mutiny – was that in the heads of the British, British troops were only to protect the lives of the British. This attitude allowed for the massacres of the Punjab during the summer of 1947.[72]

It should be noted that some senior Indian officers felt betrayed by independence and the rapid pace at which it took place. Ismay was told by an old friend and senior officer of the Indian army that 'We soldiers have trusted you for forty years and now you are going to betray us.'[73] Mountbatten's acceleration of the independence programme was a major problem and it is certain that Auchinleck would have preferred far slower progress and achieved a better result for the division of the Indian army between Pakistan and India. There were suspicions that Auchinleck, like many British army officers, preferred Muslims to Hindus but he was prepared to ensure equity between the two faiths and peoples in the disposal of the post-British Indian army. Nehru and Baldev Singh were on the verge of refusing to accept Auchinleck as Supreme Commander, but Mountbatten managed to negotiate this away.[74] The latter also got caught up in some of the in-fighting around the break-up of the Indian army. He feared that Baldev Singh and Auchinleck would not work together and so asked Nehru to select another candidate as Indian Defence Minister, but Baldev Singh and Auchinleck proved that they would work together. Unfortunately, in the meantime, Nehru had selected a man who Fred Burrows, a former trade union official and now the governor of Bengal, described as being 'so low that a snake could not crawl under his belly'. Mountbatten had to quickly return to Nehru and claim that perhaps Baldev Singh was the right man for Defence Minister after all.[75]

The situation was often quite fraught as the baggage of British imperial rule in India was beginning to become quite awkward, while a number of Indian political actors were hardly respectable or trustworthy. The rapid independence programme had a whiff of British panic about it as inter-communal violence began to break out across India. It would seem that the British, on the whole, had had enough and just wanted to go home and leave India to sort itself out.[76] For decades, leading Indians had pressed for independence and now they were about to get it but not in the circumstances that they might have wanted.

Any dismissal of Auchinleck might have pandered to the vanity of some of the Indian negotiators, but probably not as the problem was that the Indians had achieved independence but still found that some aspects such as the redistribution of assets including the military were still withheld from them. However, the assets were British, and it was unlikely that the Indians and Pakistanis would agree over anything regarding weapons as by September there had been enough blood spilt as a result of Partition.

General Ismay wrote to Auchinleck and told him that the entire episode connected to the question of the Supreme Commander had reached an impasse.[77] It was on that day that Mountbatten had to write 'probably the most difficult letter' that he had ever written in his life. He argued his letter of Auchinleck's dismissal in the most diplomatic of terms, using flattery and guile. He described the resentment of Indians regarding the presence of a high-ranking officer such as Auchinleck in the Supreme Headquarters. He discussed Auchinleck's ability as 'a man of your very high rank and great personal prestige and reputation'. Mountbatten described how he tried to persuade senior Indians that concerns about Auchinleck's impartiality were without foundation, but this issue was due to be raised in the Joint Defence Council. In the past Auchinleck had told Mountbatten that he was quite willing to disappear from the scene, so Mountbatten asked him if he could now 'take advantage of your selfless offer'.[78]

Auchinleck was quite willing to leave India discreetly and so he began to tie up loose ends, which as ever meant reports and advice. He made his own report to the Cabinet and Chiefs of Staff in London on the situation in India and Pakistan and was critical of Pakistan. His observation was that the Pakistani government had 'removed themselves from Delhi with almost indecent haste and proceeded to establish as far as possible at Karachi'. Auchinleck was of the opinion that if the Pakistanis had stayed in Delhi it might have been possible to have prevented the slaughters of Partition.[79]

He was probably right in his observations of the Pakistani government; they had withdrawn swiftly to their own capital and were not really negotiating with the Indians. Of the two peoples, the Indians and the Pakistanis as they had become in 1947, Auchinleck understood the Pakistanis better owing to his service with the by then former Indian army.

Whether a closer relationship between the two governments would have prevented the slaughter on the frontiers will have to remain a moot point; who knows? From the information gleaned from Mountbatten, Ismay and Auchinleck it can be assumed that neither of the two governments that had emerged from British India were willing to truly work together and merely sought to score off one another and try to gain as much of the ex-Indian armed forces as possible.

In the second part of his report, Auchinleck gave further information concerning the situation in independent India. The first thing he stated was that there was a risk of war between India and Pakistan at very short notice.[80] This was an astute judgement as the following month war did break out between India and Pakistan over the disputed Kashmir area; this war lasted through 1948. This was just the beginning of a number of conflicts over Kashmir; indeed, at the time of writing this book in 2019, India and Pakistan are fighting over Kashmir once again.

Auchinleck was very concerned about the safety of British civilians who were still in India and the need to protect them. However, there were few British troops left in the country and each month their number was being reduced. He explained the situation in India since Independence Day and wrote:

> Since the 15th August the situation had steadily deteriorated and the Indian leaders, cabinet ministers, civil officials and others have persistently tried to obstruct the work of partition of the Armed Forces. I and my officers have been continuously and virulently accused of being pro-Pakistan and partial, whereas the truth is that we have merely tried to do our duty impartially and without fear, favour or affection. That we have done this is universally acknowledged by all fair-minded people. This campaign continues and grows stronger and more vicious every day. The Governor-General, Lord Mountbatten, is subjected to the strongest and unceasing pressure to abolish my headquarters so that the one impartial body remaining in this country could be removed.

Auchinleck claimed that the motivation of the Indians was to try to deny the Pakistanis their fair share of military equipment in India. According to him, 'the attitude of Pakistan on the other hand, had been reasonable and co-operative throughout. This is natural in the circumstances, as Pakistan had practically nothing of her own and must obtain most of what she wants from the reserves of stores etc now lying in India.' He reported that the massacres had sickened most British officers and that they had lost faith in their men of whom they were so proud only two months earlier. Auchinleck also placed the blame on the Sikhs, of whom he said were 'the worse'. The situation, according to Auchinleck, was appalling as

> It is commonly believed that the rulers of the Sikh States in the Eastern Punjab have been behind the campaign of extermination, for such it is, the East Punjab. They certainly do not appear to have done anything to stop it, in spite of their protestations. Today, there is an organised system of information and control which enables Muslim refugee trains to be attacked with impunity. A few days ago, 1,500 helpless refugees are said to have been massacred in one such train alone at Amritsar, the escort, including the British officer in command, being killed or wounded. On the other hand, military trains carrying troops and stores in the furtherance of Reconstitution are unmolested.

Even so, Auchinleck reported that there was so far no evidence of any general anti-British feeling or of any immediate danger to British lives or to their property. However, death threats had been issued against British officers and British women who had been helping Muslim refugees and Auchinleck considered that perhaps it was indeed time to leave India. The situation was worsening and there was clearly a fear that given time the British, as they wound down their presence in India, would fall victim to the mobs who were rampaging seeking victims. Although without doubt Auchinleck did so with a heavy heart, he did, as we have seen, advise that the British should leave and allow the Indians and Pakistanis to determine their own future, no matter how murderous it looked.

It should be noted that there was a fear for the safety of British civilians living in the Kashmir region in the city of Srinagar as it was thought that Pathan tribesmen were advancing towards the city. Auchinleck had pleaded to be allowed to send British troops to the area. Mountbatten considered that this would be improper. Auchinleck said to Mountbatten: 'Those people will be massacred, and their blood will be on your head.' Mountbatten replied: 'I shall have to take responsibility, but I could not answer for what might happen if British troops became involved.' However, the Indian army intervened and intercepted the marauding tribesmen, thus preventing any trouble for the British residents in Srinagar.[81]

The situation in India post-independence was unravelling fast, while the situation for Britons was becoming more dangerous by the day. There was intelligence suggesting that the Sikhs were also trying to get their own independent state with Simla as the capital of the proposed state. Auchinleck, in his report on the state of India, identified the Maharaja of Faridkot as 'in this business up to his neck'. He accused the Maharaja of having told 'poor old Miss Hotz to get rid of all her Muslim servants overnight from Wildflower Hall – which she managed to do, though there were six corpses on the road outside her gate next morning.' He also reported that possibly Sikh units – former INA and troops of the Sikh states (ex-Indian army) – intended to march on Lahore and retake it and as much of Eastern Punjab as possible.[82]

Few of the British could have considered that Indian independence could ever go so badly wrong. The violence and hostility were on a scale that could not have been anticipated and the threats against 'poor old Miss Hotz' were unconscionable, yet other individuals were also targeted. This aspect of Indian independence and Partition was often recorded at the time and is often a feature of fiction in which some of the story takes place around the time of Partition.

As with the collapse of any power, the subject nations will always try to make a land-grab. The collapse of the Central European empires in 1918 is an example of this from history and accounted for the lack of stability in the region during the inter-war period. India was just another example, as the Sikhs also tried to obtain an independent state, something which had not been negotiated. Auchinleck had to try to control the situation – which was no longer his to try to control – if only to try to protect those Britons still resident in India after August 1947. The use of ex-INA troops and Sikh troops in the proposed march on Lahore further complicated an already dangerous situation. It also seemed that the new Indian government was making concessions to the Sikhs as the ban on them wearing the kirpan (a small symbolic dagger) or ceremonial swords was rescinded. Auchinleck saw this as a weakness of the Indian government and said so. Mountbatten also was very clear that the Sikhs had a leading role in provoking the inter-communal riots and leading the massacres of Muslims, but neither man wanted to make an already horrific set of circumstances worse.[83]

Mountbatten was also aware of the irregular use of ex-INA officers in foreign service as military attachés for the Indian diplomatic service and he voiced his objections to Sardar Baldev Singh on 24 October 1947. He wrote the following:

> I have noticed from the Minutes of the Cabinet Meeting held on 15 October that it is proposed that ex-INA Officers should be considered for appointments in the Foreign Service as Military Attaches and should be given commissions for other purposes such as appointments in the Railway Auxiliary Force. This matter is, of course, purely for the Cabinet to decide upon. But I thought that you might not be averse to hearing my comments, in my capacity as ex-Supreme Allied Commander, South-East Asia, who commanded the Indian forces against which the INA fought. I believe that you are fully aware of my views that no members of the INA except those who committed atrocities which should be punishable under any law, should be penalized for what they did beyond or being paid by the Government of India whilst fighting the regular army of India. In this I include particularly those officers who, in joining the INA, thought that they would thereby the more quickly achieve independence of their country (although on what grounds they based their hopes that a fascist nation like Japan would ever grant India independence, I do not know). This all leads me to the opinion that to give ex-INA officers commissions in the Regular Army at the present stage and particularly to appoint them as military attaches in any Allied country (or indeed in any country except, of course, Japan) would be a step likely to bring not only the Regular Army itself but also India as a whole into disrepute. Surely, in any case,

> the shortage of regular Indian Officers is primarily in the technical arms and not the Infantry and larger corps. I would have thought that the appointment of regular Army officers as Military Attaches would have been far more suitable. Ordinarily, Military Attaches to foreign Embassies are selected from Army Officers with good records. If these posts of pride are taken away from the Army and given to the INA, there will certainly be discontent amongst our officers. I repeat that these views are based on my experience as Supreme Allied Commander, South-East Asia, and that I have no wish to suggest that ex-members of the INA should be penalized as such, but I do not consider that they should be given posts which could bring India into disrepute or upset the loyal officers of the Indian Army.

This was also sent to Pandit Nehru.[84] These were wise words coming from Mountbatten, which is surprising given that he is not often credited with being overly bright, but it was of course his own experience of how people react to such situations. However, the Indians seemed very determined to do their own thing and so Baldev Singh sidestepped the issue and observed that the military attaché postings were not military postings and suggested that the real problems would be future commissions in the newly-independent Indian army.[85] There may have been an element of truth in what Baldev Singh said, but he was overlooking how many countries might have viewed post-independence India. As Mountbatten had pointed out, many countries would have been very uncomfortable, if not hostile, towards diplomats who had turned traitor in their eyes and fought with the Japanese against the Allies. The Japanese had a reputation for cruelty, especially towards their prisoners. This was not forgotten in 1947 and therefore it followed that those who had collaborated with them would be viewed as being the same and not to be trusted. It seemed that some of the new Indian authorities were determined to exasperate the British, who in their turn just wanted to leave once they saw law and order breaking down in India and hostilities beginning to break out between India and Pakistan.

The former Viceroy, Field Marshal Archibald Wavell, wrote to Auchinleck on 20 November 1947 expressing his sympathy for the tragedy that was unfolding in India and 'the disruption of the Indian Army and the apparent destruction of your [Auchinleck's] work.' Yet as Wavell remarked, 'What can one do?'[86] Indeed, what could one do in 1947? The Indian people, having thrown off British rule, began to divide into their religious groupings as well as slaughtering one another. It must have appeared to the likes of Wavell and Auchinleck that the people they had known had taken leave of their senses, but of course the resentment was always there; not only religious resentment against those of different religions but also against the British. Yet they feared to do much against them, possibly because the British were obviously leaving India.

It is interesting that in an undated paper, Auchinleck considered that many of the problems in India of 1947 had their roots in 1857.[87] His father had witnessed the events of 1857, the so-called Indian Mutiny or First Indian War of Independence, which probably caused his son to want to prevent the huge loss of life that had occurred at that time, especially among women and children, both British and Indian. A book written shortly after the Indian Mutiny was quite clear about the mistakes made by the British in 1857. The author – a British officer, Major C.N. North – wrote of a lack of understanding of the Indian population by the British authorities. North considered that the brigadier in command of him humiliated those about to be executed by their being made to mop up the blood from the floor of the house of 'martyred country-women…where they were sacrificed'. In other words, they had to clear up the blood of murdered British women; true, murdered by Indians but vindictive nevertheless. North also noted the humiliation of the 'novel mode of punishment, which is utterly antagonistic to the prejudices of the people and is attended with the forfeiture of caste.'[88] The forfeiture of caste was essentially the removal of the identity of an Indian, which was viewed as their birthright and their very being.

Another instructive exercise was noted in 1904 in a study of the Indian Mutiny which was still very much in living memory as the author observed that much of the revolt had its roots in religion, especially Islam and the slaughter of Christians in what is today Pakistan. As this statement ran, 'within a few hours the authority of England in Allahabad was overthrown and a green flag waving over the Kotwali (police station) proclaimed the restored supremacy of Islam.'[89] Ninety years later, Indians slaughtered one another along religious lines; therefore it is no surprise that they killed British people in 1857 along the same lines as well, in addition to killing those who were occupying their country.

Nine decades after the observations of the good Major North, Auchinleck was partially successful in 1947 as there were few Europeans killed, but the death toll among the native population was horrific, even if the deaths of Indians were not inflicted by the British. However, in 1947 the British were no longer in control, it was an Indian problem and they seemed to lack the ability to control their people, or else they feigned the lack of ability to take control. Adams notes that Gandhi was quite willing to see civil war in India in negotiations in the past with the British, which left the British horrified.[90] Gandhi considered that the long-standing lesson of 1857 was that violence would not expel the British who would always remain militarily the stronger.[91] It was observed that in the early twentieth century it was not British strength that had kept them in India but Indian weakness, and blind self-interest was what had kept the British in power. Gandhi's attitude was somewhat questionable, while his ideas for non-violence were totally unrealistic. This included giving in to Hitler's aggression.[92] Major General Shahid Hamid, who as a younger man was private secretary to Auchinleck between 1946 and 1947, remarked that Gandhi was a dreamer and did not deal with reality. This self-deception left India split between Hindus and Muslims.[93] This is a clear suggestion that Gandhi was largely responsible for the slaughter during Partition and not part of the official mythology regarding him.

Auchinleck's final major decision of his career as a soldier on 28 October 1947 was one that prevented war between India and Pakistan. As the two new states began to square up to one another in the Kashmir region, Auchinleck realized that to prevent war, he needed to threaten to remove instantaneously those British officers from the commands and all staff appointments from the service of both Pakistan and India. This worked and war was averted, for a while at least.[94] The fear was that not only might an unwanted war break out; there was also the fear of British officers being pitted against one another. As Auchinleck warned the Pakistani authorities, if all the British officers left the Pakistani army, it would fall apart.[95]

Auchinleck remained a popular figure as he oversaw the transformation of the ex-Indian army to that of the new national armed forces of Pakistan and India. Mountbatten remarked that once Auchinleck was 'going', the Indians began to express regret at his passing and were in full admiration of his work in India following independence.[96] As the date for Auchinleck's departure from India loomed large, both Indian and Pakistani governments wished him well with Nehru, Baldev, Gopalaswami Ayyangar, Liaquat Ali Khan and Malik Ghulam Muhammad all sending him greetings and their best wishes for the future. The Pakistani leader, Muhammad Ali Jinnah, wrote to Auchinleck on 18 December 1947 and said:

> I do not know how to thank you for all your good wishes. I wish that I had been able to see you at least for a few minutes before you left, but really I was unable to do so owing to my disposition, and I could not also reply earlier to your letter as I was not well. I wish you a well-earned rest, and all happiness and prosperity.[97]

Jinnah, a heavy smoker and suffering from tuberculosis since the 1930s, died in September 1948. It was the British Prime Minister Clement Attlee who summed up the success of Auchinleck's final years in India and wrote to him, saying:

> You may feel that your job ended in little but frustration, but the fact that the Army held together as well as it did, that re-constitution went through so smoothly and that both India and Pakistan now have disciplined Armed Forces at their command, is clear proof of the real and lasting success of the work you did.[98]

This was a fitting tribute to the long, hard years that Auchinleck had worked and served in India. However, White-Spunner disputes this and considers that Auchinleck left India a saddened man. As he presided over his last C-in-C conference, Auchinleck reflected that there was nothing that would prevent war between India and Pakistan, which was a sad admission from a man who had spent his career in India and in the Indian army. He refused all honours, perhaps because he felt that they were tainted by the possible intercession of Mountbatten or Attlee, had a quiet meal with Mountbatten, not because of the man but because of his office of governor general, and then without any show, Auchinleck left India. White-Spunner considers that Auchinleck was without doubt too harsh on himself, but does consider that he could have done more to have prevented the massacre in Punjab in 1947.[99] Shahid Hamid claimed that it was only Auchinleck who held India together as it moved towards independence and Partition.[100]

This is a matter of opinion because it seemed that nothing could have prevented the inter-communal slaughter that typified Partition, especially in Punjab. If Auchinleck had used British or Gurkha troops against rioting Indians, without doubt those on the left of politics or anti-imperialists would have accused the British of trying to retain India using armed force. Sometimes one cannot win, no matter what steps are taken to try to avoid further violence at a time when nobody could really restore order until the fighting factions were ready to cease their violence.

*Chapter Ten*

# The Twilight Years: 1948–81

After finally finishing his work in India Auchinleck retired from military service but his life remained interesting, which was a consequence of his taking an interest in people and life in general. He may have retired but he was not a retiring type of person. Warner suggests 'A Long Sunset'.[1] This is probably accurate, but one must not filch ideas! There was still plenty to do in Auchinleck's life, still fireworks in his literary battles with Montgomery, but thankfully no invading armies, shell or rifle-fire, just a few frayed nerves and the occasional loss of temper.

At first Auchinleck moved to Italy but not for long and despite never having been really comfortable in the UK, he moved to London before relocating to Beccles in Suffolk during 1960. As Warner wrote, the early years of retirement in the UK were not very happy; immediate post-war London was a very depressing place for him to go to. The city had been frequently bombed and later attacked by V-1 and V-2 rockets over the six years of the Second World War and there appeared to be shortages of many things or rationing of many essentials of life.[2] This included bread, which ironically had not happened during the war years. Auchinleck took a flat in Mayfair and had many interests as well as many friends. He also took up a number of appointments on various boards as well as being governor of his former school, Wellington College, between 1946 and 1959.

However, in the late 1950s and well into the 1960s a considerable amount of Auchinleck's time was spent in trying to ensure that the historical record was kept straight in the light of Montgomery's memoirs which came out in 1958 in which the latter tried to reduce, if not remove, Auchinleck's influence during the North Africa campaign during 1942. Auchinleck's reputation was largely defended by Brigadier Eric O'Gowan, known to his intimates as 'Chink' but born Eric Dorman-

Smith. During a short period in 1942 – 16 June to 6 August – O'Gowan, then still Dorman-Smith, was a full colonel but was Auchinleck's chief of staff and held the temporary rank of major general. The above period was extremely important in the Auchinleck story because as we have seen it was the time of the First Battle of El Alamein which serious military historians credit to Auchinleck, as well as being the turning-point of the North Africa campaign with the halting of Rommel's advance towards Alexandria and the Suez Canal. This was something that Montgomery tried to ignore or at least belittle. He did not want a rival to his own North African laurels as he claimed that his battle during October to November 1942 was the only battle of El Alamein.

The problem was one of credibility. Montgomery was the flamboyant and well-known general, later field marshal, a rank shared by Auchinleck, who as we have seen was remembered by those who had served under him and well-respected but lacked the high profile of Montgomery. Auchinleck had not written a memoir and never did, but in 1958 Montgomery's autobiography was published. His account of the later battle of El Alamein suggested that it was the only battle of that name and that prior to his succeeding Auchinleck in the Middle East, Auchinleck was very much on the back foot in the fighting against Rommel's troops. It was very much a matter of one man's word against another's. General Brian Horrocks wrote to O'Gowan stating that Montgomery was not 'a liar' and that there had been a misunderstanding between Auchinleck and Montgomery back in August 1942. Montgomery was determined that Auchinleck had plans to withdraw back into Egypt and to the Nile Delta; something denied by Auchinleck.[3] In his turn, a month earlier Auchinleck confided to O'Gowan that he had interviewed Montgomery in August 1942 as the latter was about to take over from him in Egypt, but he had not kept a record of the discussion. As he wrote to O'Gowan: 'Stupid, I suppose, but I never did keep any. I am, I fear, too trustful to expect malice and evil when no cause appears to exist.'[4] This certainly showed Montgomery in a different light to that of how Horrocks saw him. However, the real problem was that Montgomery resented any reference to a 'first Alamein' as O'Gowan noted in a letter to Auchinleck.[5] In O'Gowan Auchinleck had the most loyal of allies as he knew from a letter which he had received from O'Gowan nearly a decade earlier in which O'Gowan wrote that he was determined to make the British public recognize the First Battle of El Alamein.[6] O'Gowan's point was that Montgomery had built on Auchinleck's work during the summer of 1942 and was reaping the glory with his autobiography which exaggerated Montgomery's role in North Africa. O'Gowan also felt quite aggrieved at how Auchinleck and those on his staff in Cairo in 1942, including O'Gowan, felt about their treatment by the British government or, realistically, Churchill. O'Gowan felt that they had been scapegoated even years after the end of the war.

To deal with the first point that Montgomery exaggerated his role in North Africa during 1942, O'Gowan, terrier-like, refused to allow his former boss's role to be diminished and led a campaign for the recognition of the First Battle of El Alamein and the successful tactics of Auchinleck which denied Rommel the victory that many thought was bound to happen. O'Gowan returned to the historical record of operations between 25 June and 15 August 1942. A piece of evidence in support of Auchinleck came from the testimony of General Fritz Bayerlein, who served as a staff officer with Rommel in the Afrika Korps. Of the period 10 to 17 July 1942, Bayerlein said

> …all of Auchinleck's counter-attacks were tremendously successful. If Rommel had not been beaten then he would have advanced deep into Egypt. When Rommel lost Tel el Eisa and Rweisat, he and all of us knew we were lost. It is a pity that no one in Britain recognised the marvellous though smaller battles that Auchinleck won.[7]

This was what O'Gowan was talking about as he defended Auchinleck and began to try to raise his former chief and friend's profile. O'Gowan was determined to highlight exactly what had been the role of Auchinleck in the desert campaign during 1942.

O'Gowan recalled the times when the Middle East had been endangered by drawing on the historic account of events. The first thing to be noted was that later General Alan Brooke, in his role as CIGS, wrote that it was a good thing Hitler had failed to recognize the importance of Persia (Iran) and Iraq, so wasted his resources at Stalingrad.[8] However, Auchinleck had long realized the importance of the two countries as he had considered the lengthy supply line which in his mind ran from India to the Middle East via Iran and Iraq. Hitler always considered that he was better than his own general staff and finally decided operational matters for the German armed forces; he was a dictator and therefore could do so. Churchill also tried this but as he was working within the legal constraints of a democracy found that he could not do as he liked and had to listen to his service chiefs, but few had realized the overall importance of Iran and Iraq and that the supply line ran from India and not vice versa.

During June 1942, the war in Libya and beyond was beginning to shape up. On 14 June 1942, Richard Casey, an Australian appointed as Minister of State, Egypt, argued that Auchinleck should take personal command in Cyrenaica as the British army was retreating towards Egypt from the Gazala line following an enemy counter-attack on 11 June. On 22 June, Auchinleck returned from a visit to the Eighth Army. As a result of his visit he realized it was unlikely that its commanding officer, General Neil Ritchie, was able to carry on. Auchinleck's view was reinforced by Air Marshal Tedder who on 24 June 1942 from a similar visit openly expressed his consideration to Auchinleck that both Ritchie and Brigadier Whitely, who was the brigadier general staff, were both exhausted. On the previous day, Auchinleck had already suggested to the CIGS that Ritchie should be removed from his command. It was clear that Auchinleck felt awkward about this suggestion and insisted it was not that he felt Ritchie was incompetent but had instead 'lost originality'. This appeared to make him look unlucky and unsuccessful in his command. However, a change was needed and Ritchie's fatigue – he also had the added command of his remaining field forces as well as his already heavy burden of responsibility – should be relieved without delay. On 25 June 1942, Auchinleck appointed General Corbett as deputy commander-in-chief but left him in Cairo. Major General Dorman-Smith was appointed chief of staff and then departed to Eighth Army HQ at Baguish that evening. Once there he sent Ritchie on leave and then assumed command of the Eighth Army.[9] Connell notes that Auchinleck should have intervened earlier and of course Ritchie had been given a task vastly beyond his experience and capability. The consequences went beyond their immediate responsibilities and were paid for by both

Ritchie and Auchinleck and by those under their command.[10] People tend to forget this as they often forget the 'little people'.

It was the results of these events that later made O'Gowan somewhat bitter. This is a theme to which we will return later. In the dying days of June 1942, under the subtitle of 'cohesion and confusion', O'Gowan reported the history of the time, writing

> in the event, as will be seen, things did not turn out as badly as might just be anticipated on this gloomy 28th June, since Rommel was, in fact, halted at El Alamein on 1st July, and the need to fight him further to the east did not arise. But few would have banked on the 8th Army's power to halt Rommel at El Alamein on 28th June. Auchinleck intended to pursue his original intention for a decisive battle at El Alamein so long as there held the least chance of success. But El Alamein need not necessarily be the last fight for the Middle East.[11]

The point about this statement was that Montgomery was trying to ignore the Battle of El Alamein during the summer of 1942 and the fact that Auchinleck, rather than retreating headlong towards Cairo and beyond, was indeed doing quite the opposite and was actually making a stand and halted Rommel in his tracks. For some reason this was unknown to any save for those who had been involved in the fighting, including the Germans who praised Auchinleck and his tactics. Indeed, Desmond Young, in his work on Rommel, noted that Auchinleck had no more intention of abandoning El Alamein than Churchill ever had of abandoning London.[12] This seems fairly conclusive.

On 30 June 1942 Auchinleck issued his first 'Order of the Day' to all ranks of the Eighth Army. He observed and ordered that 'the enemy is stretching to his limit and thinks we are a broken army. He hopes to take Egypt by bluff. Show him where he gets off.' However, the higher echelons of command were not too sure and noted that 'continued defeat erodes resistance'. General 'Straffer' Gott was perturbed by the dispatch of the acting commander of the New Zealanders to their Delta base. This was provisionally to plan the evacuation of the Delta area and not, as General Corbett appeared to imply, that 'the worst possible case' was that

Egypt might be evacuated. Gott incautiously passed this information to the New Zealand Division's acting commander and added erroneously that he wanted to fight regardless but the South Africans did not. Warner discusses those panicky days in Egypt at the end of June 1942 and 'The Flap' in Cairo following the retreat from the Gazala line, the so-called 'Gazala Gallop'. There was confusion in Cairo as it was thought that the Germans were unstoppable and that Cairo was to be abandoned, and this gave way to a real panic. Extremely frightened officials, including those at the British embassy, behaved with a complete lack of dignity and so official papers were burned in such prolific quantities and with such haste that 1 July 1942 was known as 'Ash Wednesday', while towards the end of June, much of the British fleet left Alexandria owing to the German threat but said nothing to Auchinleck before sailing away.

Corbett, as Chief of the General Staff, Middle East was later held responsible for the lack of dignity of that time. It was also alleged that he had approved the order that all officers should carry revolvers at all times, as well as putting the centre of Cairo out of bounds from 8.00 pm to 7.00 am. These and other orders might have been sound if they had been accompanied by reassurances, but these were not forthcoming so panic was allowed to continue. To many local Egyptians and many of the British living in the Egyptian capital city, it seemed that Rommel's entry into Cairo was just a matter of time. Corbett was blamed for the panic and he, of course, was an Auchinleck appointee.[13] This was to matter within a few weeks when Auchinleck would not give Churchill what he wanted, which was another offensive.

At El Alamein, the commander of the 1st South African Infantry Division, General Daniel Pienaar, openly criticized Auchinleck's decision to fight west of the waterline (the River Nile). This opinion was shared with the French General de Larminat, who on the same day gave Dorman-Smith a paper stating his view that Auchinleck was 'insensitive' to fight west of the Nile. General Norrie – who was on the point of being sacked by Auchinleck – was in closer touch with his commander and was completely confident in what was going ahead. However, one of Auchinleck's main problems throughout July 1942 was how to re-establish confidence in his command among the senior ranks.[14] This account gives a good impression of the steps leading up to the fighting of the First Battle of El Alamein and the confusion. Auchinleck was not one to panic, even if some of his staff and other commanders were prone to do so. Part of the problem was that many Allied commanders and those serving under them were in awe of Rommel and seemed to consider him as being some form of superman. This was something that Auchinleck cautioned against.

At the beginning of July 1942 even Churchill was pessimistic about the situation in North Africa. In the House of Commons he said: 'We are at the moment in the presence of a recession of our hopes and prospects in the Middle East and in the Mediterranean unequalled since the fall of France.' In Washington DC, General Marshall warned Roosevelt that Rommel might be in Cairo by 10 July. Curiously, it was Rommel who wasn't so certain of a German victory in Egypt. He had quickly realized that he was facing Auchinleck and not Ritchie as he reported that Auchinleck 'was handling his forces with very considerable skill and tactically better than Ritchie'.[15] Auchinleck's actions following his assumption of command of the Eighth Army put paid to Rommel's operation known as AIDA. It was said that Auchinleck's tactical successes at Tel el Eisa and at Rweisat 'vitiated' the Axis grand strategy for the Mediterranean campaign, as they not only checkmated AIDA but also stopped Operation HERCULES, the German invasion of Malta. His tactics meant that Rommel was to be committed to a new 'dubious offensive' sometime in late August against a 'rested, reorganised, reinforced 8th Army'. It was declared that for Rommel 'the future did not look very bright'.[16]

It was the next stage of the defence of Egypt that became contentious in the 1950s once Montgomery had his autobiography published and tried to ensure that Auchinleck's role in Egypt was reduced in the narrative of events there in the summer of 1942. The record, however, showed that Auchinleck was determined that the 'Battle for Egypt' should be fought by a mobile Eighth Army to the west of the waterline (the River Nile) and if possible the enemy should be held around the Alamein gap.[17] It was at this time that General Montgomery arrived in North Africa ready to take command of the Eighth Army. Montgomery was to be under the command of Auchinleck until 15 August 1942. On 12 August, Auchinleck had his infamous meeting with Montgomery of which he did not keep notes as we have seen, while Montgomery tried to twist events in order to try to further enhance his popularity. As we can see above, Auchinleck had no intention of abandoning Egypt and was determined to fight away from Cairo and the Suez Canal. During the meeting, Montgomery claimed that 'if Rommel attacked in strength, as was expected soon, the Eighth army would fall back to the (Nile) Delta, if Cairo and the Delta could not be held, the army would retire southwards up the Nile.' O'Gowan commented that it was unlikely Auchinleck said anything of the sort and Auchinleck certainly denied that this was ever said. It was stated that on 14 August 1942, Montgomery had accepted Auchinleck's defensive policy of fighting west of the River Nile.[18]

During August 1942 the record is quite clear that Auchinleck and Churchill were not agreeing over the situation in North Africa. Churchill saw Egypt as the springboard to seize North Africa and threaten southern Italy. Auchinleck saw it somewhat differently. To him, Egypt was on the western flank of the Middle East theatre; this flank extended from Afghanistan, through Persia and Syria and then to Cyrenaica. Auchinleck considered that the greatest threat to this flank was a German offensive from the north-west from the Caucasus against oil instillations in the Persian Gulf on which the entire effort east of Suez depended. Even though it was desirable to drive the enemy from North Africa, a military vacuum should not be created in Iraq or Iran.

Once Auchinleck had taken over from Wavell on 1 July 1941, Churchill pressed him to undertake an offensive in the Western Desert in order to relieve Tobruk, recapture Cyrenaica and then advance to Tripoli. It was all sound, but Auchinleck rejected it as he decided to attack only when his forces were ready. There had been disagreements before between Churchill and Auchinleck, notably the appointment of the commander of the Eighth Army at the time of its creation. Churchill had wanted General 'Jumbo' Maitland Wilson while Auchinleck wanted General Cunningham. Four months were to lapse between Auchinleck and the launching of CRUSADER. Of this delay Churchill said 'so late and alike a mistake and a misfortune', but agreed that the offensive could not have been launched earlier. It was also observed that Ritchie had lost his nerve at Tobruk.

On 14 June 1942 Churchill recommended that Auchinleck should reverse his instructions about Tobruk not being held if the main force of the Eighth Army was withdrawn for future deployment. Ritchie recommended the pre-CRUSADER situation with Tobruk being reinforced or 'reinvested'. Auchinleck was not aware of the situation and replied that El Adan should be reinforced and Tobruk defended without investment. He did not know on 11 June 1942 that at El Adan there was only the 29th Infantry Brigade Group which was vulnerable to concentrated attacks from Rommel's mobile forces. Churchill's only reply to Ritchie would have been that in the circumstances the entire Eighth Army must be concentrated in the future and Tobruk abandoned, but Auchinleck was not aware of what was going on. Churchill knew that Auchinleck could not take both eyes from the very real danger that was threatening Syria, Persia (Iran) and the oilfields. The latter was in Cairo between 3 and 4 August 1942 and told Churchill that a major offensive was not possible before mid-September. Even then, any such offensive was dependent on the situation in southern Russia and the Caucasus, basically in the hope that there would not be a German breakthrough in that region. This angered Churchill as he clearly wanted an offensive sooner rather than later; however, in conversations between him and his CIGS on the command of the Eighth Army held during the same period, the question of Auchinleck's removal from that command was not raised.[19]

More than ten years later as the repercussions of Montgomery's autobiography began to make themselves felt, O'Gowan continued to make his case for Auchinleck. The account of events in North Africa during the summer of 1942 by O'Gowan had been made public and he went further. In a letter to the editor of the *Guardian*, he recalled that on 28 July 1942 Auchinleck had visited Eighth Army HQ and had seen for himself that the army was not aggressive enough to carry out another offensive. This was part of the basis of a plan of action for August-September 1942. On 30 July 1942, new plans for further operations against Rommel were being considered at a corps commanders' conference. O'Gowan asserted that there was absolutely no reference to a possible withdrawal of the Eighth Army in the event of Rommel attacking. On 6 August 1942 the approach to further operations was also explained to General Wavell who was visiting the Eighth Army and he agreed to their soundness.[20] These, without doubt, were the plans to rid Egypt and North Africa of Rommel and his forces. However, a new operation, let alone plans, could not come quickly enough for the ever-impatient Churchill and this allowed Montgomery to try to denigrate Auchinleck's role in North Africa in July 1942.

O'Gowan understood Auchinleck and how he thought; pointing out that he had been closely associated with him since a brief period in 1938–39 when he was deputy chief of general staff in India and O'Gowan was the director of military training in India, and then during those six crucial weeks in June-July 1942 when they both served in the Middle East and halted Rommel's advance into Egypt. O'Gowan identified that Auchinleck should have been left in India instead of being sent to the Middle East in July 1941. O'Gowan gave two good reasons why. The first was that the Middle East veterans, such as they were, never took to the 'sepoy general' as C-in-C. This of course was with reference to the fact that Auchinleck was part of the Indian army rather than the British army and that much of his service career reflected that. The second reason was an excellent observation as O'Gowan asserted that if Auchinleck had been left in India and not replaced by Wavell, he might have been better placed to deal with the Japanese attack when it came. Auchinleck had, during 1938, studied the Japanese problem and the possibility of a Japanese invasion of British possessions in South-East Asia. Auchinleck's posting to the Middle East meant that he had to learn everything from scratch.[21] However, it should be considered that perhaps this wasn't such a bad thing given that when Auchinleck first arrived in Cairo during July 1941, he found himself in charge of a mostly impotent army which had been severely disorganized by the fiasco in Greece and the departure of General Wavell. O'Gowan also stuck his neck out and stated that Auchinleck should have been made viceroy as he might have been able to prevent the massacres that sadly accompanied the transition period as India and Pakistan became independent.[22]

It might well have been the case that veteran generals of the Middle East might not have been able to think beyond the immediate problems of the Middle East while Auchinleck, as we have seen, saw the supply line to the Middle East somewhat differently to many conventional thinkers as he saw it originating in India and stretching out to the Middle East rather than the other way around. He was also aware of the German threat as the German army advanced into southern Russia and threatened the Caucasus. If they had not been distracted by Hitler's fatal attraction to Stalingrad, the Germans may well have broken into the Middle East from the north and then perhaps have moved eastwards towards India and to their Japanese allies. Auchinleck was aware of this probability. Therefore, it was fortunate that he was in the Middle East when he was and prevented Rommel from taking Egypt. Whether Auchinleck could have done something about the Japanese remains a moot point, but as he had already studied them and their techniques he was probably in a better position than most. Warner observed that Leo Amery, at the time of the exchange of Auchinleck and Wavell, told Churchill that he felt Wavell should come home and someone else take over in Cairo. Amery told Churchill that he feared India would feel that she was being given a failed general in Wavell at a time of a massive threat from Japan. Amery considered that it might have been better if Auchinleck was retained in India as he had the necessary drive to face the impending threat from the Japanese.[23]

Barnett also comments on the perceived problems of Auchinleck in the Middle East. There was a definite rivalry between the British and Indian armies with the British looking down on the Indians as 'frontier soldiers' which was resented. India had the men and the space for proper training and preparation for war, whereas the UK had neither. Auchinleck, coming from India, did not know the reputations of officers in the British army and was therefore handicapped by a lack of knowledge when he was choosing men to serve under him. Auchinleck was ignorant of the use of armour but as Barnett says, so was every senior officer, whether they were from the British or Indian army.[24]

O'Gowan was certainly one of Auchinleck's main supporters, if not his post-war number one fan and stood by him as we have seen, but there was a reason for this. O'Gowan considered himself to be a victim of the events of August 1942 which saw the dismissal of Auchinleck and most of his senior appointees including O'Gowan. In 1944 a letter from O'Gowan complains that he had been removed from his command of a brigade 'in the interests of General Ritchie' and he admitted to being 'bitter' about this injustice and relates it to the Middle East and 1942.[25] O'Gowan was also aware that Auchinleck was unpopular with some of the army in the

Middle East and that no doubt rubbed off onto him. As in a document from 1944 to the commander of Eighth Army, O'Gowan put the case that he had been, before 'these cumulative distresses had happened', director of military training in India and then later, in 1942, had been deputy chief of Auchinleck's general staff.[26]

It is well known that Montgomery's first move on taking command of the Eighth Army was to rid himself of Auchinleck's staff and senior commanders. This began with the removal of O'Gowan who seemed to have made many enemies at the time. O'Gowan's dismissal from the Eighth Army was basically the end of his military career.[27] It was said later that Auchinleck was too tolerant of unorthodox thinkers and that his appointments of Corbett, O'Gowan (then Dorman-Smith) and Ritchie were examples of this, according to some critics. Brooke was clearly unhappy about the appointment of Corbett and had asked about him as he had never heard of him before, nor had anyone who he asked about Corbett. Warner noted that this was not necessarily to the credit of Brooke who, as CIGS, should have known his generals in case he had need of them.

Brooke thought that he might have Auchinleck to appoint someone rather than have Corbett; someone of a higher calibre, he thought. Brooke certainly did not like Dorman-Smith and wrote that he 'had a most fertile brain, continually producing new ideas, some of which (not many) were good, and the rest useless'. He also considered that Dorman-Smith had too much influence over Auchinleck. Of Ritchie, Brooke considered that even though he was 'steadfast' as he had been during CRUSADER, where Auchinleck had been present to guide him, overall Ritchie was too young and too inexperienced to command a large army during a crisis. At Gazala, Ritchie had been overconfident and that had ended badly. Ritchie, as we know, was sacked by Auchinleck, while Dorman-Smith and Corbett were replaced at the same time as Auchinleck.[28] Dorman-Smith was certainly influential in his work with Auchinleck as the latter had, indeed, made contingency plans for a retreat in Egypt (as a good general will do if everything fouls up) in order to keep his forces together, while there was another set of plans that were completed by Dorman-Smith on 27 July 1942 for the strengthening and defence of the El Alamein line as well as plans for an offensive once Auchinleck's force had had a chance to retrain and refit.[29] There is an early reference to Dorman-Smith's plan as when his own brother, Sir Reginald Dorman-Smith, governor of Burma at the time of the Japanese attack, attended a luncheon with Auchinleck and Eric Dorman-Smith, among others, on 14 June 1942, the latter was asked by Auchinleck to give Sir Reginald a 'full picture' of what lay before them in North Africa.

Several interesting things came out in this talk by Eric Dorman-Smith. The first thing was that he spoke of the shortages of men and machinery that plagued them. This was followed by his assessment of Rommel and Ritchie and he claimed that Rommel had 'imposed his mind so much on Ritchie' and that Rommel was always going to come out on top of Ritchie. Sir Reginald asked his brother why Auchinleck did not sack Ritchie and was told that Auchinleck did not like dismissing people. In sacking Cunningham, Auchinleck had reached the end of his sacking ration. This shook Sir Reginald. Eric asked his brother to tell Whitehall of the grave shortages of just about everything in North Africa. Next, Sir Reginald asked his brother if he thought Rommel could take Cairo. Eric considered and then replied: 'Provided the Auk accepts the plan which I am putting up to him we can tie Rommel up into knots, but we cannot stage an all-out offensive unless and until we have more men and machines.' Indeed, Eric Dorman-Smith was so confident that he also told his brother of troops who were down because of reverses in North Africa, 'their tails will get right up once they know that we can defeat Rommel, which we will do if Auk listens to me.'[30]

This was the very confident Eric Dorman-Smith who defied Churchill, lost his career due to his loyalty to Auchinleck which was to carry on to the end of Dorman-Smith's life, but also was the man who in reality scared orthodox military thinkers such as Montgomery. It should also be noted that on 18 June, Auchinleck went with Dorman-Smith to Richie's HQ. Once there, Dorman-Smith was struck by the air of failure and the apparent belief that Rommel was virtually unstoppable and would take Tobruk at his leisure.[31] Connell gives a list of ideas from Dorman-Smith that were to be used in the defence of Egypt. Auchinleck certainly approved of these ideas and was grateful for the freshness and originality of Dorman-Smith.[32] Auchinleck, at the time of the mass sackings of August 1942, was angry; not for himself but for others. He considered that the sackings were beyond the remit of Churchill and that the prime minister was afraid of Dorman-Smith.[33]

It was the imagination and breadth of understanding of the task before Auchinleck and Dorman-Smith which so vexed Montgomery, who was brilliant in himself but refused to share the success of the North African campaign then, and then later in the 1950s. As for Churchill, he had a lot to worry about and needed to illustrate clearly to Stalin that the British were still committed to the war and not leaving the fighting to the Red Army. Equally, Auchinleck was not afraid of Churchill, the War Cabinet or the Germans; he just wanted to do the right thing and the fair thing.[34] He was certainly no career-minded officer and in the end it did him no harm to stick to his guns. Connell observed that Churchill had a few problems though, which included a distrust of generals and an acute dislike of India and the Indian army.[35] These three prejudices certainly covered Auchinleck.

Brooke, editing his diaries after the war, was once quite supportive of Ritchie. He wrote that Ritchie had served well in France in the fighting that led to the evacuation at Dunkirk in 1940 and had grown fond of him and was dismayed to find that Ritchie had lost his command of the Eighth Army. Brooke was presumptuous enough to tell Ritchie that in his opinion much of the blame lay with Auchinleck as Ritchie had never commanded a division in action before, far less an army in the field. Brooke told Ritchie that the best way forward was to get his confidence back and command a division at home in the UK and that once he had regained his confidence, Brooke would give him a corps to command. This indeed came to pass.[36]

On the same day, 15 July 1942, if one follows Brooke's post-war commentary, he wanted to go to the Middle East on his own but needed permission from Churchill and that was difficult, if not impossible. Brooke considered that he needed to be in the Middle East in order to see what was going wrong there and he did not want Churchill interfering in this. However, Brooke was realistic enough to know that it was unlikely Churchill would sanction his going alone, citing that he could not manage alone. The real reason was that Churchill wanted to go as well. Brooke also wanted to see what was going on with the Eighth Army as Auchinleck was considering giving its command to General Corbett.[37]

During this period Brooke mentioned that he had to discuss a proposed draft of a telegram urging Auchinleck to hurry up and begin his attack.[38]

However, Auchinleck had already started his attack and on 23 July 1942, Brooke complained that he wasn't very happy with its progress.[39] At the COS meeting of 27 July, which Brooke wrote in his diary was to be about new planning for operations in North Africa, it was learned that Auchinleck had started a new offensive.[40] The next day, Brooke revealed that Churchill was depressed that Auchinleck's new attack was being repulsed and was questioning just how Auchinleck was running the operation while not giving him any credit for anything. Brooke considered that it was 'heart-breaking' to work for Churchill, but admitted that he found it difficult to defend Auchinleck from the prime minister as Brooke wasn't too sure what Auchinleck was doing.[41]

Brooke flew out to North Africa and was in Cairo by 3 August 1942. He went to GHQ and interviewed Corbett who Auchinleck was considering for the post of commander of the Eighth Army. Auchinleck was against the appointment and after a long talk with Corbett, Brooke decided against Corbett as being totally unsuitable and 'a very small man'. After the war Brooke enlarged on his decision back in 1942 and wrote:

> One interview with him [Corbett] was enough to size him up. He was a very, very small man unfit for the job of CGS [Chief of General Staff] and was totally unsuited for command of 8th Army, an appointment which the Auk [Auchinleck] had suggested. Consequently Corbett's selection reflected unfavourably on the Auk's ability to select men and confirmed my fears in that respect.

The arguments between Brooke and Churchill continued. Churchill wanted Auchinleck to leave command of the Eighth Army and return as commander of the Middle East force from Cairo. That was exactly what Brooke had argued previously, but then Churchill began to think of alternatives and even suggested that Brooke should take command of the Eighth Army. Brooke noted that he would have been highly unsuited as he had never been desert-trained. Working with Churchill was without doubt an extremely frustrating task.[42] The next day there were more meetings regarding the situation in the Middle East and how important

Egypt was as opposed to the oilfields of Abadan in Iran, but it was agreed that Abadan was more important. In his edited post-war remarks Brooke noted that all 'motive power' at sea, on the ground or in the air throughout the Middle East, the Indian Ocean and India was wholly dependent on oil from Abadan (an area familiar to Auchinleck from the First World War), and that if this supply was lost, the shortfall could not be made good from American sources. Therefore he concluded that if this oil was lost, it would have meant the loss of Egypt and command of the Indian Ocean, while the entire Indian-Burma campaign would have been endangered.[43] This was something already anticipated by Auchinleck.

During an afternoon meeting it was decided that Montgomery should be the new commander of the Eighth Army. In his post-war amendments Brooke admitted he was surprised that Auchinleck accepted the appointment of Montgomery as commander. Brooke had fully expected Auchinleck to argue about it and then he had reservations as to whether the two generals would work together. Brooke was worried that Auchinleck might try to dominate Montgomery and might then put him 'out of his stride'. This was at a time when Brooke was most anxious to see Montgomery commanding the Eighth Army. Therefore Brooke decided that there was a need to move Auchinleck elsewhere and away from Montgomery; this was all added to Brooke's diaries after the war.

In the late afternoon of 4 August 1942 there was yet another conference of inter-service senior commanders chaired by Churchill with the question of Middle Eastern operations being discussed. Finally, Churchill pressed Auchinleck about a new offensive. Auchinleck, as we have seen, would not begin a further operation until he was ready and this angered Churchill who demanded an earlier date.[44] Brooke remarked on the removal of Auchinleck and his staff and found that he could not agree with Churchill who wanted to use Gott and Wilson, but Brooke argued that Gott was too tired and Wilson too old. Churchill maintained the line that Brooke was failing to make use of the best men before admitting that he knew neither of them and that it was Eden, the Foreign Secretary, who had told him so.

As we can see, there was a sense of scapegoating in Cairo once Montgomery took over the Eighth Army and indeed, the author of the first comprehensive biography of Auchinleck, John Connell, gave over an entire chapter – that is Chapter 24 and more than thirty pages – to his 'Scapegoats in Cairo'. Part of the reason for the dismissals of Auchinleck and Dorman-Smith can be found in Connell's work. On 5 August 1942 while Churchill was in the Middle East, Auchinleck and Dorman-Smith met him in the operations caravan. Once there, Churchill looked at the wall map and began to thrust his thumb and fingers across it as if they were 'battle-tested formations'. Then he demanded that there should be attacks, before trying to become persuasive. Churchill observed that the 44th Division had just arrived in North Africa from the UK and demanded to know why it was not being committed immediately to the offensive.

Politely yet firmly, Auchinleck stood his ground and told his prime minister why he was not putting a fresh, unacclimatized division, untrained in desert warfare, straight into battle. Churchill was furious, but Auchinleck stood his ground and so the British prime minister rounded on Dorman-Smith, who had supported his boss in the argument with Churchill. Connell noted that because Auchinleck had defied Churchill and Dorman-Smith had backed him up, the 44th Division was not wasted on the battlefield and so many lives were saved but it was the end of Auchinleck's and Dorman-Smith's active military careers.

Churchill left the caravan and the meeting. Mid-evening he wrote to Attlee, the leader of the Labour Party and deputy prime minister, and told him that he had made enquiries in the Middle East and after lengthy consultations with Field Marshal Smuts (the South African prime minister), CIGS and the Minister of State and concluded that the Middle East command needed to be reorganized into two separate commands as we have seen earlier in this discourse. Much of it was reshuffling, but it was obvious that Auchinleck had been reduced in his role (which he refused to accept), while Generals Corbett, Ramsden and Dorman-Smith were all dismissed. Much of this was to do with defying Churchill, especially as Auchinleck, supported by his doughty Dorman-Smith, refused to commit the Eighth Army to a premature offensive, which left Churchill furious. Connell admitted that Corbett, Ramsden and Dorman-Smith alongside Auchinleck were definitely scapegoats for the mess that was the Middle East.[45] However, in late January 1942, Brooke had noted that Dorman-Smith, even before he became Chief of

Auchinleck's General Staff, was a problem. During this period Brooke was beginning to get messages coming from Auchinleck's office which were beginning to 'upset Brooke and he was becoming suspicious of Dorman-Smith as being a bad influence'. He noted that Wavell had made use of Dorman-Smith who, as we have seen was quite brilliant but had managed to use only the good and dump the bad. Brooke was of the opinion that Auchinleck was incapable of doing this and so fell too far under Dorman-Smith's influence. This, according to Brooke, was possibly the major cause of the fall of Auchinleck and his staff in 1942.[46]

This is an interesting admission and suggests that Auchinleck made a mistake in his choice of staff, but how can this be if the First Battle of El Alamein was a success and prepared the ground for Montgomery's offensive, the Second Battle of El Alamein, which was the beginning of the end as far as Churchill was concerned? It might be the case that the British army did not look favourably on genuine talent – it has been known – and there were other prejudices such as Auchinleck being the 'sepoy general' as some of the hind-bound traditional officers of the British remarked, while Dorman-Smith was Irish and Catholic and therefore suspect in the collective minds of the British officer corps. There is the added spice that Montgomery detested Auchinleck, something that goes back to India, if not before.

Once the wartime memoirs began to be published in the 1950s it was obvious that the recollections of Montgomery would be sought after and one of the more interesting. Montgomery was a hero, and everyone wanted to know what he had done and how he thought. Without doubt, veterans who had campaigned with Montgomery also wanted to read about their own war and how their commander had overseen operations in which they had taken part. However, once these memoirs were published, as we have seen, Auchinleck's role was reduced and there was a major discrepancy in how Auchinleck remembered the meeting between him and Montgomery in Egypt during August 1942. It is insinuated that Montgomery lied in his version and that was why Dorman-Smith, by then O'Gowan, stood by his former boss and demanded that Auchinleck's role be recognized. O'Gowan may have been many of the things that Brooke suggested in 1942, but he was also a very loyal friend and a good one to Auchinleck. O'Gowan was also driven by the fact that he considered the premature end of his service career and of others from Auchinleck's staff was a grave injustice; he said so in 1944 and continued to pursue it into the 1950s. His complete dissatisfaction with the British establishment and perhaps the UK itself became quite obvious when he became involved with the Irish Republican Army, the IRA, later in his life. He may have been Irish and discontent with the British, but few Irishmen, no matter how angry, join the IRA. What is amazing is that Auchinleck doesn't mention this apparent disloyalty.

Auchinleck carried on with his life in retirement, and an interesting aside was his decision prior to leaving the UK to lodge his personal papers with the University of Manchester. Asked why he had chosen Manchester, Auchinleck replied: 'I think that it is a good thing to spread these things around a bit. I'm all for these younger universities taking their place.' The University of Manchester was founded in 1851 but this answers a question this author had for an archival assistant when I first consulted the Auchinleck papers at the John Rylands Special Collection at the University of Manchester library.[47] It might also explain the O'Gowan papers being lodged there as well. There were also others who continued to support Auchinleck as Major Alexander Greenwood, his longest-serving ADC, had not only helped with financial activities once Auchinleck retired but also wanted his wartime contribution recognized further.

In 1977, Greenwood wrote to Mountbatten with the suggestion of honouring Auchinleck further. Mountbatten gently rebuffed Greenwood, citing that Auchinleck had in the past refused all honours including a peerage. Furthermore, in the past, Auchinleck had asked Mountbatten not to try to get him any further honours than the ones he had achieved in his service career. It is considered that if his sovereign had offered him a peerage he might have accepted it, but to have accepted it via Attlee or Mountbatten was unthinkable and linked in his mind to the premature Partition of India.[48] Zeigler noted that Mountbatten tried to champion the cause of Auchinleck even when he himself had retired.[49] Yet what can you do with a man who refuses to be recognized, honoured or even live in the country of his birth?

However, overall it would seem that Auchinleck was quite bored with his long retirement, especially when he was still an active man, but financially was quite poor in so many ways. Auchinleck had been a soldier for all of his professional life and had fought in two world wars as well as minor colonial campaigns and now, after forty years, was expected to settle down as a half-pay field marshal. He had not saved that much during his career with Jessie spending much that he had earned, so his monthly salary was spent almost as soon as it arrived. In common with many service officers, Auchinleck thought that his pension would be sufficient to live off once he left the army. It was not, and the interest from his bank account was insufficient to support him if he wanted to lead a full life in the UK. Within six months of retiring, he was bored and poor. He decided to leave Italy as he was also lonely.[50]

With the aid of Field Marshal Earl Wavell, Auchinleck found a home in London, a flat that was close to his favourite London club. However, he remained restless and continued to be bored with his new life. He travelled a bit in Rhodesia (modern-day Zimbabwe), as well as taking advantage of travelling and staying in Pakistan. There was an interesting interlude when Queen Elizabeth II was crowned, as on her coronation day all field marshals who could were expected, on horseback, to lead the ceremonial parade through the streets of London, field marshal baton in the right hand and reins in the other. Auchinleck, aged 69, practised and rehearsed with his friend Field Marshal Alexander and all went well on the day.[51]

His years in London saw Auchinleck taking more interest in what was around him and in seeing his friends. In 1954, he went with Field Marshal Alexander to Portugal on a tour of the battlefields of the Peninsular War. Both men relaxed by painting while they were there. Auchinleck also travelled to Norway for fishing; he loved the country and its people.[52] Surely he must have also thought of those days in 1940 when he commanded the expedition there. In 1957, Auchinleck had his appendix removed. He was by then aged 73; he made a rapid recovery and soon returned to his life in London clubland.[53]

The spat with Montgomery during the 1950s was of some limited interest to Auchinleck, but only because he was trying to ensure that the historical record of events in 1942 was accurate and not versions put about by Montgomery and up to a point by Churchill. It is interesting to note that at a time when Montgomery was trying to reduce the role that

Auchinleck had played in the victory in North Africa, one of his foes, General Fritz Bayerlein, wrote to O'Gowan praising Auchinleck and how he commanded his forces in North Africa. Later, the son of Rommel, Manfred, wrote that even Erwin Rommel thought a lot of Auchinleck and did not believe that he would be able to re-organize his forces as he had at El Alamein and out-manoeuvred the Germans in July 1942 during the fighting in the El Alamein area. Manfred Rommel confirmed that most senior German commanders admitted this, including his own illustrious father Erwin Rommel.[54]

Between 1960 and 1967, Auchinleck lived in Beccles in Suffolk. His great friend, the artist Edward Seago, lived only a few miles away at Ludham in Norfolk. Auchinleck's seven years in Suffolk was the longest period he had ever spent in one place in his entire life. During this period Auchinleck still spent time in Pakistan visiting his old regiment and the Staff College as well as the North-West Frontier, but this was his last visit to Pakistan. The short war between India and Pakistan dismayed Auchinleck who remarked to a friend, Shahid Hamid, that the Sikhs were 'good soldiers, but they are born intriguers and care too much for money'.[55] This was without doubt a comment on India and the country it had become nearly twenty years after independence, but does reveal that he was more sympathetic towards Pakistan as was often the charge against him during the period 1946 to 1948.

In January 1966 Auchinleck went on holiday to Morocco. On his return he wrote to Alexander Greenwood of his enthusiasm for the country:

> Morocco was wonderful – climate, scenery, and atmosphere. I fell for it. It is a country of great space and tremendous horizons, very lovely I thought. I am sorry to leave it to come back to this country where everyone is always in a hurry or some fuss or other! Senile decay I suppose, but true.[56]

Auchinleck was trying to find somewhere that reminded him of the India he loved and of course living in Morocco was much cheaper than living in the UK. The following year he returned to Morocco and spent January and February there and once more was entranced by the country. This time he wrote to Greenwood:

> Chiefly in Marrakech. I enjoyed the climate, the scenery, the food and the people. It is a wonderful place for a simple holiday, without frills, wireless, T.V., or other modern nuisances! I am now up to the eyes in dealing with letters, reports, etc., etc. which are piled up on my desk.

As Greenwood notes, Auchinleck was still accepting appointments which took their toll on his time and money.[57] The problem was that Auchinleck was too generous with his time and cash, and things were beginning to become difficult for him. At the beginning of 1968 he simply informed Greenwood that he had emigrated to Morocco. Greenwood believes that there were three reasons for Auchinleck leaving the UK. The first was the taxation policies of the Labour Party at that time with the claim that Auchinleck could not live on his pension in the manner to which he was accustomed. The second was the climate – Auchinleck was used to living in a sunny, dry climate and the UK is far from that – while the third was that of attitude. Auchinleck was more Celtic than English and didn't really connect with the latter.[58] It is quite clear from Greenwood's narrative that he didn't like the Labour Party; we have no idea whether Auchinleck did or not, but the climate issue certainly makes sense and he had never really lived in England so it would have been hard for him to settle there.

Auchinleck clearly began to enjoy life in Morocco as Greenwood could testify when he visited him in 1969. Even so, he still travelled quite widely, taking in Europe and the USA. In 1971 he was in the UK for the unveiling of a monument in Saint Paul's Cathedral commemorating the 2 million men from the Indian army who had served in the Second World War. Auchinleck attended Queen Elizabeth II on that occasion and then kept a further appointment the same afternoon. In 1972 he was once more in the UK for a prostate operation. As the 1970s progressed, as with all old people, Auchinleck's friends began to die, including Seago who passed away in 1974. During this year Auchinleck reached his 90th birthday and once more he was in the UK for a special luncheon to mark the occasion. He was interviewed by David Dimbleby.[59] Apart from a stay with his cousin, Lieutenant Colonel Clive Auchinleck, in Norfolk in 1976, this was the last time that Auchinleck visited the UK. He didn't attend the funeral of Montgomery in 1976 but why should he have done so? In early 1981 he met Queen Elizabeth II for the last time when she was in Morocco on a state visit. Auchinleck died on 23 March 1981, three months short of his 97th birthday.[60]

Auchinleck had been granted a long and full life, and even though it would seem that from the time of his retirement his life began to decline, this is not the way to understand the man. He had never had things easy, whether financially or in his career. His personal life was painful as his wife Jessie left him for a fellow officer, but little got him down for long, if at all. Even the dispute with Montgomery in the 1950s was for the historical record and not for himself. Auchinleck clearly loved living in Morocco even if he did travel outside of it quite a lot, but he had found a place to lay his head, reflect on his long life and finally pass away. The old warrior had returned home.

# Notes

### Introduction

1. Patrick French, *India: A Portrait* (London, Allen Lane, 2011), p.284.

### Chapter One

1. Philip Warner, *Auchinleck: The Lonely Soldier* (London, Buchan & Enright, 1981), pp.7–8.
2. A.A. Greenwood, *Field Marshal Auchinleck* (Durham, Pentland Press, 1981), pp.19–21.
3. John Connell, *Auchinleck: A Critical Biography* (London, Cassell, 1959), pp.16–30.

### Chapter Two

1. Ibid, pp.31–50. Greenwood, pp.28–45.

### Chapter Three

1. Warner, p 36.
2. Roger Parkinson, *The Auk: Auchinleck, Victor at Alamein* (London, Granada, 1977), p.41.
3. Ibid, pp.46–67; Connell, pp.51–75.

### Chapter Four

1. TNA, FO 371/56341 1946 Norway, File No. 11144, Letter from Major General P.J. Mackesy, Commander of 'Rupertforce' to Permanent Under Secretary of State, The War Office, 15 May 1940.
2. The Auchinleck Papers, GB 133 AUC, John Rylands Library, Special Collections, University of Manchester, AUC/3, May 1–16, 1940, Items 3,25, Climatic Conditions, 2 May 1940.
3. Ibid.
4. Ibid.
5. Ibid.
6. TNA, PREM 3/328/5, 1941 Norway, Operations in Northern Norway from May 13 1940 to June 8 1940. Cabinet Papers, Lieutenant General C.J.E. Auchinleck, GOC C-in-C, North-Western Expeditionary Force.
7. Ibid.
8. Winston S. Churchill to Lord Cork, telegram, Admiralty Papers, ADM 199/1929, 22 April 1940, (personal), *Churchill 1*.
9. John Rylands, AUC, File III, May 1–16 1940, Auchinleck to General Dill, 14 May 1940.

10. TNA, PREM 3/328/5, 1941.
11. TNA, PREM 3/328/5, Section 11, The Capture of Narvik.
12. Ibid.
13. TNA, PREM 3/328/5, 29 May 1940.
14. TNA, PREM 3/328/4, FO (Flag Officer) Narvik to Admiralty in Naval Cipher (NAR) by W/T, 4 June 1940.
15. TNA, PREM 3/328/4, From C-in-C, Home Fleet, to Admiralty, First Sea Lord and First Lord, 26 May 1940.
16. TNA, PREM 3/328/4, Admiralty to FO, Narvik, 24 May 1940.
17. TNA, PREM 3/328/4, FO, Narvik to Admiralty, 25 May 1940.
18. Winston S. Churchill, *The Second World War*, Volume IV, *The Hinge of Fate* (London, Cassell, 1951), p.511.
19. Ibid, pp.510–511.
20. John Rylands, AUC/70–120 Southern Command, File V, June 1–30 1940, Items 63–73, MUL 63 HQ NWEF to Colonel Graham, Base Command, TROMSO, 1 June 1940.
21. Ibid.
22. John Rylands, MUL 74, File VI, July 1–31 1940, Items 74–83, Copy of Letter Addressed to the Admiral of the Fleet, the Earl of Cork and Orrery from the Admiralty, 3 July 1940.
23. Ibid.
24. John Rylands, MUL 77, Auchinleck to Cork, 7 July 1940.

**Chapter Five**

1. Greenwood, p.101.
2. *The Ironside Diaries, 1937–1940*, Roderick Macleod & Denis Kelly (eds) (London, Constable, 1962), p.352.
3. Warner, p.59.
4. Ibid, p.61.
5. Greenwood, p.102.
6. Warner, pp.60–61.
7. Ibid, p.108.
8. John Rylands, MUL 97, Auchinleck to Montgomery, 19 October 1940.
9. John Rylands, MUL 98, Auchinleck to Lieutenant Wemyss, 19 October 1940.
10. Greenwood, p.111.
11. I.S.O. Playfair, *The History of the Second World War. The Mediterranean and Middle East*, Volume 2 (London, HMSO, 1956), pp.177–178, hereafter referred to as *Playfair 2*.
12. Stephen Bungay, *Alamein* (London, Aurum Press, 2003), pp.8–9.
13. *War Diaries, 1939–1945. Field Marshal Lord Alanbrooke*, Alex Danchev & Daniel Todman (eds) (London, Weidenfeld & Nicolson, 2001), p.141, diary entry, 17 February 1941.
14. Greenwood, p.122.
15. John Rylands, MUL 131, General Dill to Auchinleck, 13 March 1941.
16. John Rylands, MUL 133, Cornwallis, Baghdad to FO, 3 April 1941.
17. Greenwood, p.128.

18. Ibid, p.130.
19. John Rylands, MUL 149, Air HQ Iraq to HQ RAF Middle East, 30 April 1941.
20. Greenwood, p.132.
21. Ibid, p.133.
22. Ibid, p.136.
23. Ibid, p.139.
24. Correlli Barnett, *The Desert Generals* (London, George Allen & Unwin, 2nd edition, 1983), p.77.

**Chapter Six**

1. John Rylands, Auchinleck Collection, File XVIII, July 1–July 29 1941, Items 275–291, MUL 275a, Churchill to General Auchinleck, 1 July 1941, Private for C-in-C.
2. John Rylands, MUL 279, Personal for CIGS from C-in-C (Auchinleck), 2 July 1941.
3. Ibid.
4. John Rylands, MUL 280, Auchinleck to Churchill, 4 July 1941.
5. John Rylands, MUL 281, Churchill to Auchinleck, 6 July 1941. Referring to Auchinleck's telegram 4/7/41.
6. *Playfair 2*, p.22.
7. Ibid, p.197.
8. John Rylands, MUL 282, Auchinleck to Churchill, 15 July 1941.
9. John Rylands, MUL 283, Letter from Sir John Dill to Auchinleck, 16 July 1941.
10. John Rylands, MUL 285, Amery, India Office to Auchinleck, 19 July 1941.
11. John Rylands, MUL 288, Churchill to Auchinleck, 20 July 1941.
12. John Rylands, MUL 289, Auchinleck to General Sir John Dill, 21 July 1941.
13. *Playfair 2*, p.254.
14. Greenwood, pp.147–149.
15. Warner, pp.82–83.
16. Roy Jenkins, *Churchill* (London, Macmillan, 2001), p.658.
17. Correlli Barnett, *The Desert Generals* (London, George Allen & Unwin, 2nd edition, 1983), p.7.
18. Ibid.
19. Ibid, pp.78–79.
20. Greenwood, p.150.
21. John Rylands, File XVIII, August 5–August 31 1941, MUL 292, Auchinleck to Dill, 5 August 1941, 16 August 1941.
22. Greenwood, p.150.
23. *Playfair 2*, pp.255–256.
24. Ibid, p.262.
25. Ibid, p.285.
26. I.S.O. Playfair, *History of the Second World War. The Mediterranean and Middle East*, Volume 3 (London, HMSO, 1960), p.3. Hereafter referred to as *Playfair 3*.
27. Ibid, p.6.
28. Greenwood, p.152.
29. John Rylands, File XIX, September 2–September 10 1941, MUL 310, General Sir Claude Auchinleck, 6 September 1941.

30. John Rylands, MUL 316, n.d.
31. John Rylands, MUL 318, Office of C-in-C, Mediterranean Station. Personal for C-in-C, MEF, 9 September 1941.
32. Greenwood, p.153.
33. Ibid.

**Chapter Seven**

1. Ibid, pp.153–154.
2. *Playfair 3*, p.7.
3. Greenwood, p.151.
4. John Rylands, File XXI, September 18–September 30 1941, MUL 343, Churchill to Auchinleck, 18 September 1941.
5. Greenwood, p.151.
6. John Rylands, MUL 346, Auchinleck to Churchill, 21 September 1941.
7. John Rylands, MUL 378, Churchill to Auchinleck, 14 October 1941.
8. Greenwood, p.154.
9. Ibid.
10. Ibid, pp.154–155.
11. John Rylands, File XXIII, October 16–October 21 1941, Items 381–400, MUL 382, Churchill to Auchinleck, 16 October 1941.
12. *Playfair 3*, pp.120–121.
13. John Rylands, File XXIV, October 22–October 31 1941, MUL 403, Auchinleck to Churchill, 23 October 1941.
14. *Playfair 3*, pp.4–5.
15. John Rylands, MUL 408, Dill to Auchinleck, private letter, 25 October 1941.
16. *The Maisky Diaries. Red Ambassador to the Court of St James's 1932–1943*, Gabriel Gorodetsky (ed.) (London, Yale University Press, 2015), p.399.
17. Ibid, p.401.
18. John Rylands, MUL 414, General Wavell to CIGS, Cipher Message, 30 October 1941.
19. John Rylands, MUL 417, CIGS from General Auchinleck, 31 October 1941.
20. John Rylands, File XXV November 1–November 19 1941, Items 419–438, MUL 426, Field Marshal Jan Smuts, Prime Minister South Africa to Auchinleck, 6 November 1941.
21. Greenwood, pp.158–159.
22. Ibid, pp.160–161.
23. Ibid, pp.161–162.
24. Barnett, p.113.
25. Ibid, pp.115–116.
26. Greenwood, p.162.
27. John Rylands, File XXVII, November 25–27 1941, Items 457–480, MUL 458, Auchinleck to General Sir Alan Cunningham, 25 November 1941.
28. John Rylands, MUL 459, Auchinleck to General Sir Alan Cunningham, letter, 25 November 1941.
29. John Rylands, MUL 463a, Mideast to Troopers (Auchinleck to Churchill), 25 November 1941.

30. John Rylands, MUL 464, Auchinleck to Churchill, 25 November 1941.
31. Ibid.
32. John Rylands, MUL 465, Auchinleck to Churchill, 25 November 1941.
33. John Rylands, MUL 466, Auchinleck to Churchill, 25 November 1941.
34. John Rylands, MUL 469, Churchill to Auchinleck, 26 November 1941.
35. John Rylands, MUL 475, Auchinleck to Churchill, 27 November 1941.
36. John Rylands, MUL 476a, Auchinleck to CIGS, 27 November 1941.
37. John Rylands, MUL 477, Churchill to Auchinleck, 27 November 1941.
38. John Rylands, File XXVIII, November 28–30 1941, MUL 482, Auchinleck to Churchill, 28 November 1941.
39. John Rylands, MUL 483, CIGS to Auchinleck, 28 November 1941.
40. John Rylands, MUL 484, Auchinleck to CIGS, 28 November 1941.
41. John Rylands, MUL 485, Cunningham to Auchinleck, letter from hospital, 28 November 1941.
42. John Rylands, MUL 487, Medical report, 30 November 1941.
43. John Rylands, MUL 489, Churchill to Auchinleck, 29 November 1941.
44. John Rylands, File XXIX, December 1–December 6 1941, Items 504–526, MUL 505a, Auchinleck to Churchill, 1 December 1941.
45. John Rylands, MUL 515, Extract from Field Censorship Summary No.6, 4 December 1941.
46. John Rylands, MUL 518, General Arthur Smith to Auchinleck, 4 December 1941.
47. John Rylands, MUL 526, Auchinleck to General Arthur Smith, 6 December 1941.
48. John Rylands, MUL 537, Churchill to Auchinleck, 9 December 1941.
49. John Rylands, MUL 539, General Sir Alan Brooke (CIGS) to Auchinleck, 10 December 1941.
50. John Rylands, MUL 544, Auchinleck to Air Chief Marshal Sir Charles A. Portal, Chief of Air Staff, 11 December 1941.
51. John Rylands, MUL 549, Churchill to Auchinleck, 12 December 1941.
52. Greenwood, pp.163–164.
53. John Rylands, File XXXI, December 13–December 21 1941, Items 551–569, MUL 551, General Neil Ritchie to Auchinleck, 13 December 1941.
54. John Rylands, File XXXII, December 22–December 26 1941, Items 570–586, MUL 570, Ritchie to Auchinleck, 22 December 1941.
55. John Rylands, MUL 573, Auchinleck to Churchill, 24 December 1941.
56. John Rylands, MUL 575, Ritchie (ADV HQ Eighth Army HQ) to Auchinleck.
57. John Rylands, MUL 578, Amery to Auchinleck, 24 December 1941.
58. *Playfair 3*, p.70.
59. Greenwood, pp.167–168.

**Chapter Eight**

1. John Rylands, MUL 580, Auchinleck to CIGS, 25 December 1941.
2. John Rylands, File XXXIII, December 27–December 31 1941, Items 587–601, MUL 591, Churchill to Auchinleck, 27 December 1941.
3. John Rylands, MUL 596, Copy of a letter from Brigadier Scott-Cockburn, DSO, to Commander 13 Corps, 29 December 1941.

4. John Rylands, MUL 597, Field Marshal Smuts to Auchinleck, 29 December 1941.
5. John Rylands, MUL 599, Armed Engagement South of Agedabia on 27th December 1941, Ritchie to Auchinleck, 30 December 1941.
6. www.youtube.com/watch?v=yqSiwQoAf21, accessed 11 July 2018.
7. John Rylands, File XXXIV, January 1–January 10 1942, MUL 603, Auchinleck to Ritchie, 1 January 1942.
8. Barnett, p.75.
9. The 8th Army in North Africa, www.youtube.com/watch?v=h_glHd662v0 accessed 11 July 2018.
10. John Rylands, MUL 608, Field Marshal Smuts to Auchinleck, 2 January 1942.
11. John Rylands, MUL 614, CIGS to Auchinleck, 4 January 1942.
12. John Rylands, MUL 617, Auchinleck to CIGS, 7 January 1942.
13. John Rylands, MUL 619, Ritchie to Auchinleck, 8 January 1942.
14. John Rylands, MUL 623, Churchill to Auchinleck, 11 January 1942.
15. John Rylands, MUL 625a, Ritchie to Auchinleck, 11 January 1942.
16. John Rylands, MUL 627, Auchinleck to Churchill, 12 January 1942.
17. John Rylands, MUL 628, Auchinleck to Churchill, 12 January 1942.
18. John Rylands, MUL 640, Auchinleck to CIGS, 15 January 1942.
19. John Rylands, MUL 647, Brooke to Auchinleck, 21 January 1942.
20. John Rylands, MUL 653b, Churchill to Auchinleck, 25 January 1942.
21. Parkinson, p.55.
22. John Rylands, File XXXVII, MUL 656, Auchinleck to Lieutenant General Sir Arthur Smith, 27 January 1942.
23. John Rylands, MUL 660, Field Marshal Smuts to General Theron, 27 January 1942.
24. John Rylands, MUL 670, Auchinleck to Churchill, 30 January 1942.
25. John Rylands, File XXXVIII, 1 February-9 February 1942, Items 673–695, MUL 679, From Chequers, 'Pug' to Auchinleck, 1 February 1942.
26. John Rylands, MUL 688 CIGS, General Sir Alan Brooke to Auchinleck, 6 February 1942.
27. John Rylands, MUL 692, Auchinleck to Field Marshal Smuts, 8 February 1942.
28. John Rylands, File XXXIX, 10 February-15 February 1942, Items 696–711, MUL 696, Auchinleck to Ritchie, 10 February 1942.
29. John Rylands, File XXIX, 1December-6 December 1941, MUL 520, Auchinleck to General Arthur Smith, 5 December 1941.
30. John Rylands, MUL 700, Auchinleck to Ritchie, 11 February 1942.
31. John Rylands, MUL 706, Auchinleck to Brooke, 14 February 1942.
32. John Rylands, MUL 720, Ritchie to Auchinleck, 17 February 1942.
33. John Rylands, MUL 725, Auchinleck to CIGS (General Brooke), 23 February 1942.
34. John Rylands, File XLI, 1 March-9 March 1942, MUL 741, Auchinleck to CIGS (General Brooke), 6 March 1942.
35. Warner, p.125.
36. Ibid. pp.125–126.

37. John Rylands, File XL, 16 February-27 February 1942, Items 712–730, MUL 715, Extract from Signal to Secretary of State for Air from AOC-in-C, reference Air Estimates Speech, c.16 February 1942.
38. John Rylands, MUL 717, Auchinleck to Secretary of State for Air, 17 February 1942.
39. John Rylands, MUL 750a, Auchinleck to CIGS, 12 March 1942.
40. John Rylands, MUL 753a, Churchill to Auchinleck, 15 March 1942.
41. John Rylands, File XLIII, 20 March-31 March 1942, Items 761–772, MUL 762, Auchinleck to Field Marshal Smuts, 20 March 1942.
42. John Rylands, MUL 763, Cripps to Churchill, 20 March 1942.
43. John Rylands, MUL 764, Memorandum by Auchinleck, Libya, March 1942.
44. *Playfair 3*, pp.213–215. See also Timothy Harrison Place, *Military Training in the British Army, 1940–1944. From Dunkirk to D-Day* (London, Frank Cass, 2000), pp.128–152.
45. John Rylands, MUL 765, Auchinleck to General Ritchie, 22 March 1942.
46. John Rylands, MUL 772, Alan Brooke to Auchinleck, Private Letter, 31 March 1941.
47. John Rylands, File XLIV, 2 April-10 April 1942, Items 773–794, MUL 774, Letter to Auchinleck, 3 April 1942.
48. John Rylands, File XLV, 11 April-21 April 1942, Items 795–815, MUL 811, CIGS (Brooke) to Auchinleck, 17 April 1942.
49. John Rylands, MUL 812, Auchinleck to CIGS, 17 April 1942.
50. John Rylands, MUL 823, From Middle East to Air Ministry Special Signal Office – For Chiefs of Staff from Commanders-in-Chief, c.24 April 1942.
51. John Rylands, MUL 824, Tehran to FO, 29 April 1942.
52. John Rylands, File XLVII, 1 May-12 May 1942, Items 830–846, MUL 834, Auchinleck to CIGS, 3 May 1942.
53. John Rylands, File XLVIII, 13 May-22 May 1942, Items 847–866, MUL 852, CIGS to Auchinleck, 16 May 1942.
54. John Rylands, File XLIX, 23 May-31 May 1942, Items 867–887, MUL 876, Rommel's Order of the Day. Captured version issued to the Italians.
55. Jenkins, p.690.
56. John Rylands, MUL 882, Amery to Auchinleck, 28 May 1942.
57. John Rylands, File L, 1 June-7 June 1942, Items 888–907, MUL 888, Auchinleck to Churchill, 1 June 1942.
58. Greenwood, p.192.
59. John Rylands, MUL 890, Smuts to Auchinleck, 1 June 1942.
60. John Rylands, MUL 892, Auchinleck to Smuts, 2 June 1942.
61. John Rylands, MUL 893, Message from King George VI, 2 June 1942.
62. John Rylands, MUL 896b, Auchinleck to Ritchie, 3 June 1942.
63. John Rylands, File LI, 8 June-14 June 1942, Items 908–924, MUL 923, Churchill to Auchinleck, 14 June 1942.
64. John Rylands, MUL 924, Auchinleck to Field Marshal Smuts, 14 June 1942.
65. John Rylands, File LII, 15 June-20 June 1942, MUL 925, Auchinleck to Churchill, 15 June 1942.
66. John Rylands, MUL 937, Auchinleck to Field Marshal Smuts, 19 June 1942.

67. John Rylands, File LIII, 21 June-22 June 1942, Items 943–948, MUL 943, Middle East Defence Committee to Minister of Defence and Defence Committee, 21 June 1942.
68. Churchill, pp.373–374.
69. Warner, p.148.
70. John Rylands, File LIV, 28 June-30 June 1942, Items 949–962, MUL 950, Auchinleck to CIGS, 23 June 1942.
71. John Rylands, MUL 961a, Auchinleck to CIGS, 28 June 1942.
72. *The Real 'Dad's Army'. The War Diaries of Colonel Rodney Foster*, Ronnie Scott (ed.) (London, Penguin, 2012), p.177, diary entry, 21 June 1942.
73. Connell, p.593.
74. *Playfair 3*, p.275.
75. Parkinson, p.9.
76. *Playfair 3*, p.286.
77. Ibid, pp.286–287.
78. John Rylands, File LV, 1 July-13 July 1942, Items 963–977, MUL Auchinleck to Field Marshal Smuts, 1 July 1942.
79. Bungay, pp.2, 45.
80. *Playfair 3*, p.96.
81. Parkinson, p.196.
82. John Rylands, MUL 965, Amery (India Office) to Auchinleck, 2 July 1942.
83. John Rylands, MUL 967, Churchill to Auchinleck, 3 July 1942.
84. Warner, p.158.
85. John Rylands, MUL 968, General Corbett to Churchill, 3 July 1942.
86. John Rylands, MUL 970a, Field Marshal Smuts to Auchinleck, 6 July 1942.
87. John Rylands, MUL 971 from VCIGS to General Corbett, 6 July 1942.
88. John Rylands, MUL 973, Auchinleck to CIGS, 8 July 1942.
89. John Rylands, File LVI 14 July-31 July 1942, MUL 978, CIGS to Auchinleck, 14 July 1942.
90. John Rylands, MUL 980, Auchinleck to Churchill, 14 July 1942.
91. John Rylands, MUL 981, Field Marshal Smuts to Auchinleck, 15 July 1942.
92. John Rylands, MUL 982, Auchinleck to Field Marshal Smuts, 16 July 1942.
93. John Rylands, MUL 988, Auchinleck to Brooke, 25 July 1942.
94. John Rylands, MUL 989, Churchill to Auchinleck, 27 July 1942.
95. John Rylands, File LVII, 1 August-31 August 1942, Items 990–1000, MUL 990, Churchill to Auchinleck, 8 August 1942.
96. Parkinson, p.216.
97. Ibid, p.225.
98. Warner, pp.161–162.
99. Warner, p.166.

**Chapter Nine**

1. John Rylands, MUL 990, Churchill to Auchinleck, 8 August 1942.
2. *Playfair 3*, p.205.
3. John Rylands, GOW/1/26/15, Churchill in Cairo, 1942, 20 October 1964.

4. John Rylands, MUL 994, General Tom Corbett to Auchinleck, 14 August 1942.
5. John Rylands, MUL 995, General Zając, C-in-C Polish Forces, ME, to Auchinleck, 19 August 1942.
6. John Rylands, MUL 997a, Auchinleck to Lord Linlithgow, 24 August 1942.
7. John Rylands, File LVIII, 1 September-31 December 1942, Items 1001–1017, MUL 1001, Amery to Auchinleck, 2 September 1942.
8. Connell, p.730.
9. John Rylands, MUL 1003, Lord Birdwood to Auchinleck, 6 September 1942.
10. John Rylands, MUL 1011, Amery to Auchinleck, 9 November 1942.
11. John Rylands, MUL 1012, Q to Auchinleck, 14 November 1942.
12. John Rylands, MUL 1014, Victor Cazalet to Auchinleck, 24 November 1942.
13. John Rylands, File LIX, 1 January-31 May 1943, MUL 1019, General Anders to Auchinleck, 22 February 1943.
14. John Rylands, File LX, 1 June-31 August 1943, Items 1024–1034, MUL 1026, Arthur Smith to Auchinleck, 21 June 1943.
15. John Rylands, MUL 1032, Linlithgow to Auchinleck, 26 July 1943.
16. *The Diaries of Sir Alexander Cadogan, 1938–1945*, David Dilks (ed.) (London, Cassell, 1971), pp.375–382.
17. Greenwood, p.235.
18. *The Harold Nicolson Diaries, 1907–1963*, Nigel Nicolson (ed.) (London, Weidenfeld & Nicolson, 2004), diary entry, 6 November 1942, pp.269–270.
19. John Rylands, GOW/1/21, Auchinleck to O'Gowan, 5 July 1963.
20. Greenwood, pp.235–236.
21. Connell, p.747.
22. Ibid, p.241. For the eccentricities of Wingate and the prowess of the Chindits and their long-range activities see Francis Pike, *Hirohito's War: The Pacific War, 1941–1945* (London, Bloomsbury, 2015), pp.680–690.
23. Ibid, pp.272–273.
24. Greenwood, p.241.
25. Ibid, p.243.
26. Barney White-Spunner, *Partition: The Story of Indian Independence and the Creation of Pakistan in 1947* (London, Simon & Schuster, 2017), pp.106–107.
27. Ibid, p.249.
28. Ibid, p.250.
29. *The Real 'Dad's Army'*, pp.311–312, diary entry, 26 November 1944.
30. Greenwood, p.253.
31. Warner, pp.184–185.
32. Sugata Bose, *His Majesty's Opponent: Subhas Chandra Bose and India's Struggle Against Empire* (Cambridge, Massachusetts, The Belknap Press of Harvard University Press, 2011), pp.4–5.
33. Warner, p.262.
34. Ibid.
35. Warner, pp.192–193.

36. Bose, p.242.
37. John Rylands, File LXVI, 1 November-31 December 1945, Items 1109– 1125, MUL 1113, 15 November 1945.
38. John Rylands, MUL 1114, Major C. Charles M. Cockin to Colonel K.S. Himatsinhji, GHQ (1) New Delhi, 19 November 1945.
39. John Rylands, MUL 1125, report of sympathy for INA in the Indian army, 29 December 1945.
40. Connell, p.794.
41. John Rylands, File LXVIII February 1–25 1946, Items 1136–1141, MUL 1137a, Report by Auchinleck, 12 February 1946.
42. Ibid.
43. John Rylands, MUL 1138, Colonel K.S. Himatsinhji (VII Rajput Regiment) to Auchinleck, 17 February 1946.
44. John Rylands, MUL 1140, Wavell to Auchinleck, 20 February 1946.
45. John Rylands, MUL 1149, Nehru to Auchinleck, 4 May 1946.
46. John Rylands, File LXXI 1 June 1946–30 June 1946, Items 1159–1187, MUL 1159, Amery to Auchinleck, 1 June 1946.
47. John Rylands, MUL 1170, *The Times*, 1 June 1946.
48. John Rylands, MUL 1176, *Daily Mail*, Douglas Kay, 3 June 1946.
49. John Rylands, MUL 1187, G.E.B. Abell, private secretary to viceroy, to Auchinleck, 17 June 1946.
50. Nisid Hajari, *Midnight's Furies: The Deadly Legacy of India's Partition* (Stroud, Gloucestershire, Amberley, 2015), p.7.
51. Alex von Tunzelmann, *Indian Summer: The Secret History of the end of an Empire* (London, Pocket Books, 2007), p.139.
52. Ibid, p.254.
53. John Rylands, File LXXII, 1 July-31 August 1946, Items 1188–1192, MUL 1188 COS (46) 765 (JPC [46] 11) Appreciation of the Strategic Value of India to the British Commonwealth of Nations (Final Paper).
54. John Rylands, MUL 1192, Policy Note No.17 Provision of Personal Weapons, Auchinleck, C-in-C India, Field Marshal, 5 August 1946.
55. John Rylands, File LXXIII, 1 September-31 December 1946, Items 1193–1204, National Indian Armed Forces, MUL 1198, List of INA personnel who are in prison in October 1946.
56. John Rylands, MUL 1204, Nehru to Baldev Singhji, 25 December 1946.
57. John Rylands, File LXXIV, 1 January 1947–31 January 1947, Items 1205 – 1213, MUL 1205, Auchinleck to Sardar Baldev Singh, 6 January 1947.
58. John Rylands, MUL 1208, Wavell to Auchinleck, 9 January 1947.
59. John Rylands, File LXXXVII, 1 June-31 June 1947, Items 1228–1238, MUL 1229, Auchinleck to General Lord Ismay, Viceroy's House, 11 June 1947.
60. Hajari, p.102.
61. John Rylands, MUL 1230, Terms of Reference of the Armed Forces Reconstitution Committee, 5 July 1947.

62. John Rylands, MUL 1232 Auchinleck to Viscountess Mountbatten of Burma, 9 July 1947 – re: letter from her from Mrs Kiani, MUL 1231, Viscountess Mountbatten of Burma to Auchinleck, 8 July 1947.
63. John Rylands, MUL 1235, Jawaharlal Nehru to Lord Mountbatten, 19 July 1947.
64. John Rylands, MUL 1236, Auchinleck to Sir George Abell, Private Secretary to HE the Viceroy, 21 July 1947.
65. John Rylands, File LXXVIII, August 1–9 1947, Item 1239–1244, MUL 1234, Auchinleck to Mountbatten, 9 August 1947.
66. Ibid.
67. John Rylands, File LXXIX, August 11–August 31, 1947, Items 1245–1251, MUL 1251, Report by Major General J.B. Dalison on the attack by Sikhs on the 3 UP Frontier Mail at Maur at about 0950 hours on Sunday, 24 August 1947.
68. John Rylands, File LXXXI, 15 September 1947–30 September 1947, Items 1260–1262, MUL 1260, Mountbatten to Auchinleck, 26 September 1947.
69. White-Spunner, pp.267–268.
70. Phillip Ziegler, *Mountbatten: The Official Biography* (London, Collins, 1985), p.463.
71. Ibid, p.464.
72. Ibid, pp.268–269.
73. Ibid, p.390.
74. Ibid.
75. Ibid, p.424.
76. Ibid, pp.372–373.
77. John Rylands, MUL 1261, 'Pug' Ismay to Auchinleck, 26 September 1947.
78. Zeigler, p.464.
79. John Rylands, MUL 1262, Report on the Situation in India and Pakistan by Field Marshal Sir Claude Auchinleck for the information of the Cabinet and the Chiefs of Staff in the United Kingdom, September 1947, 28 September 1947.
80. John Rylands, MUL 1262, PART II for the personal information of the Prime Minister, the Chief of the Naval Staff, the Chief of the Imperial General Staff and the Chief of the Air Staff only, 28 September 1947.
81. Zeigler, pp.446–447.
82. John Rylands, MUL 1263, Auchinleck Report, 5 October 1947.
83. Zeigler, p.436.
84. John Rylands, File LXXXIV, 1 November 1947–21 November 1947, Items 1278–1289, MUL 1279, Mountbatten to Sardar Baldev Singh, 24 October 1947.
85. John Rylands, MUL 1279, Baldev Singh to Mountbatten, 2 November 1947.
86. John Rylands, MUL 1287, 'Archie' to Auchinleck, 20 November 1947.
87. John Rylands, File XC, undated papers, Items 1332–1333, MUL 1332, Armies of India.
88. C.N. North, *Journal of an English Officer in India* (London, Hurst & Blachett, 1858), pp.125–126.
89. T. Rice-Holmes, *A History of the Indian Mutiny and of the Disturbances Which Accompanied it amongst the Civil Population* (London, Macmillan & Co. Limited, 1904, 5th edition), p.217.

90. Jad Adams, *Gandhi: Naked Ambition* (London, Quercus, 2010), p.5.
91. Ibid. p.25.
92. Ibid. pp.128–129, 229.
93. Shahid Hamid, *Disastrous Twilight: A Personal Record of the Partition of India* (London, Leo Cooper, 1986), p.4.
94. Connell, pp.930–932.
95. Nisid Hajari, *Midnight's Furies: The Deadly Legacy of India's Partition* (Stroud, Gloucester, Amberley Publishing, 2015), p.194.
96. John Rylands, File LXXXVI, 1 December 1947–31 December 1947, Items 1300–1305, MUL 1301 'Dickie' Mountbatten to Auchinleck, 2 December 1947.
97. John Rylands, MUL 1304, Jinnah to Auchinleck, 18 December 1947.
98. John Rylands, MUL 1305, Attlee to Auchinleck, 30 December 1947.
99. White-Spunner, pp.329–331.
100. Hamid, p.178.

**Chapter Ten**

1. Warner, p.227.
2. Ibid. p.228.
3. John Rylands, GOW/1/20/51, General Brian Horrocks to O'Gowan, 29 November 1958.
4. John Rylands, GOW/1/21/19, Auchinleck to O'Gowan, 19 October 1958.
5. John Rylands, GOW/1/29/12, O'Gowan to Auchinleck, 1 July 1967.
6. John Rylands, GOW/1/29/24, O'Gowan to Auchinleck, 23 November 1958.
7. John Rylands, GOW/1/32/1, General Bayerlein, July 10–July 17 1942.
8. John Rylands, GOW/1/32/32, The Middle East in Danger.
9. Ibid.
10. Connell, p.613.
11. John Rylands, GOW/1/32/5, Cohesion and Confusion, 28–29 June 1942.
12. Desmond Young, *Rommel* (London, Collins, 1950), p.164.
13. Warner, pp.161–162.
14. John Rylands, GOW/1/32/7, Prelude to Battle, 30 June 1942.
15. John Rylands, GOW/1/32/8, Check to 'Aida', 1 July 1942–2 July 1942.
16. John Rylands, GOW/1/32/12, Checkmate to 'Aida' and to 'Hercules'.
17. John Rylands, GOW/1/32/13, The new defence of Egypt.
18. John Rylands, GOW/1/32/26, General Montgomery with the 8th Army, 15 August 1942.
19. John Rylands, GOW/1/32/29, Auchinleck and the Prime Minister, Cairo, August 1942.
20. John Rylands, GOW/1/20, O'Gowan to the editor, The *Guardian*, 22 October 1958.
21. John Rylands, GOW/1/20/38, Auchinleck in India.
22. Ibid.
23. Warner, p.80.
24. Barnett, pp.77–78.
25. John Rylands, GOW/1/33/1/22, 3 March 1944.

26. John Rylands, GOW/1/33/2/2, Commander 8th Army from Brigadier E. Dorman-Smith.
27. Robin Neillands, *Eighth Army: From the Western Desert to the Alps, 1939–1945* (London, John Murray, 2004), pp.158–159.
28. Warner, pp.173–174.
29. Ibid, p.166.
30. Connell, pp.570–571.
31. Ibid, p.587.
32. Ibid, p.617.
33. Parkinson, p.231.
34. Warner, p.174.
35. Connell, p.643.
36. Alanbrooke, p.280.
37. Ibid, pp.280–281.
38. Ibid, pp.283–284, diary entry, 22 July 1942.
39. Ibid, p.284, 23 July 1942.
40. Ibid, p.286, 27 July 1942.
41. Ibid, 28 July 1942.
42. Ibid, pp.289–290, diary entry, 3 August 1942.
43. Ibid, p.290.
44. Ibid, pp.290–291, 4 August 1942.
45. Connell, pp.702–703.
46. Alanbrooke, p.224, notes to diary entry 29 January 1942.
47. Warner, p.230.
48. Ibid, pp.264–265.
49. Zeigler, p.671.
50. Greenwood, p.287.
51. Ibid, pp.291–292.
52. Ibid, p.292.
53. Ibid, p.293.
54. John Rylands, GOW/1/25, letter, General Bayerlein to O'Gowan, 13 January 1950. Manfred Rommel, 22 September 1954.
55. Greenwood, pp.294–295.
56. Ibid, p.295.
57. Ibid.
58. Ibid, p.297.
59. Ibid, pp.302–303.
60. Ibid, pp.305–314.

# Index

**Military Units and Operations**